A JOURNEY THROUGH
TIME

NEWTON MUDAKI KIMIYWI

Worlds Unknown Publishers

ISBN: 978-1-7349822-2-0 (Paperback)
ISBN: 978-1-7352874-2-3 (Hardcover)
ISBN: 978-1-7352874-3-0 (Ebook)

This book is a work of fiction. Names, characters, places, and incidents are either the product of the author's imagination or are used fictitiously, and any resemblance to actual persons, living or dead, business establishment, event or locales is entirely coincidental.

Printed in the United States of America.
First printing edition 2020.

Worlds Unknown Publishers
2515 E Thomas Rd,
Ste 16 -1061
Phoenix, AZ 85016-7946

www.wupubs.com

DEDICATION

To my mum, a special gem, your presence, dedication and love will forever be felt. To my wife Debbie and the Harveys you are my world. Thanks for everything that you have been to me. This work could not have been possible without your constant motivation.

CHAPTER ONE

E ven in the rare moments that he wasn't angry, Uncle Matata was intimidating—a sharp-tongued man who towered above everyone. A feral animal with the body of a beer keg. The volcanic folds on his gargoyle face neutered any chance of a smile, and he was always at risk of erupting.

On the evening that he kicked us out of the compound, he definitely erupted, drenching every one of us with the hot lava of his wrath.

"Get *out!*" he seethed.

To demonstrate his anger, he hoisted up the huge water pot, which usually sat conspicuously in the corner of the kitchen, and dropped it outside. Our ancestral pot. It exploded into shards! It was like witnessing a brutal murder. That pot had been part of our family for as long as I remembered.

I watched in horrified fascination, the dismay I felt almost overshadowing my fear.

I surely was going to miss that pot. It always had cool water that refreshed and quenched our thirst.

"Matata, what have you done? Why have you shattered our family?" Mum cried out.

"When you rattle a snake be ready for its bite!" Matata shouted.

"And what do you want with these *sufurias*? Haven't you done enough harm?" she asked bitterly as Uncle Matata crushed an aluminum container under his heel.

Uncle Matata pushed Mum, and she fell into a puddle of murky water that was fast forming in the heavy rain. He then tore through the house and threw out as many of our earthly belongings as he could. Having done so, he slammed the door shut and locked it.

His compound had two houses: one that he had built himself for his family and the other one that my elder brother, Isate, Mum and I, lived in. This had belonged to our late grandmother, Guuku Azbeta.

Uncle Matata was her only son. 'Our house', therefore, was his. It was his inheritance, and he incessantly reminded us of this. Guuku Azbeta, when she was still alive, had tried to make Uncle Matata see sense, but he was completely blind to the truth. He couldn't love us. Grandma had ultimately given up trying to convince him, and the heartbreak of it all must have hastened her journey to that mysterious place beyond.

The house seemed as ancient as time itself. It was clinging to its life just as Guuku Azbeta had towards the end of her long, eventful journey. The roof was caving in. The frames and wooden beams that held the roof in place had been chewed away by determined termites, making them look like the legs of a malnourished child. We were always afraid that one day it would crumble on us. Still, we loved this four-roomed house, as it was the only place that we could call home.

The sitting room had a large table and several armchairs made of bamboo and sisal reeds. My brother, Isate, and I slept on the earthen floor in one of the rooms while the other room was Mum's. There was a small kitchen area with a hearth. Long black sooty strings hung precariously from its roof. Whenever Mum cooked, the whole house would become a chimney. Somehow, she survived the smoke to fix us meal after meal, day after day—it was a total sacrifice. A rare skill. And as the food was always limited, she served us first, and the little that remained on the cooking pot is what she gladly took. We came first, and she came last.

Now Uncle Matata had pushed us out of the house into the rain. Mum hadn't taken it lying down, but her feeble struggles were no match for the immense strength of the furious giant that her brother was. When Uncle Matata threw her outside, we followed Mum like dogs would their master.

"I don't want to ever see you here again! Take your little brats, and go to your husband!"

"Which husband? You know I don't have—"

"Find one! Try those at Mudete! Tomorrow is a market day, you know!"

"Matata! How many times will you do this to us? You heartless man! Did we really come from the same womb?" Mum cried.

"A cow that calves twins better be ready with enough milk! I am tired of all of you. Filthy ticks! If I see you again, I will crush you!" His lips were trembling, and his fists were clenched.

He turned and stamped away angrily. I could hear the ground tremble with his every step. We watched his gigantic silhouette until it disappeared into his house.

We moved into the eaves of the house. Our upper bodies were sheltered, but the rains licked at our feet. My teeth were chattering uncontrollably. The ruthless cold cut straight to the bone. Isate suddenly burst into loud wails, unable to hold back his emotions any longer. I wasn't any better. The thought of spending yet another night in the freezing cold filled me with so much despair. I joined Isate in the wailing match. The rain beat the rusty iron sheets like a violent drum, dwarfing our cries, which soon subsided to sobs and sniffs that eventually died out too.

My entire body was shivering from the intense cold, and my teeth were chattering piteously. Mum placed her hands around my shoulders and those of Isate, trying to comfort us and at the same time, keep us warm. We huddled against each other, as if our collective miseries were going to warm our bodies and souls for the night.

The rain kept on licking at our feet, and as it subsided, men and women trooped to the euphorbia fence to see what the commotion had been all about. Even if they had come earlier, they couldn't have done much more than watch. Who would dare challenge Uncle Matata? His fiery temper made him untouchable. He had turned himself into a leprous island.

They mumbled, clucked their tongues, shook their heads, and eventually slipped back into their respective warm houses, leaving the cold all to us.

"When will this ever stop, Mum!" I sobbed miserably.

"One day, Baraka. One day . . ."

"But this has to stop, mum. We cannot continue living like this!" Isate shouted heatedly.

"Calm down, Isate!" Mum said. "What do you want me to do?"

'No, Mum! Uncle Matata is right. We need to go to our father! Who *is* our father?" he thundered.

Mum ignored Isate, just like she always did when we asked about our father. We couldn't bring her to discuss this topic. It hurt us that she couldn't tell us who our father was. She seemed to hurt too whenever we treaded anywhere near that forbidden territory.

Although I was still quite young, I could understand why the topic was so painful to her. I had overheard the taunts and backbiting that were constantly being cast her way—mostly at the village square. Our village square always had a "panel" of backbiters—an open jury that meted judgment with utmost cruelty. It was a syndicate of lazy minds that discussed other people's issues and offered solutions to them—solutions that never really reached the victims. Mama was never part of them, but deep down in her soul, she knew that she was a constant victim of these gatherings. She was their favorite item on the menu—juiciest of all.

Though she was of slight build, I knew Mum was strong. However, tonight her head hung low. We silently sat in the darkness, and the gloom couldn't have been more complete. I tried to look at her eyes but I couldn't see them. Maybe they were blank, staring into space, or red from silently crying. Usually, she would retain a slight smile as her mind crafted—some way out of the latest tight spot. At that moment, Isate and I knew we would not be going to any of our neighbors to ask for help. We had done that enough times to become a general nuisance. Even if they couldn't tell us to our faces, the behavior spelt it out clearly enough.

As we huddled together in our misery, willing morning to dawn and bring with it sunshine to warm our frozen bones, we were suddenly startled by Uncle Matata's heavy footsteps. Was he coming to push us around some more? I clung to Mum fearfully. However, Uncle Matata's heart seemed to have softened.

"I am a good man. I will allow you to use this house as you plan to move away from here." He unlocked the padlock and purposefully strode away; like an invincible demigod that could give and take life at will.

CHAPTER TWO

I t was a big relief to be back in the house, but the whole incident had taken its toll on Mum. She looked wearily at the shards of the broken water pot. Something inside her had shattered as the pot was dashed to pieces by her brother.

She didn't breathe a word all morning. The only sound was the occasional breaking of dry sticks as she gathered firewood and put it on the hearth. I glanced furtively at her drawn face as we all tried to thaw out our limbs at the feeble flames of the fire she lit. It seemed like everything we ever had was just as feeble as those flickering flames.

Mum had struggled, burning her candle from both ends to ensure Isate joined form one in a local institution, Kisangula Secondary School, but she couldn't raise enough money to feed us and at the same time manage Isate's school fees.

We depended mostly on the charity of the neighbors— so much so that we seemed to be forcing it through.

However, it was Mum who put to a stop our pattern of begging, which usually started with an argument of shame when we could no longer stand our hunger. Many were the nights we had these difficult choices in our hands.

"Baraka, yesterday I borrowed flour from *mama* Adagala. Today, you should go borrow some from Ainea!" Isate would suggest, not wanting to go himself.

"I don't think that's a good idea. They seem to have discovered our little secret," I would say. I did not want to go either.

"Stop that nonsense. You are not going anywhere tonight. You better teach your stomachs to adjust. You should not make your plans based on someone else's fortunes, my sons!"

"This hunger is too much!" Isate would mourn. "The aroma of ugali cooking in Adagala's house is not helping. That virtual diet will not fill our stomachs! Let me go and . . ." Isate said, and even before he could finish the statement, he was on the way out.

Mum grabbed and tried to restrain him, but Isate was too swift for her. I called out, "Isate, you forgot the bowl." I flung the bowl and he grabbed it mid-air. Evading Mum, as he disappeared into the night. When he came back, we both would endure a caning that would bite more than the hunger we experienced. To add to the punishment, she would typically make us clear a part of the small field that she farmed or some other similar piece of work.

Only Uncle Matata's numerous squabbles with Mum would somehow save us from the tedious toil at such times. The smell of the tobacco that he sniffed usually hit our noses before we could see him.

"Here he comes again!" Mum would say, apprehensively sniffing the air.

"You plough, but you reap nothing! A poor man's cow only calves bulls" he would taunt and laugh sarcastically. "Look at these thorns and thistles that you toil for everyday!"

"Leave us alone, Matata! What else are you good at apart from fighting me?"

"I will fight you again and again. Whatever is bad must be spat out. Look at my bananas. They bend with the heaviness of the huge clustered bunches! My sugarcane is juicy and succulent. That is what a husband would provide for you! My barns are full of cassava and maize from the last season! Now, this part of the farm that you are clearing is exhausted, and the soil needs rest. So, stop clearing it."

Mum would continue working.

"Hey, I am talking to you, woman!"

Mum would stop working and walk past Uncle Matata. Isate and I would run after her. Uncle Matata seemed to be ever-present, ready to soil whatever little happiness we ever had.

There was the day, for instance, when I came home with my report card. I had performed very well at school. I was in Class 6. Mum was in a good mood, and I took advantage to ask a question that had been bothering me.

"Mum, why does Uncle hate us so much?" I asked.

"He doesn't want us to stay here any longer. You are boys, and you are growing fast. Maybe he worries you will ask him for inheritance—land. Even so, don't worry. One day you will have your own home! Just keep working hard, and we shall soon be out of this misery. Don't worry about Matata. This is just for a season that will come to pass."

"I heard you calling me. Here I am!" Uncle Matata shouted as he stormed into the house.

I ran to him full of excitement and showed him my report card. Uncle Matata grabbed my report card and shoved me aside. I watched in horror as he tore it, shredding it into confetti.

"Stupid boy! You will never amount to anything!" he barked.

Mum flipped.

"Leave my son alone, Matata! It's your daughter Clara that is foolish, I heard she is always last in class!"

"I studied up to form six, and I have my grades to show for it. And you, Matata? Did you ever see a classroom?" Mum thundered.

"Why are you here if you went to school! You think people eat grades? Go cook your good grades, and serve them for dinner! Foolish woman!"

Matata kicked a plastic tin that was near him and stormed out, leaving me in tears as Mum consoled me.

That was the kind of dog's life that our uncle provided for us.

When Mum, at last, spoke that afternoon, it was nothing short of a bombshell that she dropped.

"I am going to Nairobi to search for a job! We can't all die here in this village! I have a friend who I am sure will help me get a job."

I felt a sense of panic. I was only ten years old, how on earth were Isate and I going to survive all by ourselves in that hellhole?

CHAPTER THREE

The following few days were somber with little talk in the house. Then one morning, she held our hands tightly and prayed for us. It was clear from her long-winded prayer that the time had come. She was going to leave us solely in the care of the good Lord above.

"How are we going to stay in this huge house alone? What of uncle Matata? Who will protect us from him?" we cried but Mum's mind was definitely made up. She was going to leave anyway.

Sure enough, she sneaked out of the house early the following morning before we could even figure out that what we feared most about what was happening.

Now it was just Isate and I; and then Isate went back to school to beg his teachers to allow him to continue studying. I was left to somehow fend for myself with no idea how I was going to do that.

My young mind went to work, conjuring up a plan. Mum and Isate had left me, an arid man in the fast-darkening desert of life, and the silence was ready to consume my very being. All I could see were mighty sand dunes that were ready to cover me. I had dreams, but as I stood there, all I could hear were the winds ready to blow me away like the sand motes in a desert tempest

Finally, I walked to a man who sold sugarcane at Mudete market and offered to help him keep his workplace clean in exchange of a few pieces of sugar cane. He agreed, and at the end of the day, he gave me five pieces that he had not sold. I took them, and that weekend I started selling sugarcane at Kigama Secondary school gate. The students bought my sugarcane, and with the money that I got, I bought more sugarcane for the following day. Later, I added avocados to my stock. I stole those from Uncle Matata's avocado trees in the wee hours of the night. It did not occur to me that it was wrong. I was just doing my best to survive in the situation as it was. I ate some of the avocados and sold the rest. I needed the money to buy food and books. I could only dream of paying school fees. Still, I went to school.

I found myself praying that the winds could carry me beyond the horizon, but then a still voice reminded me that I needed to start the walk of hope because the grounds were about to shift, and sooner or later, I would be buried by the sands of time, completely forgotten. So I set off on a journey—a journey through time—knowing very well that I had to fight hard to go past the dunes to learn the language of the wind. Stumbling on an oasis would be a miracle.

***

I was sent home from school many times for tuition fees, but I always returned empty-handed, begging the teachers to let me stay, as I had no one to pay my school fees. They sent me away again and again, but I never gave up. I walked out of the school compound and then walked right back in. I loved being in school . . . reading books. Books were an escape from my current reality. This made Mr. Wanyonyi, our English and Science teacher, take interest in me.

Mr. Wanyonyi was my best teacher, and he became a father figure to me. He took particular interest in my studies, as I always performed well in his subjects, English and Science. He knew my mother as well, and he knew I was living alone, so he had taken it upon himself to inquire from time to time how I was managing the issues of my little life. I loved him, as he made such a huge difference in my life. He encouraged me to work hard and taught me life skills, especially when I ran out of sugarcane and avocados.

Over time, I learned that I could negotiate with a neighbor to sweep his compound in exchange for a meal or to go to the stream to fetch water in exchange for flour that would last me for a few days. This exposure built my tenacity and shrewdness in business and my overall approach to life. It gave me confidence to rebuild my self-esteem and self-worth that had deteriorated to rock bottom. It gave me the confidence to try even bigger ventures. However, this did not ease the pain of living alone. I would have given anything to have my mother back. I missed her every day.

In school, my rival for the top marks in class was Mwenesi, the math whiz. He was a true bookworm. We loved and hated each other in equal measure. In time, our academic bond grew into a strong friendship, which also meant that Mwenesi would share some of his packed lunch with me, and that kept me going but it wasn't always enough to calm the hunger pangs. Nonetheless, time went by and soon we were in Class 8.

Life was not exactly good, but things were somehow settling into a steady, bearable flow that I was getting used to. Then another unexpected storm arose and stirred things around once more. One evening I was feeling so hungry, and after scouting the area of the property that I was allowed to farm, I found that there was nothing edible—only thorns stared back at me. Uncle Matata's farm, on the other hand, blossomed with green leafy vegetables, maize, and cassavas that beckoned enticingly. I knew his caretaker guarded the farm with his own life, but I stealthily went in and uprooted a few stems of kale in a hurry, fearing that if I plucked them, he was going to catch me in the act.

What I did not know is that Uncle Matata himself was on patrol. He saw me and screamed at me. I sprinted back to the house, but he was too fast for me. I found him standing right there at my door as if he had zapped himself over there by some kind of mysterious magic. I dropped the stems that I was holding and turned to run, but as usual, he was nightmarishly fast. He grabbed me by the scruff of my neck and shook me until my teeth rattled against each other, then proceeded to thrash the living daylights out of me. My brother Isate, who had been sent home for school fees that evening, heard my cries and came out. He found Uncle Matata stepping on me like someone who was dealing with a lethal snake and uttering his usual obscenities.

"Today you must leave this compound," he roared.

Matata stormed into the house and came back with my books. He then went back to fetch Isate's and lumped the whole lot of them into one pile.

"Yeah! clever boys, huh? let me see who is clever now!"

I cried as my books were consumed by the fire he lit. My dreams and my hopes were literally going up in flames. Before long, they had turned up into a pile of ash!

Isate blew his lid off. "What do you think you are doing? Are you mad?" he shouted at Uncle Matata.

"Today you must leave or I will burn down this house!" Uncle Matata yelled back.

"We're not going anywhere. Where do you want us to go this late in the night?" Isate asked defiantly.

Uncle Matata turned to Isate and gave him a few good lashes of his cane before Isate could run off. Isate, out of rage, ran into the house and came out brandishing a cooking stick which he swung into action. The huge stick missed Uncle Matata's head by a whisker but landed across his shoulders. Isate gave Uncle Matata several whacks that left him wailing in pain, and his shirt was soon soaking in blood. Isate pushed him over and pounded his left leg in rage, causing him to scamper with a limp into his backyard. It all happened in a blur, and the true gravity of what we'd done hadn't even registered in our minds. We were still standing there, panting, with the adrenalin coursing copiously through our veins when Uncle Matata came back with his two vicious wolves of dogs snarling at his side. The growls of these two monsters grew more vicious as he sicced them at us.

In a fraction of a second, I felt teeth sink into my right thigh, and the pain was unlike anything I had ever felt before! I screamed and struggled to disentangle myself, but the dog's grip was too tight. I gave her one resounding kick forcing her to step back. At that moment, I knew I had to run. I didn't know where to, but I had to run. One of the dogs was in hot pursuit as I ran past the gate through the roadside bushes and down towards the valley that led to the stream. I couldn't stand another set of bites, so I kept running. I could hear my brothers' wails as he fought off the other dog. I could feel a warm rivulet of blood trickling down my leg as I sprinted for my very life, with my brother hot on my heels and the murderous dogs not very far behind us.

I jumped into the shallow stream and could hear Isate jumping in after me. We waded across, leaving the dogs barking angrily at us across the stream. I continued forward and soon got to a hut on the other side, panting, almost out of breath in the darkness that now embraced the night. While we ran, thick clouds had covered the lazy moon.

Isate joined me as I frantically shook the door, calling out for help. It was the only place we could think of that might offer us shelter at such a desperate hour. Every other door in that village would surely be slammed in our faces if we ever turned up there.

The owner, a wizened old woman who knew us, finally opened the hut with a kerosene lamp in her hands. Her name was Anguzuzu. She recognized my voice first and said, "Baraka, what is wrong? Why are you coming here this late tonight?"

"We have been chased away by Uncle Matata," I said, gasping for breath.

"What? Come in! Matata will kill you one day. He is so wicked! I truly hope that one day you will understand how his wickedness has caused your mother such pain!" she said as she ushered us into her grass-thatched cone hut. It had three rooms, a sitting area that was an open space, a room where she slept that was full of rags that made up her bed, and a small space with three cooking stones and a few tiny, sooty *sufurias* that served as a hearth. We stayed the night at her hut.

In the morning, we couldn't bring ourselves to ask for anything to eat. We could see the kitten, her faithful companion, was fast asleep right at the centre of the three cooking stones, a clear sign that nothing had been cooked.

The deep wound in my right thigh hurt badly, so Anguzuzu went to the bushes along the river and came back with tiny, green leaves that she squeezed into our wounds. The sap only elevated the pain, but she reassured us that that was the only medicine.

"We must go back to Uncle Matata; he must take you back in!" Anguzuzu said.

"No! he will kill us!" Isate muttered, his voice choked with emotion.

"I'm not going back to those dogs—not again!"

"I have nothing here to offer. Matata must help you. Come on, let's go!" our host insisted.

She had a lot of convincing to do because we stayed put in her hut, the trauma of being battered by Uncle Matata and the scary experience of almost being eaten alive by his monster dogs still fresh in our young minds.

It was three days later that we limped into Uncle Matata's compound in the company of Anguzuzu.

To our utter shock, he had burned everything that belonged to us and demolished the house to ensure we never went back. In turn, he'd reported the assault to the area's assistant chief, so we didn't have anywhere we could seek redress. All my books and notes had been burned, and Isate's school work was gone too. I may as well have lain down and died. It seemed like it all was over for me.

"What brings you back to this compound?" Uncle Matata's coarse voice reverberated. I was now clinging onto Anguzuzu, every nerve in me alert.

"You are evil, Matata. Why have you done this to these little boys? You are fully aware that Baraka is . . ." Anguzuzu's shrill, tremulous voice rose in admonition.

Uncle Matata wasn't listening. He wasn't ready for any talks. He had gone back to his backyard, and I could hear the dogs barking. I didn't wait for a second signal. I limped towards the gate with Isate and Anguzuzu right behind me. It was definitely back to her forlorn little hut with us.

Coupled with the fact that he had been forced to repeat form two since he couldn't afford the school fees, he decided to drop out of school soon after that incident and started soliciting for menial jobs at Mudete market.

One of the irreplaceable treasures that had burned up with our house was my favorite album of newspaper cuttings, which was my most treasured possessions. I had collected tons of pictures from magazines and newspapers that I picked by the roadside, most of which having been used to wrap beef and other products in the market place. Whenever I picked one that I found interesting, I cut off the juicy stories and glued them into my album using the sticky sap from Uncle Matata's euphorbia fence.

I walked to school as soon as the dog bite on my thigh healed somewhat and scabbed over. It was a wonder that I hadn't caught rabies or something from that dog. Either Uncle Matata had vaccinated it, Anguzuzu's herbs had worked, or someone big somewhere up there was watching out for me. I narrated to Mr. Wanyonyi what had happened.

I was now a candidate. Mr. Wanyonyi counselled me against dwelling on the goings-on at home. "You have excelled in your studies despite all the odds, Baraka. All that you need to do is pass your final examination. Forget all that happened to you, and focus on making your future great!" he said. He put one hand on my shoulder and gazed earnestly into my eyes.

"Promise me you will do this for your mother, to make her proud!" he beseeched me.

I hesitated, then said to him before nodding uncertainly. "Yes, I promise."

I don't know how that is going to happen, I thought.

Mr. Wanyonyi took me in, relieving me, at last, of the worst of my worries.

We still had two terms, and so I continued to study with Mwenesi, borrowing his notes and preparing hard for the forthcoming exams.

Even though a lot of the weight I had been carrying around had been lifted by Mr. Wanyonyi, I still thought of Mum every day and longed for a reunion. It gave me such a terrible feeling. I longed for that day when I could reach out to her and see her again. A year had gone by since the time she had sent a message through Mukombozi, a neighbor, whose sons were living in Nairobi. She had sent him with a telephone number that we could reverse call at the community booth at Mudete. I put this aside and concentrated on preparing to sit for my final primary school examination.

Immediately after finishing the Kenya Certificate of Primary Education (KCPE), I felt a big burden lift off my shoulders. Suddenly the urge to call Mum returned. I wanted to join her in the big city, Nairobi. I had never been to Nairobi, but I had heard of the high life and the skyscrapers that dotted the city and I wanted to see the glamour for myself. I was excited and anxious at the same time. I hardly slept.

The following morning, I snuck from Mr. Wanyonyi's house and went to the telephone booth in Mudete. It was still early morning, but I found eight people already queuing at the booth. I joined the queue amid curious looks from the mostly old folks on the line who were waiting to talk to rich relatives, sons, or daughters that lived in Nairobi. Their faces said, *who in the city would talk to a scruffy looking boy like you?* Most relatives migrated to the cities to search for jobs. I waited patiently in the queue as most people were turned away, their heads hung in disappointment after the operator failed to connect them to the people they wanted to talk to. There was a middle-aged man who banged the phone with such anger I thought the booth was going to crumble. This was after it had swallowed all his coins that he had carefully lined on the coin slot. He left cursing the phone, frustrated.

My turn finally came, and by that time, six people were already behind me, urging me to be fast.

I dialed 900 and waited anxiously as the dial tone reverberated in my eardrums. After some time, a gentle voice answered, "Hello," said the woman, "and thank you for calling the operator. What can I do for you?"

I was so excited, I quickly answered, "Please, kindly give me a reverse call."

"Where to?" she asked

"Nairobi."

"Can you give me the number and your name please?"

I read her the number that Mum had written to me; I had kept it for more than a year.

"And what's your name and the name of the person you would like to reverse call you?" she asked

"My name is Baraka Uside, and I would like to place a reverse call to Jane Uside"

She asked me to replace the receiver and wait.

I gently replaced the receiver and waited for another five anxious minutes, fighting off a huge wave of impatience from the other people in the line, who were convinced the operator wasn't going to call back.

The phone rang after about six minutes later, and I didn't wait for a second buzz. I grabbed it, and on the other end of the line was the most beautiful voice—one that tickled my nerves and made my heart skip. It was the voice of my mother. We had not spoken for more than a year, and here we were brought together by the wonders of technology.

I talked on and on with my mother. I didn't care what the other people in the queue thought. It was my mother, and the whole world could wait. Twenty minutes later, there were shouts from the people in the queue, and I could hardly hear what Mum was saying. I bid her farewell and promised to board the bus that very Saturday to Nairobi—a land of dreams and possibilities.

"I will pay your bus fare on arrival. Remember, the very last station of the bus, Baraka. Don't alight anywhere else," she insisted. There were, of course, no mobile money transfer services then. That would have made things so much easier.

I was super excited. I had called her on Monday, and I was going to Nairobi on Saturday of the same week. The few days that I had to wait seemed like an eternity.

I sat in the banana plantations on Wanyonyi's farm and smiled to myself as I tapped the loose soil with the stick in my hands, allowing my mind to wander into the great fortunes that lay ahead of me in Nairobi. The wound on my right thigh was still sensitive. It seemed that it was going to stay with me for the rest of my life. The thought of Isate at the marketplace scared me stiff. I dreaded bumping into him, but nothing was going to stop me. No one was going to stop me! My heart raced with excitement as I daydreamed about jumping into my mother's loving arms. But still I had to convince Wanyonyi, as he didn't want to release me to the city on my own.

He reacted exactly the way I had expected him to when I asked for his permission to travel.

"I can't allow you to leave alone, Baraka. It's too dangerous!" he shook his head firmly.

"No, I will manage. Mum will pay my fare when I arrive in Nairobi!" I argued. The thought of not seeing my mum was almost unbearable.

"But the bus conductors will not allow you on board without the money!" he reasoned, his voice softening into a pleading note.

"No, they will. Mum will pay them! I will ask Mum to pay them extra money!" I shot back heatedly.

Mr. Wanyonyi would hear none of it. He wasn't going to allow me to leave on my own.

I was going to go anyway, and indeed I left soon after.

The chilly breeze tore through the perforations in my tattered shorts as I hurtled towards Mudete market, racing against time. Wanyonyi would soon realize I was missing, and he would be looking for me. I flew through the roadside bushes and through to the gravel road, unaware of the stones that were trained to cut through my bare soles. My heart was pounding, and my breath was erratic when I arrived at the bus station, my lungs threatening to explode. I was now holding tightly to my nylon paper bag that contained a half-torn t-shirt and a rugged pair of blue shorts.

Suddenly a wave of fear engulfed me. How was I going to start the conversation with the bus conductors? *Mr. Wanyonyi had been right. Oh, how foolish I had been not to listen to him*, I thought.

Passengers with heavy bags and sacks full of food were milling the bus station, waiting for the Mbukinya, Eldoret, Express, and Ugwe buses to arrive.

Before long, the whole bus station was a beehive of activity. The Mbukinya bus was the first to arrive about an hour later, and the driver seemed high on something, honking as if to wake up the whole village to come and board. Two Eldoret Express buses were right behind in the same madness. They pulled up to the bus stop, and passengers started boarding in a hurry, the conductors jostling for customers and rushing them onto the bus.

"Hey you! There's no time to waste!"

"Hurry up! *Wewe mama kuja hapa!* 'The lady the tout was talking to moved closer to the bus.

"Beba! Nai Twende!"

"Jaza, faster oya! Wewe!" He continued to call on passengers to board to Nairobi.

It was chaotic.

I took the step and timidly went to Mbukinya. I stepped into the bus and made my way in, just as I was about to sit the second conductor who was seated at the entrance seat asked, *"Wewe Kijana uko na Nani?"* The conductor demanded to know whom I was traveling with.

"I am alone!" I said timidly.

"Ongea wewe! He wanted me to speak up.

"Where are you going?"

"To Nairobi!"

"Lete pesa yako!" His hand was right in my face demanding for the bus fare.

"My Mum said she will pay you."

"Where is your mum!"

"In Nairobi, she will be . . ."

He didn't wait for me to finish my statement. His eyes suddenly turned red and, in a rage, he gave me a resounding whack across my back and pushed me out of the bus, kicking me as hard as he could. Losing control, I spilled over the staircase, scraping my knees.

"Kwenda huko kabisa! Peleka mchezo mbali, shenzi!" he shouted, calling me a fool and imploring me to take my games and stupidity elsewhere—away from his bus.

As he shouted, I wasn't hearing his voice. It was Uncle Matata's voice that I was hearing.

"Stupid boy! You will never amount to anything!"

It seemed weird that even a stranger knew I was stupid! But was I?

As I got back to my feet, tears milling in my eyes, I almost fainted. Was I seeing ghosts? From a distance, I could see Matata limping towards the bus in the company of Wanyonyi.

I looked at my wounds, I remembered the dogs, and thought to myself, *No way am I going back!*

They were now closer. "I told you these brats are a nuisance," said Uncle Matata. "And the whole village thinks *I'm* the problem. Now see for yourself, Wanyonyi." They were almost close enough to grab me at this point. I locked eyes with my uncle, and at that moment, I knew I only had one option! To run!

Ugwe bus had just arrived at the station and the conductor was letting in passengers in a hurry, trying to catch up with the other three buses that had just left the bus station. Another Eldoret Express bus was busy with passengers.

Uncle Matata was now holding my hand firmly, "Baraka, see what your brother did to my leg? You must pay for it! You are going back with me!"

I gathered all the strength in my bones and disentangled myself from his grip and started running away from the bus station, heading back home. My mind was a jumble of chaotic thoughts. I looked back, and Wanyonyi and Uncle Matata were right behind me in hot pursuit, Uncle Matata's stomach swinging like a pendulum.

Passersby watched the chase in amusement, not knowing what was going on. Uncle Matata stretched his hand to grab my shirt, but I made a quick turnaround, causing him to lose his balance and come down with a thud, shaking the whole ground beneath him like an earthquake.

I ran back to the bus station and hid behind Eldoret Express bus, then stepped into the humongous crowd of passengers that was at the station.

I slid past a woman who was struggling to carry her two children and her bags at the same time.

"Let me help you Ma'am!" I said to her as I took one of her bags and entered the bus.

"Ahsante sana kijana yangu, she thanked me respectfully as her son as I passed by the conductor into the bus!

She was right behind me, and the conductor shielded us as he hung onto the door's metal bars, banging the bus and shouting at the driver to leave.

"Twende, Twende! Dere!"

The bus zoomed from the bus station, and peering out the window, I locked eyes with Uncle Matata again. He looked at Wanyonyi, who was equally startled, then looked at me again, eyes blank.

It was going to be the start of yet another journey—a journey through time.

CHAPTER FOUR

The issue of the fare did not arise until several kilometers away, when we were already past Kapsabet town, some fifty kilometers away. The conductor had probably assumed that I was part of the brood of the lady whose bag I had helped to carry. Now that I thought about it, how on earth did my mother imagine that the bus crew would be so understanding as to allow me to travel, with just the promise of their money when we arrived? Perhaps people as kind-hearted as her thought that all humans were like them.

Besides, there were no means, then, for her to send me the bus fare. She would have to wait for a long time for a trust worthy relative who would be coming home, and she could send her with the money, but this was urgent. I needed to join her, and none of us could have waited.

I will pay your bus fare on arrival. Remember the very last station of the bus Baraka, don't alight anywhere else. Her words on phone kept ringing in my ears.

I had been worried sick that the conductor would ask for the bus fare as soon as we left Mudete and when he discovered I was a stowaway, throw me off the bus. This did not happen. Still, I was really worried, and my heart was in my mouth by the time he was asking the lady for my bus fare.

'*Wapi fare yake?*" the conductor poked the lady I had helped with the bag.

"Why are you asking me for his fare?" she protested with a puzzled look on her face.

"Aren't you together?" the conductor's face turned into a cloudy sky, ready to rain a storm.

"*Harakisha kijana!*" His rugged hands outstretched right into my face, urging me to hurry up and pay.

"My mum will pay you when we get to the bus station in Nairobi!" Now it didn't sound as reasonable and clever as it had sounded inside my head. I knew I was definitely in great trouble.

"What! Stop joking I don't have time to waste!" His finger, thick as a sausage, was almost poking out my left eye—that's how close he thrust it into my face.

"Your fare now! Or I throw you out of the bus!"

He was now holding my t-shirt twisting it by the neck suffocating me. He was breathing heavily over my face, his eyes reddened and almost dripping blood. He yanked me out of my seat and descended on me with kicks and blows.

"Hey, you! Leave the boy alone! Do you want to kill him?" one man seated across the passageway shouted as I cried out for help and gasped for air, tears flowing down my cheeks.

"Here, I will pay half of his bus fare!" one woman shouted. The conductor loosened the grip on my windpipe.

"We will all alight if you touch the boy again!" another old man warned.

"I will leave him alone only after he has paid! *Lipa gari!*"

"Leave him alone. Don't you have children yourself?" the woman said as she handed the conductor some coins and an old note.

"This is not enough. *Dere shukisha huyu!*" he shouted at the driver to stop so that he could kick me out.

The driver slowed down.

"*Hatashuka! Akishuka na sisi tunashuka!*" a passenger shouted.

He gave in to the pressure from the crowd as everyone joined in and threatened to disembark if he decided to leave me anywhere on the road before we arrived at our destination.

I sat on the edge of the seat, stealing frequent glances at the conductor and hoping that he wouldn't descend on me again.

The six-hour journey to Nairobi was treacherous. I had never sat in a bus for such long hours. I had heard about Eldoret town, but seeing it with my eyes was mind boggling. After about an hour, we arrived in Nakuru, and its tall buildings tuned my mind to adventure. Then came Naivasha. Multiple flower farms on the expansive road were a sight to behold. The beautiful countryside sped by in a beautiful mirage, and the soft winds caressed my head, making me forget the discomfort of the bus. We survived the potholes and the crowded bus that stank of sweat, vomit, and dried fish. As the anxiety over the fare and my fear of the conductor faded away, I managed to enjoy the rest of the journey.

I rubbed my eyes in an attempt to improve the visibility, but I still couldn't clearly see anything outside.

I leaned closer to the lady who was seated next to me and asked, "Can you see outside? I can't see anything!" It suddenly looks like morning again! What's happening?"

She laughed heartily, then responded, "This is Limuru! That's the normal weather for this place."

Most of the women had now covered their children in loose heavy fabrics and *lessos*, and the passengers sitting next to the windows were now complaining, as half the windows had no glasses, sending a chilling breeze into the bus, causing us to fold our hands in an effort to stay warm. The visibility outside was almost zero. With the fog obscuring everything, it was a mystery how the driver managed to maneuver the almost ten-kilometer stretch with very limited visibility of the pothole-infested highway.

'*Kangemi! Kangemi oya!*" the conductor shouted. "Hey move closer to the door. No time to waste!" Kangemi was the first bus stop.

Half the passengers jostled towards the door, dragging and holding tightly onto their bags.

"Next bus stop! Westlands? Westlands *oya?*" *Twende dere!* He shouted, urging the driver to leave.

There was no one who alighted at that place for some reason. The conductor was now hanging precariously on the metal bars of the door, his unbuttoned shirt dancing in the wind like a flag.

"The next bus stop is going to be Machakos country bus," he shouted.

My heart skipped a beat. I was almost there! I could feel my breath coming faster. It had been a six-hour long journey, and I couldn't wait to see my mother who would be waiting for me.

Was I dreaming? I started seeing huge buildings glamorously rise into the sky, and I was now craning my neck to get a better view. The buildings zoomed by in a confusing mirage. It was mind-boggling: hordes of people milled by with hundreds of traders shouting out their prices in noisy, uncoordinated choruses. Hundreds of public-service vehicles, the *matatus*, zoomed by—some rusty and rugged and others beaming with fresh colors, playing loud music and honking as they sped by dangerously, swerving to avoid hitting smaller cars on the road.

The streets were flowing with masses of people. I had never seen such large numbers of people in one day. I trained my eyes on one bus driver as he negotiated the corners, the roundabouts, and the numerous streets of Nairobi. I wondered how one person could master all those roads and be able to drive. The bus finally came to a halt, and all I could see around me were dozens of buses with commuters picking their bags. Some conductors and their handymen were lifting what looked like heavy sofa sets and bags onto the roof racks of the buses. Other buses were offloading their overhead carriers. It was a chaotic station that breathed heavily of diesel from the revving engines. The handcart entrepreneurs pulled their wares.

'*Mwisho! Mwisho!* Machakos Country Bus station!" shouted the driver, informing us that this was the end of the journey. He shouted as he pounced hard on the door as if hitting a big stubborn drum.

He quickly turned to me, "Where is your mother?"

"I can't see her!" I said.

"You foolish boy! Look for your mother!"

"You can't escape with my money!" He was holding my hand tightly now as we alighted.

We waited at the bus station for about thirty minutes, but Mum was nowhere to be seen.

The conductor was pacing up and down in a rage, still holding my hand and murmuring to himself.

My mind was swirling in a big whirlwind of people!

How did Mum expect me to locate her in this sea of people! I thought to myself.

"*Leo utaona!* Today I will teach you a lesson," the conductor said, his eyes swollen and popping out of their sockets.

He finally lost his mind and descended on me with kicks and blows hurling me to the ground, stepping on me as if he was trying to kill a venomous snake. It was Uncle Matata all over again. Was this my life's destiny? Were the fates aligned against me?

The conductor hit me severely on the head and broke my nose. My nose was now bleeding profusely when another conductor came to my rescue and shoved him away. He led me to an improvised stone seat that had a carton on top of it and ushered me to sit down. The other conductor who had beaten me up hurled insults at me as he walked away.

Mama! Mama! I cried in pain as my sight grew hazy and flooded with tears. My t-shirt was soaking in blood.

"Yes, call your mother! You stupid boy! You think I'm your mother!" he shouted as he walked away.

I was still clinging to my nylon paper bag hysterically sobbing and wondering how I was going to locate Mum in the massive crowds of people that streamed endlessly in all directions like busy ants. My heart sank deeper with every thought. The world around me was drowned in its own apocalyptic frenzy.

After about another thirty minutes, a stout hand grabbed me by the hand and quickly pulled me up. I looked up, and right there before my very eyes was Mum!

My brain shattered for a moment, and for an instant, my heart forgot to beat. It was as if I was learning how to breath, taking in several breaths erratically.

Mum! Mum! I called out. She was pulling me through the crowds, almost breaking into a run. "Let's get out of here! Quickly!" she said, hustling through the multitudes of people. In a few minutes we were swallowed by the enormous crowds.

I opened my mouth in awe and I forgot to close it.

We were out of the bus station when Mum stopped with a sigh of relief.

"Huh! Baraka that was close!" she at last said, "Welcome to Nairobi . . ."

"I helplessly watched as the man mishandled you and beat you up, but there was nothing I could do, Son." She said in a sad voice.

But why! I gasped unbelievingly.

"I didn't have the money to pay him for your fare!"

She looked at me as she wiped the blood that had now clotted on my nostrils.

Her words came as a shock to me. I was bewildered.

You mean you saw all that, Mum?

"Yes, Baraka. I have been here since noon when the first bus arrived, and I have been keenly checking at a distance all the buses from Mudete as people alighted. My heart skipped with tremendous joy when I saw you alight, but I was worried when I saw the conductor holding your hand. I knew you were both looking for me, but I didn't have the money, so I waited patiently, testing how long he was going to hold onto you. I knew you were in trouble!"

"Mum, that tout could have killed me!" I was a little angry.

She didn't answer. We were off the hook, and maybe that had been her worst worry. Her hand tightly holding mine as we walked on, we trekked for about one hour, my legs getting sore, the evening quickly giving way to night. We passed several estates and massive buildings with many people also trekking and seemingly minding their business, not talking to each other. We trudged on.

I had been told that Nairobi was a haven of peace, of tranquility, and of dreamers ready to achieve their dreams. That careers were made in the city. That I would forget all my troubles and sleep on a king-size bed with a heavy mattress and a soft duvet to shield me from the cold night. That I would eat bread for breakfast spread with blue band and pea nut butter and a fried egg and a piece of sausage, and I would enjoy *pishori* rice and fried chicken. That I was going to enjoy hamburgers and chips, and soda and chapatis would be aplenty. I was lucky, and I skipped in joy as I thought about these things that were now becoming a reality. Indeed, we passed several fast food shops that had chicken and chips displayed in their large glass windows.

Clara had been right. I recalled all the stories that she had narrated—the way her dad, Matata, always treated her to a plate full of chips and a quarter chicken.

I was hungry, but I knew my mum was smart, and she understood this too well and that she was soon going to stop into one of those shops, and we would grab and enjoy a huge piece of chicken. I kept my hope alive, but we kept walking until finally there were no more shops.

We suddenly took a turn that led onto a murram road that was heavily crowded with human traffic, with hordes of people on every side of the street, peddling their merchandise at the top of their voices. Crowds of people were all over the place, haggling desperately.

The murram street was soggy, and we paddled through the mud like intelligent ducks. There were hundreds of makeshift kiosks loaded with different wares. We kept walking until we got to a mass of houses that were made of corrugated iron sheets bearing the dark brown of rust. It was a cryptic maze of turns that confused my feeble mind. Above the houses were low and loosely hanging electric cables that looked like a spider's web. There were hundreds of aerial TV antennae's that swayed in the air, and dozens of women were selling vegetables and sardines.

I saw a bunch of men selling what looked like tasty barbecues coiled and roasting on raised *jikos* with people milling around, buying, and eating them with a pinch of salt spread on wooden plates. As they swallowed, I too subconsciously swallowed my saliva, which hurtled into my empty stomach.

We had been walking for the last two hours, and we seemed to bypass the houses. We went farther down to what looked like the end of the road, and then my Mum announced that we were very close to our house.

Suddenly I could smell a strong stench of raw sewage, and I could hear something that sounded like a raging river. Mum made yet another turn, and we arrived at a shanty patched with pieces of corroded iron sheets. There was a narrow passageway that we all had to bend to enter. It looked like a cage. There were doors that faced each other, and I counted five on either side. Mum reached one door on the left at the end of the corridor. It had been loosely closed with an old tri-cycle padlock with multiple metal brands heavily patched onto the door. She simply pulled the padlock open without using any keys. How she did that was one of the many questions I silently decided to save for another day. There was a whole lot for me to process as it was.

We entered the one room house and mum triumphantly announced we had finally arrived home.

"Welcome to our home Baraka!" she said, calmly looking into my face.

I looked around through the light from the smoky kerosene lamp that she lit as soon as we entered. There was hardly anything in this room. There were no chairs and no table—only a lonely stove that sat in one corner of the room, a few sooty *sufurias*, and several plastic cups and plates. There was a small bed and a sisal mat spread on one side of the room and an old blanket folded into a crumbled heap. I could see a small, green suitcase in one corner of the room, and a line had been drawn down the center of the chamber. A plain, blue sheet was hanging, half folded on the line. I guessed it acted like a partition turning the room into two rooms, a bedroom which also served as a kitchen and the sitting room which ideally was an empty space.

My dreams were suddenly shattered, and my world crumbled at the horrid sight. My hopes for a better life had been thwarted by the miserable life that Mum lived.

I wanted to sleep, but my stomach grumbled in its emptiness. Mum lit the stove and warmed a plate of *githeri*, a mixture of beans and maize, which she served with a cup of plain water. I could count the number of beans on the plate, and the hard grains of maize stubbornly dominated every spoonful that I took. They were as hard as a stone and I trained my teeth to chew them cautiously. That's all we ate that night. As I munched the *githeri* that Mum had clearly cooked several days ago, I imagined the chickens that my cousin Clara had talked about—the *chapatis* that everyone had mentioned—and my heart sunk.

We slept on the hard surface of the cold floor, as the sisal mat was very thin. We shared the same blanket, and I quickly realized how tall I had grown in the recent past. The blanket couldn't cover us from head to toe, and we braved the cold night as the wind threatened to blow the flimsy iron sheets away and carry us along into the river that was raging right behind us.

Nevertheless, morning came. I had had a grueling day and couldn't imagine just how much I had experienced in a single day. It was horrific.

I was feeling pressed, and I urgently needed to use a toilet. I remembered Clara's words: *You sit on the toilet and flush your frustrations away with one swoop at a handle!* It sounded scary yet exciting, and here was a chance to experience it. Toilet matters were always guarded secrets and were rarely spoken about, especially between children and their parents—only in hushed voices.

"Mum, where is the toilet?" She looked at me with embarrassment and defeat all over her face.

"Is it too bad or can it wait?" mum asked

"I have been holding onto it since yesterday mum! I can't hold it any longer!"

"Okay, come. Let's go!"

She walked me outside of the shanty that early morning.

"Mum! What's that smell! "I said while holding my nose, trying to block my nostrils.

"We are next to this dirty river? It's very smelly!" I shouted, and as I stepped back into her arms,

I made the gruesome discovery that our shanty was the very last one bordering a river, that breathed raw sewage. There was a small, open field next to the river with long grass.

I looked at the river, and for an instant I missed the *Wakikuyu* river back in my village that flowed gracefully, unadulterated. You could see the beautiful pebbles lying with grace on its belly.

"Are we the last ones among these houses, Mum?" I said while craning my neck to scan the environment.

"Stop asking so many questions, Baraka!"

"Relieve yourself there quickly, and let's go back to the house!" she said to me as she pointed at the bush in front of me.

"I have never done it in the bush, Mum! It's not a short call, Mum. It's the other one!" I stuttered.

"Even that one! Just do it, Baraka. Be quick!" she said with a noticeable tinge of impatience and embarrassment in her voice.

I walked towards the field, and with every step my dignity was torn away, just as you would peel a banana—fast and furious. My heart was troubled. I had never defecated in the bush, so why was I going to do it for the first time in Nairobi? A city of dreamers? I took off my shorts, but the biting cold froze my bowels, and I couldn't empty them.

I went back to Mum who was standing there in guard, waiting for me. Shame and guilt enveloped both of our faces.

"Mum, it has disappeared!" I said, with a childish whine to my voice.

"When it comes back, you know what to do!" She said in a stern voice.

I soon realized there was no clean drinking water like what we had back in Kisangula village. There was no food to eat, no friends to play with, and the playgrounds were the narrow maze of streets. If you hit a ball hard enough it would unceremoniously invite itself into a neighbor's bed. There was no one to talk to, no neighbor to borrow anything from, no warm blankets, and no avocado trees to climb. We were all alone—isolated. I thought longingly about Mr. Wanyonyi's house, and he hadn't even wanted me to leave! Had I done something I was going to deeply regret?

"I am going to work Baraka. Stay indoors, okay?" Mum said once we were back at her shack. She tied her headscarf at the nape of her neck and nodded.

"Yes, Mum!"

"This is Nairobi, not Kisangula. You can't just go anywhere as you like," she admonished.

"There is an extra plate of *githeri*. That will be enough till I come back."

I remembered the many times I could get to my uncle's mango tree and pluck raw mangoes to wade off the hunger pangs. Now that option wasn't available. I remembered how I used to dig for a sweet potato that had failed to grow and turn it into a meal. I remembered how I would work for a neighbor to get a tin of maize that I could mill and get some flour for a plate of *ugali*. Now that was all behind me. I wanted to go back home, but the mention of the word home scared me. Where was my home anyway?

I was in Nairobi with Mum, and she was family. I felt at home around her. She was all I had. I sighed, reaching some kind of resolution.

The sun's rays had fully permeated the four walls of my dwelling, and I listened as the iron sheets began to make rattling sounds in response to the sweltering heat waves. My whole body was now soaked in sweat, and I couldn't stand it anymore. I walked outside the shanties and sat on a stone. The smell of raw sewage fanned the air, filling the bushes, the crevices, the corridors, and the air above. Every particle was heavily soaked with a pulsating stench. Even the dust particles smelled of raw sewage.

I saw several people go in and out of the bush, their heads still high, as if nothing bothered them at all. They had normalized indignity and learned how to live with it. Children too easily mixed with the adults and old men in a field that they had turned into a public utility.

Women too walked beside men and relieved themselves in any of the open spaces that were available. The people had to jump over raw mounds of human waste that looked like tiny ant hills— some of which fresh, having been downloaded minutes before, and others dry. The stench was defiantly consistent.

***

By the third day, I had joined the fray and jumped the mounds too. I did so with a miserable smile, and every time I did that, a part of me died. On the third day while I was getting out of the field, I bumped into a voluptuous woman who was busy relieving herself. I was totally startled, but she simply smiled and let me move by, it was normal for her. I came to appreciate the value of a latrine—a place to relieve yourself in private. It wasn't a need any more. It was a right that everyone was entitled to, and it was very unfortunate that we didn't have this right. I remembered the many times I had lamented the dirty, acrid, smelly latrines we had in school—the ones with graffiti dotted all over the walls. I thought of the many times I had launched a rocket down the hole and waited for the bomb to explode. It was always an exciting experience, and I was now denied that opportunity. Instead of the bomb, I had to watch my own waste build up like bad luck.

Two weeks flew by in quick succession, and I could count the number of days I had had a real meal. Some evenings, Mum returned home carrying chicken innards, gizzards, chicken legs and chicken heads that were deep fried in sooty pans along the sewage lines. These chicken delicacies were meant to be dumped. They had been sourced from the eateries in the central business district, but they found their way into our stomachs. Mum had to save for a week to afford those scraps.

My mother faced all this with the steady stoicism she had maintained all her life. Then, just as I was getting used to the steady humdrum routine of my new home, fate dealt us yet another blow.

One evening, Mum was away working late. It was raining heavily. and gusty winds threatened to pull off the roof of our humble abode. I bundled myself in a corner of the room, tightly holding onto the main frame that secured the thin walls in place. The water kept lapping at the edge of our house until, finally, one of the not-so-clever old sheets gave in, and a huge torrent of water gushed through our abode.

The slum was on a riparian land. The river beside had endured so much defilement and pollution, and it had come to reclaim its rightful path. Before I knew it, the room was half-filled with water, and I was starting to feel as if I was being carried away. Everywhere there were screams, but I had learned that on this side of life, we were alone, and therefore it really didn't matter how loud one screamed. No help would be forth coming. We all needed help, so there was no one to help the other.

So I hung onto the frame as I watched the patched door get washed away by the raging waters, our sisal mat was clinging onto the doorway. I made a simple prayer to God to preserve it, but my prayer was intercepted by the evil winds. I watched helplessly as it was swept away towards the river. Our stove and all the utensils had already been swept away. I cried my heart out, devastated at how Mother Nature had decided to whip us—to punish us further.

Suddenly something hit my head hard, and I briefly lost consciousness.

CHAPTER FIVE

W hen I regained back my senses, the reality hit me hard. All hell had broken loose, and we were all definitely going to die. At last, God seemed to have heard the prayers screamed, moaned, and sobbed out to him from the several shanties, because the torrent eventually eased and subsided.

It had been a terrible storm, lasting at least two hours, and I was lucky that the raging waters had not swept me away. I waited for about one hour as I watched the water level go down. With the wisdom of a duck, I waded through the waters to check the damage and find out if my neighbors had survived the deluge. Everyone had suffered massive losses, as their household items swept away into the river.

There was no price tag on what the storm had swept away. There'd been papers that were the only evidence that some of them could ever show as proof of having attained an education, birth certificates they had toiled to receive from the government—the only true certificate in their lives—and family photos they had clung to for years, passing the memories from one generation to the other.

Panic swept through the already stressed-out throng of humanity, when Achieng', one of the neighbors that was a friend of my Mum, suddenly came from where she had sheltered from the storm. She hadn't been able to identify her one-room house amongst the half-submerged shanties, and her haunting wails further chilled our bones.

"My baby!" she wailed, "I left him in my house. Has anyone seen my baby! My baby, Ryan! Oh, my baby! Where is my baby?"

A buzz of alarm stirred the small crowd as people made all kinds of weird sounds to express their sympathy, sadness, or shock.

"I must find him," Achieng screamed, rushing towards the river bank. Several voices rose in unison to dissuade her.

"What? You'll be swept away too!" someone shouted coarsely.

"There is no use for that, my sister. It's too late," a more sympathetic voice pointed out as several hands restrained the grieving mother. Everyone was milling around trying to console her in the drizzle, but she was inconsolable. She ran towards the river in a bid to look for her son, but everyone knew that was a run towards the arms of death.

Two men ran after her and grabbed her as she fought and pleaded to be allowed to go but everyone knew it was an act in futility. Her baby, like many others before him, had gone for good.

Mum came much later in the evening, as she had been restrained by the rains. She found us clustered together like a bunch of sheep, ready to brave the evening cold. Njoroge, a middle-aged man, managed to light a bonfire with old tires, and we warmed ourselves in silence. It reminded me of that rainy night when we were thrown out by Uncle Matata. It was only that this time the situation was even more dire— but there were so many more of us in the same situation.

At the break of dawn, the slum was busy, men trying to repair their houses with any available materials from cartons to scrap metal. It brought back to my mind something that

I must have picked up from Mr. Wanyonyi: that one man's rubbish is another man's treasure. What other people 'higher up' had discarded was so valuable to that crowd of derelicts. Few of the people moved around with long faces, sobbing or beating their breasts with bitterness. Actually, a buzz of conversation steadily continued as we worked, helping each other in every way we could. There was the occasional sound of laughter too, as the people made fun of themselves and each other and their situation.

"How is your mansion coming along!" a neighbor hissed.

"At least all the spiders have been washed away!" another one responded.

"The bed bugs have survived with us!"

The chatter cheered us on.

My mother held a half-rotten piece of timber in place as I hammered a rusty nail into it with a piece of rock to hold our rickety door in place. At one point, I hit my forefinger and danced around in pain as my mum pleaded with me to let her look at the finger. It wasn't injured much, and the pain soon passed, leaving a darkened bruise.

Most of the little shanties had been restored to, more or less, their previous condition. The cheerful banter had grown even louder as the people's spirits picked up.

"Twende swimo!" one boy suddenly shouted, urging the rest to join him to go swimming, and many of the boys and young men excitedly agreed. I had never swum before but wondered where the swimming pool had been hidden. I tagged along eagerly, drawn by their palpable excitement. I badly needed a distraction from the previous night's scary events.

The "swimming pool" was an abandoned quarry that naturally filled up with water after heavy torrents like the one last night.

Looking at the excitement from those boys, I understood that behind every adversity there is always something to learn or to celebrate. It takes a lot to kill the indefatigable human spirit.

When we got to the mouth of the quarry, I was astounded at its size; it *was* like a huge, natural swimming pool. I quickly learned that whenever it rained, water could collect inside, and people would go in to have fun. It was one happy community. In misery and joy, we were bound at the hip.

It was going to be such fun! Some of the boys wasted no time in stripping into their birthday suits, plunging right into the quarry and swimming around like a crowd of weird humanoid fish.

The quarry was full to the brim, but no one seemed to care! They threw themselves in with the same lack of inhibition with which they'd stripped.

Then, all of a sudden, a scared scream rose above all the other voices. Everyone froze wherever they were.

"Help!" the person yelled once more. Tragedy. There was bound to be tragedy after so much exuberance. There had been too much joy to go unpunished.

It was Maiko, the scruffy cross-eyed boy that lived just two shacks away from my mother's house. He had been enjoying himself with his brother, Sami, and the others when the daredevil streak in him inspired him to swim to the deeper end.

His calls for help grew more frantic as his head kept sinking and bobbing up again.

Sami, seeing that Maiko was in trouble, was calling for help and swimming out to his brother with the agility of a dolphin. Maiko's hand was now quickly disappearing under the expansive waters, and Sami reached out for him as the crowd watched in anguish. They were the best swimmers the slum had, and no one else would dare venture into these mighty waters, apart from their dad who also was well known to be a great swimmer.

Sami, after a tremendous struggle, reached his brother and started to help him afloat.

"Go and call Mzee Assava," one elderly man who had rushed to the scene after being drawn by the commotion shouted.

All the other swimmers were now out of the water watching helplessly from the mouth of the quarry, except the two who were fighting to remain afloat.

Mzee Assava came running to the scene in no time, and quickly dove into the deep end like a seal, fully dressed, desperate to save his sons.

Sami's mouth was opening and closing like that of a landed fish. He slipped out of his brother's hands and sank. Sami tried hard to paddle with his arms and feet, but watching from the edge, I thought he must have developed a cramp or muscle pull in his legs. He gave one scared yell, just when his father was about to grab him, and sank to the same depths that had swallowed his brother.

A whole crowd had now gathered around the mouth of the gigantic quarry wailing and crying, jumping up and down in distress. I was now sweating profusely, scared stiff.

Mzee Assava was now alone in the quarry trying to find his sons, fighting against time to save them. Twice he dove deep into the quarry and came back on the surface to catch his breath. The third time when we he went under, we waited with bated breath for Mzee Assava to rise back with his two sons in his hands, but he didn't. He had been swallowed by the quarry. The tension around the quarry was electric and the air around us could not relax it was stretched tight to the limit with anxiety.

As the seconds turned to minutes . . . and eventually into an hour, then two . . . it became very clear that indeed all was lost.

CHAPTER SIX

Kinoti had rushed to the nearby booth and called the town council for help, but they only came three hours later. The crowd of onlookers grew, swelling around the quarry as they watched the Town Hall divers. It wasn't for many hours that the three bodies were retrieved at last.

Excitement rippled among the crowd and cries of grief and pain rang through the air as many of the onlookers pushed and jostled to catch a glimpse of each body. Soon a much louder and pain-filled voice rose above all the others as Mrs. Assava arrived at last.

She had been away at the market selling her vegetables and only learned of the tragic news long after the fact.

She was wailing uncontrollably, and as soon as she saw the three bodies of her husband and her two sons she collapsed and died on the spot.

Another neighbor also fainted and had to be attended to.

It was tragic. How much were we supposed to see in less than twenty-four hours? The rest of that day was spent in a numb daze of grief and shock. No one was sure what they were supposed to do or who they were supposed to turn to. The government? The local elected leaders? Those had not been seen in that dump of a slum since the last elections.

It wasn't until the next day that officials from the town hall visited the area.

"We will launch thorough investigations into what happened here yesterday! No stone will be left unturned! The culprits who left the quarry open will be brought to book," one of the officials roared. With his voice choked by passion, he managed to sound more bereaved than us.

"Heads are going to roll," the town clerk was barking into the microphone as if the culprit was amongst us. The crowd didn't pay attention to the rhetoric. They had enough worries troubling their minds. They were thinking of how to bury their own, and they didn't have any more room left in their brains.

"*Serikali saidia!*" one drunk man shouted, asking the government to help.

"No one eats words!" Mum said with a shrug.

"The community here has heard such promises before, and we all know that nothing will happen!" she said testily.

Soon after the town council officials left, other visitors came. A group of well-dressed men and women—some in shorts with sandals and multi-colored happy socks—were streaming in with cartons of milk, bread, and blankets. Mum pointed at them and said, "And those are the neighbors who reside over the walls, my son. When you get beyond those walls one day, you will understand that they are not like us. They have everything that money can buy, and they have erected those walls to separate themselves from us."

"Who are they, Mum, and what do they want here?"

"They only come to these slums here when we are faced with a calamity like this one, but they can never come up with anything that can help prevent these tragedies from occurring in the first place. We provide labor for them, nurse their children, cook their foods, and tend their gardens, and in return they pay us the meager wages that keep us going." Mum continued "This happens here year in, year out, but there have never been any measures in put in place to prevent or manage these calamities. Here in the slums we are a forgotten lot. We are on our own, and we live each day as it comes to us." Her voice sounded helpless yet angry. "Tomorrow you will see the politicians here. They will dish handouts and give us food. They can't empower us to fish, so they bait us with the fish, and we readily bite the bait. Poverty is the ugly ghost that needs to be exorcised, my son. None of us here has a voice, and the power of choice has been stifled and stolen from us. Unless the cycle of poverty breaks, we will remain slaves for years to come, my son. We are like sheep. After being fed, we are led to the shearer's house, and we don't care about the pain as our wool is taken away so long as our stomachs don't ache from the hunger. We are fine, but then they lead us into the slaughter house—into the abattoir of life—and we blindly enter as our destinies and the future of our generations and generations to come are all killed on the altar of greed. One day you will understand this, Son," she said, her tone turning coarse.

"Mum, I now have my own blanket and a new mattress! My blanket is red. Let me see yours, Mum!"

Mum ignored my excitement. She simply looked at me and me and frowned, probably displeased that her long speech didn't seem to have made any impression on me.

The donations from well-wishers kept streaming in: foodstuff and bedding . . . strangely, condoms and sanitary pads! One lady with a hawkish beak who made a long speech after delivering the latter two kept calling them "non-food items."

As more days went by, the leaders among us organized a rag-tag committee and managed to raise some funds for the burial of the dead. The task itself was herculean. Young men had to brave vigils, begging from fellow dwellers while holding the pictures of the deceased, but these efforts only raised a few coins. Of course, political leaders chipped in—with the cameras rolling so that every act of charity was recorded for payback come the next elections. The somber mood that engulfed the short service that was organized before the bodies were sent upcountry for burial was a testament to how the slum was emotionally united together to help each other sometimes even beyond their own capabilities.

Two days after the sendoff, yet another tragedy struck. We were awoken in the dead of night by screams from the neighboring slum. This time it was fire, not water. As usual, its cause was unknown. All the houses were in flames as families ran trying to salvage whatever their hands could hold onto. We ran through the cold towards the huge inferno, but there was no running water in the slum—and no marked roads. The town hall fire engine arrived two hours later as the fire razed on. They couldn't reach the heart of the fire, but they reached the edge, their deafening sirens engulfing the air all around us, they mounted the horse pipes, only to discover the tanks were empty and they didn't have any water. Their ineptitude was truly appalling.

I turned to my mum and told her, "For sure, investigations will be done and no stone will be unturned."

She looked at me, and gave me a weak smile. "Yes, Son, you are learning fast. Yes indeed, investigations will determine why these fire engines didn't have water! Let's wait for the answers tomorrow morning, but meanwhile, let's see if we can help." she moved closer to the crowds that were still salvaging their charred items from the fire, it was an act of futility.

When morning came, hundreds of slum dwellers were homeless, still rummaging through the charred remains, looking for anything valuable that may have been spared. The scrap metal dealers were the biggest winners.

There were a dozen news anchors in their high heels and pinstriped suits interviewing the residents to explain what happened.

Mum looked at me and said, "Here, Son, we make the news, but unfortunately the news doesn't make anything for us!" Our misery appeals to the viewers. We are heavy capital and it's in the interest of many for us to remain the way we are, but we have to fight it. Some of us might not live to see the gains of the fights, but you need to live to see the gains, Son. This madness should stop!" she said, anger building in her voice.

Soon, it was over as suddenly as it had begun. The people salvaged whatever they could of their meager possessions and moved to another slum or began building other ramshackle shanties. Life stubbornly went on!

It was a tragedy to live in the slum, and I felt that every day was as unpredictable as it could get. Our lives in the slum had been loosely perched on a short pier that led into the mystic sea of life that was determined to religiously dispense its daily dosage of misery to us. It was a hotbed of misery. We lived by day in misery and went to bed with our daily dose. It wasn't meant to cure us—no. We were being poisoned and broken down over time. I didn't want to die that way. Most evenings, I could hear gun shots, and I knew that another soul had been felled either by gangsters or by the police. There was an intricate web of syndicates, and my small, timid mind couldn't unravel the mysteries.

In one dark alley, one could access marijuana and *mchele* (used by criminals to drug their victims). In another adjacent alley, one could access illicit brews—some laced with methanol that caused victims to go completely blind. It didn't matter what business people engaged in; people had to survive, and they didn't care anymore what they did for survival. Life had pushed them to their elastic limits and they couldn't retract back to their innocent selves. One didn't have to go too far to access all sorts of contraband items. They were readily available. The authorities knew about it, but they had a finger in every pie too.

Our immediate neighbor was selling *chang'aa*, a local brew, illegally, and many were the days the local authorities came to arrest her, but she always had a way of dealing with them. She had formed a friendship with them, and she could intoxicate them and bribe them with fifty Kenyan shillings each. Soon enough, they would be on their way, letting her continue with her illicit trade.

Her den was always packed with patrons, singing the whole night and drinking their lives away. As rumor had it, she had the best local brew in the slum, and the customers that flocked into her den were endless.

"Don't ever go into that house Baraka!"

'Yes, Mum! It's too smelly. I can't stand the smell of that brew!"

Curiosity killed the cat. Mama Pima's husband was the ace distiller and a gift to the slum. His brew turned losers in the slums into instant champions—poverty into sudden wealth. It calmed hunger, postponed misery, and magically elevated the revelers to the top of the world. He was a hero, and his wife was a heroine. He was loved and cherished and revered by the revelers who flocked to their tiny den in droves. They were part of the system, and the authorities had learned not to mess up with them. But he was inebriated half the time. He had a big mouth laced with venom that he readily spewed on friends and foes alike, and no one wanted to engage him in a verbal fight, as he was a rabble-rouser who seemed to suffer from acute verbal diarrhea, always spoiling for a fight. His tongue was sharp enough to fell a *mugumo* tree. His name was Pombe.

"*Wewe Kijana*! *Kuwa mwanaume*! Come and feel good!" Mama Pima teased me.

As she said that to me; three men were touting me, saying how great it felt to feel high.

"Just try this small glass!" mama Pima was now holding it very close to me.

After further hyping, I gave in and gulped the half glass quickly. It contained the bitterest thing that I had ever tasted, and I quickly wondered why they kept coming over and over again for it. One of the young men was smoking something rolled in a *kakhi* paper, and he breathed out the entire smoke into my face almost choking me. I inhaled the smoke and instantly I felt as if I was weightless.

"Sweet marijuana! You fool!" he said while blowing a second cloud of smoke into my face. After a few minutes I was feeling so dizzy and confused that I couldn't stand on my feet. I was now babbling words that I couldn't understand as I walked outside.

From a distance I could hear the men clapping and Mama Pima shouting as if celebrating some newfound victory. Had she won a lottery, I wondered? The moment I got outside, I lost balance and fell with a thud into a sewage trench. I tried to pull myself back to my feet, but I couldn't. The whole world around me was spinning, and I was totally confused and lost in my own space, then everything got quiet.

I came to the following day, only to find myself lying on my new tiny mattress with Mum beside me. She looked very frustrated.

"What happened?" I asked in a daze. "Is that you, Mum?"

She held me in her arms. She skipped work that day and took care of me, cleaning all the vomit. She was holding onto a packet of fresh milk in her hands that she had forced me to drink like a baby. I was feeling very sick. Later I collected myself and managed to explain to her what happened, and she was totally agitated with me. She threatened to leave the house and to never come back if I tried such a thing again, and I believed her. My father had left, and I couldn't afford to have Mum leave again. I would be left all alone in this world with Isate, so I promised her that I would never do it again.

Mama Pima was no beauty. She had a big mouth with heavy solid lips half burnt from the alcohol she had taken over the years, and she had a green layer that lined her teeth from years of chewing khat. When she spoke, she looked like a trumpet ready to sound. She was gabby and dowdily dressed, and she would do anything to incite Mum to fight her.

She really looked like a clown—a comedian whose existence was to make people laugh. Whenever I looked at her, I had to stifle a giggle.

My mum confronted Mama Pima, and they argued to the point of almost fighting each other. Had it not been for her revelers' intervention, they could have torn into each other with bare knuckles. But it's said that when you fight a pig, the pig gets dirty and likes it.

That evil brew had made me forget myself completely, and I vowed never to take it again in my life. I would stay away from it, I promised myself.

CHAPTER SEVEN

I had seen small boys younger than me climbing on the back of tracks and lorries carrying sand, and I had entertained the thought of hanging onto one someday to go and visit the central business district without the knowledge of my mother. One morning, I actualized my thoughts, hitchhiking onto a trailer that had taken off toward town.

I was feeling so excited to visit the city all by myself. I wandered into the streets of Nairobi, admiring the land marks and the skyscrapers. My mind was racing with questions that I had no answers to.

Nairobi was abuzz with activity. The city spread across the flat terrain—a labyrinth of arcane corridors strewn with milling masses. I looked around and observed their faces. Some were sodden, mostly frowning, and others had dark folds on their faces that formed groves like a rugged old frog—a true testament to the lives they led.

How were these tall buildings built? How did they manage to stay so high in the air?

I was scared one was going to fall on me! The feeling was scary yet exciting. There were hordes of people and a cornucopia of things to see. Everyone seemed to be rushing somewhere, and I seemed to be the only one lost in my own world. I felt like Alice in Wonderland And marveled at the fact that someone could feel so alone amongst a sea of humanity.

I stumbled into a well-padded man—portly with a huge beard—and he shoved me to the side of the street; as he angrily muttered some words over my head, complaining why I wasn't paying attention. "Do you have eyes, *kijana*," he shouted. I fell with a thud on the metal barriers by the road, hurting my back.

I turned looking around for anyone to say something or to stop to help me, but everyone sped by, lost in their own worlds. I scampered on with a bruise on my ankle and an ache on my back. At one large window, a boy was holding a big piece of round bread with what looked to be green vegetables and a layer of meat. He was bringing it to his mouth to bite when we locked eyes. I smiled at him as I took an imaginary bite at his roll. He frowned at me and turned to his mother who gave me a mean look. I winked at them and walked by thinking about how it must have felt to have such a large piece all to himself. *That must be very evil and selfish*, I thought to myself.

However, it looked weird that the boy was feeding on what looked like raw, green vegetables.

I counted myself blessed that I always had my kale cooked, and I could have whispered in his ear for him to complain if he cared to listen. At that moment, while still lost in thought, I heard a loud commotion, and looking back, I saw a huge crowd of people running in all directions. I stood there confused as the tumultuous crowd surged forward, shouting and chanting,

"Kanyoro must go! Kanyoro must go!"

I saw a police man riding on a horse chasing after the crowd, and behind him was a battery of others who were on foot chasing after the crowd. Before I could even fully process what was going on, I had been engulfed by the mammoth crowd, and I found myself running aimlessly.

The police men were now right behind us, and one of them hurled a substance that released what looked like smoke that came from Uncle Matata's kitchen. Immediately there was a pungent smell, and my eyes were very irritated. In no time, my nostrils were already watery, running like a forgotten tap. My lungs suddenly felt heavy, and I was having difficulty breathing. My sight got hazy, and I couldn't tell where I was running to, but I kept running, fearing the worst. I almost lost my balance, but the crowd swept me on, tossing me forward. I could hear the horses trotting right behind me. Several people had fallen down and had been trodden by the masses in the stampede. I took a turn into a long alley as the crowd scuttled in all directions. I kept running—running for life, skedaddling deeper into the streets. I kept turning and turning, losing breath.

Eventually I couldn't run anymore. I stopped, and in an instant, it dawned on me that I was all alone in a deep back street alley. My eyes were now dry but sore, and my view was blurred. I looked around, and there was no one. The pathway was deserted, eerie, and strangely quiet. It was dusk, and the evening was fast giving way into the night. I was suddenly engulfed with a wave of fear, and my nerves started to dance to a creepy tune. It's then that it dawned on me that I was lost and I couldn't trace my way back to the bus station. I was now gasping for breath, moving higgledy-piggledy with the night starting to creep in, which turned the dark alleys into tunnels. I felt trapped, and the night seemed to aggressively cover the skies with its thick, dark blanket bringing along a strange sense of terror to my timid mind.

I was approaching the end of the alley to make yet another turn when I bumped into two boys who were lying down carefree. They were clumsy, their hairdos unkempt and rugged. They stood up at once and blocked my way. The younger one of the two hit and kicked me, demanding that I kneel down. I obliged while begging them to show me the way out and back to the bus station. They could hear none of my pleas; they laughed it off!

"You have trespassed, and we are going to teach you a lesson!" the smaller one of the two quickly chirped.

"Please kindly spare me and assist me to get back home!" I pleaded.

The smaller boy gave me a resounding whack across my back that sent me to the ground, sprawling in pain. I was still writhing when he attacked me with kicks and blows, hurting me greatly. I could feel blood oozing from my nostrils and my vision grew fuzzy.

"Let me go! Let me go!" I pleaded with them, but he kept pouncing on me harder. They both grabbed my feet and dragged me along the murky street, scraping my back.

I was now screaming for help, but all I could hear were echoes screaming back at me. They increased the pace as they dragged me along to a barrier of sorts, and by this point, my voice was coarse. I tried to scream, but all that came out was a flaccid groan of anguish.

One of the boys forcefully grabbed a pile of bottles, and I was shocked to see the pile opening into what looked like a hideout. It was a hidden entrance perfectly camouflaged with hundreds of rags and scrap metals forming its walls. Inside the dungeon was a small fire being fed by a huge pile of cartons. From the light source, I could see more than ten faces seated around the fire with each one of them having a bottle to their nostrils. I couldn't move further. My feet were cold with fear, and I began to shiver. Through the hazy flames I could see one young man with a corrugated face that seemed to be the leader. He spoke first.

"And who is that boy, Mugweru?" he asked

"He is a spy, we found him spying on us!"

"What?" he exclaimed. His voice was coarse and stern.

"Let's kill him and throw him into the river as usual!" One of the girls shouted.

The word usual sounded like a combat knife that drew my liquid brain back into reality and gave me heebie-jeebies leaving my nerves in a wretch.

One of the three boys was already on his feet charging towards me with his fists clenched when the boy who looked like their leader shouted. "Wait a minute. "Where do you come from, and why are you here?" he asked.

My voice was trembling like a reed, and I was scared out of my wits, staring at an impending attack. There was no hope for escape, as I had no idea how I got to that place and how to get away and back home; indeed, my goose was cooked and was ready to be served.

I quickly gathered the little strength that was left and said in a low mumble, "I had come to visit Nairobi town when the police started chasing us. I kept running and now am lost." I narrated the whole ordeal that I had gone through amidst laughter from all of them except the leader who seemed to doubt every word that I said. They chided me to tell them more, and as I explained to them, they laughed and kicked me around, taking turns and seemingly enjoying every bit of it.

"We will give you a chance," said the leader, "but if you try to escape, we will kill you, ok?" He pointed a gun at me.

It was scary, but having no choice, I said, "Yes! Yes!" He spoke almost with no emotion on his face. He'd been numbed by life.

"We don't just accept anyone into this family, we have rules and they must be obeyed!" We will have to be sure you were not spying on us, and therefore I will not release you. You will have to be part of us, and you will have to be us!" He continued; "You will do what we do, eat what we eat, speak our language, and toe the line. Fail and you'll be dead meat!"

He continued, "We have seen many of you that come here in innocence and turned out to work with the police. I will not tolerate that, and the slightest hint of such will cost your useless life! Your filthy body will be good food for the vultures that prowl by the river." He quivered in a harsh rusty voice that reverberated in the silence of the night.

As he spoke, a cold shrill of fear and pain ran down my spine, and my feet grew colder, not knowing what I had gotten myself into. I slowly thought to myself, *Indeed, God is a comedian, and He has truly mastered the art of comedy. My whole life had been a joke.* It seemed like the leader was trying to play some trick on me, but his coarse voice and drew me back to the stark reality that what I was experiencing was real, indeed—no joke at all.

"You will be under my watch, you little brat. Let me find out what you've got!" he bubbled on. He grabbed my neck and hurled me to the ground. I fell with a thud into the cartons, and my hands dug deep into what felt like a paste, making my hands soggy and sticky. I smelled my hands and confirmed my worst fears that the paste had been human waste. I wanted to cut my hands off and feed them to the young man, but a look into his blazing eyes sealed my fate.

"Here there is no dignity, you little imp. We have all been stripped off our dignity. We are dead, and we live as such in this place! We live in this squalor, and eat from it, and empty our bowels into it. It makes no difference!" As he spoke, my soul was slowly dying inside. Back home, I had hated the sight of human waste so much that I gathered a tremendous skill for hopping and jumping over them, but one day I had stepped into one of the humongous mounds, and I'd proceeded to scrub my foot for days on end, so mad at myself for having allowed myself to sink that low and step into human waste. Yet, I was looking at my hands marinated in human waste. It looked filthier than I had ever imagined and its feel and texture in my hands was appalling.

My heart sank and my stomach rumbled. I felt some hot bile piling up in my stomach, and I knew I was going to vomit. The ring leader had now moved closer to me, and we were looking at each other eye ball to eye ball. He gave me a heavy slap that sent my vision out-of-focus, causing my brain to take a ride on a whirlwind. The entire world spun around me.

He shouted, "Try to mess around here with your vomit, and I will mess your messed life further!" That was a stern warning, and in the few moments that I'd been here, I quickly learned that he wasn't joking. I clutched my hands for the better part of the night, stretching them away from my body, fully aware of the filth that they carried. I knew they would never be clean again.

That night, sleep was as remote as the distant stars that I could see through the narrow openings of the dungeon. I watched as the boys told of the day's escapades, the way one had slit open a woman's throat when she had resisted and tried to fight to keep her hand bag. Another one explained how he had threatened a smartly dressed man with raw sewage, daring to smear the waste on his white shirt. The man had given him his phone and run away.

"He ran away as if I had carried an atomic bomb," he narrated, and everyone broke into hysterical laughter.

"Our human waste is such a powerful tool!" one of the boys said, seemingly giving me unsolicited advice. "It's the quickest way to empty someone's pockets on the streets" he said.

They talked on and on into the night. They all had a bottle that they were sniffing at; their eyes brazen with the color of blood.

My mind was a jumbo of chaotic thoughts sliding back and forth from my world and the reality of what I was now experiencing. Just a few hours ago I was riding on cloud nine enjoying the jostling of the city, feeding my curious, insatiable mind on the glitterati that the city of Nairobi offered, and now I was here trapped in this dungeon. I didn't know what to do. I couldn't sleep a tinge, and the pain that covered my whole body remained a stubborn reminder of the beatings that I had received from the three boys.

My mother will be looking for me, I thought to myself. She had given me express warnings never to leave alone to anywhere far away from our shanty, but out of excitement I had decided to come along alone. She had been right, and I should have listened, but now that was water under the bridge. I needed to focus and deal with my current reality.

"This is Nairobi, not Kisangula village!" Her words now stuck with me.

The night dragged by, and as the fire died down, the biting cold of the night froze my feeble legs. There was nothing to cover myself with, and the cold breeze that blew through the numerous perforations in the metal sheets, plastics, and assorted cartons that made up the walls of the dungeon gave me a chill—a deplorable embrace of sorts. Everyone was now fast asleep except the gang leader whose bulbous black eyes gazed at me like a gamblers' eye, giving nothing away and elucidating no emotion. They were cold eyes, in sync with the unnerving night. He looked at me with a strange gaze, his onion-like eyeballs bulging out. He looked like he suffered chronic proptosis, and every quick look at him caused my nerves to shrink.

Apart from the erratic sounds of frogs and insects, nothing else disturbed the loud silence that frightened me to the core. I couldn't sleep a wink. That night, I discovered the power of time, and how long an hour can last. I remembered from my Sunday school that weeping may endure for a night but joy comes with the morning. I waited for the morning that never seemed to come, but it finally came.

The first ray of light that came through the narrow openings of the gutter was a welcome sign that the night had given way to yet a new day. I told myself that the new day would bring with it hope and freedom! To my utter surprise, none of the boys woke up. They slept on, except for their leader who had stayed awake the whole night keeping vigil.

I waited for the normal, sugarless black tea that my mother prepared some mornings as other mornings even the grained tea leaves was not available, and we had to take water but it didn't come. I would go out every morning after waking up and walk towards the sewage lines and relieve myself, sometimes lingering to watch the green waste being washed down the river into a thick, grimy gel.

I sat there without that privilege. Luckily my stomach felt empty and my bladder dry. It was nature's ingenious way of reminding me that I hadn't taken any meal or drunk any liquid in the past several hours. That night, I had learned that freedom is an asset, whether you are poor or rich. Freedom is life, and without it, you're half dead. And nothing compares to waking up knowing that you are free. It was a strange feeling, being caged and waiting for instructions.

I started appreciating that in life, even poverty has cadres. I was poor. I had tasted poverty and seen it with my eyes. In turn, poverty had recognized me as its own. She knew me by name, and over time, I had come to appreciate the fact that we were enjoined at the hip, together for life.

However, what I was facing now I couldn't place it in any of the poverty bands that came to my mind. This was extreme, where you were nothing, owned nothing, lived for nothing, and had nothing to lose—except for time, and there seemed to be plenty of that. I longed to lose it, but it clung onto me, frustrating my timid mind. I could only sit and hope it would let loose and pass by. But in the loud silence, I could hear it slowly tick away, clinging on, not letting go!

Time was a nuisance.

As I lingered in the dungeon, I started to lose all sense of time, but perhaps it was the hot sun's rays, which penetrated the crevices in the makeshift hideout, that shook everyone out of their sleep. The rusty scrap-metal barriers, which bore an assortment of faded brands ranging from milks to paints, were now hot from the sun's consistent and scorching heat, and we were now sweating profusely. I could clearly see everyone inside the dungeon now, and they all looked scary with their clothes all stained and sweaty and smelling likes pigs.

I was a pig myself, but at least I wasn't a smelly one. I was a pig and had always been one, but still I had some dignity. I was amongst a drift of pigs with no dignity at all. My heart laughed out in silence.

In my entire life, I had never owned a thing, apart from the paper album that Uncle Matata had turned into flames back then, but now I had descended to a new low. We lived in abject poverty, and my mum, too, owned nothing, apart from the rags that she had held onto for years and her certificates that she had nicely stored inside an old bible that she guarded with her life. She had stored them away in a rusty metal box and wrapped it in multiple layers of nylon to be impermeable to the seasonal raging waters and our constantly leaking roof. She also owned the sisal sheet that she had slept on for years and the patched blanket that had been sewn so many times that it was fast turning into a woolen blanket.

But she had been different. She had insisted on sweeping the floor every morning, taking a bath whenever we were lucky enough to have water, cleaning the patched multicolor blanket and putting it out in the sun to scare and fry away the bed bugs. I had felt dirty, less fortunate, underprivileged, and at times useless, but sitting here, watching the lives around me, I started to hear a life-changing voice speaking to me. I started thinking about my mother who had been there for me, who spoke to me every morning and every night, and gave me the assurance to believe that I could be a better person if I worked harder. Indeed, you appreciate something more once you lose it or once it's out of sight.

A tear curved at the corner of my left eye.

The leader seemed to read my mind and he summoned everyone to sit in a circle.

"Hey guys, come here all of you!"

His voice was an unmistaken order. His words were sharp and his stare was a wild encounter. Everybody moved in a hurry and made a circle around him.

He started by introducing himself.

"My name is Kiberenge! But they call me Kibe!"

"I am the mother and father of this home! I give rules here, and what I say must be done!"

"You disobey the rules, and you are dead meat!" the girl chipped in.

I found the word home ironical.

He went on. "Everyone here has a story. Everyone here has a background! He pointed at the only girl on the team and mentioned that she was his wife. "Her name is Njoki, and she is carrying my baby."

I was now looking at Njoki directly, and for the first time, I could see half of her face was burnt and her facial skin folded into rugged layers and she had a squint in her look. Her stomach was protruding, turning her tiny frame into a spectacle.

Kibe continued. "Njoki ran from her parents' house after her dad stabbed her mother and left her for the dead. Her dad turned to Njoki and attacked her with a machete and tore her clothes ready to rape her. It's at that stage that she decided to fight for her life. She fought her dad back with the machete that he had used to stab her mother, but unfortunately for Njoki, her dad grabbed a pot of boiling beans from the fireplace and threw the pot onto her face, burning her severely. She passed out, and when she regained consciousness, she ran away from the house never to return again. She doesn't know if her mother or father are still alive."

He sighed a bit and continued. "This is Makau," he said, pointing to a sturdy, young man with a thick frame. He was well-built, looking like a tank. He was wearing a long, sooty jacket layered with such thick stubborn stains that I couldn't determine its original color.

"Makau watched his mother stab his father. He had stood up to defend his father, but he was not strong enough, and he had watched his dad helplessly breathe his last. His mum escaped from the village, never to return again, and after his dad's burial, the uncles and everyone else looked at Makau as a bad omen—a reject—and no one wanted to touch him, as he smelled the smell of death. In frustration he fled and found a home here."

He gave an account of everyone and how fate had joined them together. They all had very dark backgrounds and had experienced lives that they would probably never would go back to even if they were given the chance.

I sat there soaking in every moment in a sojourn into the world of each and every one of them, and it was the worst sojourn I had ever taken, yet the most amazing and surprisingly refreshing.

Kibe's story turned my eyes wet with frustration and anger "My dad and mum would always fight over everything and nothing, but one day one of their usual fights degenerated, and my dad had turned into an untamed animal. I was helpless as I saw my dad strangle my mum and my little sister."

"My mother pleaded and screamed for her life, but her screams were all in vain, and my little sister had died in the same hands that were meant to nurture her, to love her, and to care for her, so now it was my turn. I struggled with my father. The hands that were meant to protect me were the same hands that tenaciously held me close, not letting go, squeezing my neck. I was losing breath. With one last shove, I pushed my dad off and tried to escape, but my dad was determined to kill me, so seeing that I was at the door and I was going to escape, he threw his old car battery at me, pouring all the sulfuric acid onto my clothes burning my neck, back and shoulders. Some of the acid splashed into my eyes, burning the corners, and that's why my eyes are the way they are till today. I was only ten years old. Now I can only stare."

He paused with his unnerving signature stare, scaring me further.

I felt a strange connection with the stories that I heard in the hideout. There were strong tentacles that were now strangely entangling me to the rest of the team. I could relate to every bit of their stories, and one thing that we had in common was our having been rejected.

Our fathers had believed that we were worthless—that we didn't deserve to be part of them, to feel the warmth of their embrace, to feel loved, or to feel cared for.

Kibe continued. "Looking around you will see that we are all dead. We have nothing to lose. Dead or alive, there is no difference! You will soon realize you were born once but here you die multiple times. Living is by chance, as we come out of death daily and we trudge on. We are all dirty pigs, and even society out there doesn't recognize us as humans!"

"Our flesh stinks. Our future stinks with hopelessness. It doesn't even exist." He took a dramatic pause. "Or does it? Wherever we go, people murmur behind our backs and children run or cling to their parents whenever they see us."

"Here we find solace in each other. We thank fate for uniting us in misery, for creating a pool of people who understand each other's pain." It was Njoki.

"That is who we are," Kibe concluded.

I felt angry at myself—at my past, at my future, and at my father! I was now burning with rage and was asking myself why my dad had also disappeared from my life.

However, it felt so nice to meet others who could understand my story. We shared the same fate, and we seemed to have been cut from the same piece of rugged, rejected clothes. Oddly, we thanked nature for uniting us—to suffer together, to enjoy and soak in the misery of life together, with our souls unified to savor the vagaries that life served us every day. Strangely, it was such a fresh beginning. Kibe had called it a home, and he was right. A family home of rejected souls. A family whose diet was pain, fully balanced with daily doses of desperation. It was going to be a journey through time.

CHAPTER EIGHT

Kibe assigned me to Makau. He was swift, strong, and vicious.

"Baraka, these streets are lethal. For one to survive you are supposed to be tough. There are no better days. Every day is a struggle that you have to live through. When you venture into the streets and come back alive, it's a miracle. Here there are dynasties that rule the streets, and there are different families—weak families and strong families."

"*Eeeh! Weuuh*" I muttered.

"The street family hierarchies here determine the kind of trade you engage in. Some are hired by armed gangsters, and they make lots of money, though it's very risky. Others engage in drug trafficking syndicates where they are paid handsomely, as they can move the drugs without getting noticed. Others are hired by rogue businessmen to commit crimes, ranging from simple to highly complex assignments. When none of these opportunities arise, we end up snatching purses, phones and other valuables from motorists and people from the streets, but this is the most dangerous of all. When you're caught, you're dead meat!"

"That's scary!" I said.

"Baraka, our family is not the weakest, though we are still weak on the streets. As you saw, Kibe has a gun, and that's why we are all here, for his protection, though we cannot afford to venture on the major streets, as there are bigger and more powerful gangs controlling those streets. If you cross their paths you will be looking for an early death appointment!"

He was walking with a limp, and I was curious, so I asked him, "What happened to your leg?"

"It's a long story, but don't dare try to run away from Kibe. He will hunt you down and kill you!"

That terrified me.

"One day I tried to escape from him, and he chased me through the corridors. When I got too fast for him, he shot at me and the bullet missed my hip and hit my left leg. It's still lodged in there as a solid reminder that his threats are not empty. He dragged me back into the den and I learned my lessons since then!"

He continued with the orientation:

"So, we mostly beg for food in the restaurants around here on river road for the leftovers. On the street's hierarchy, begging is at the base of the pyramid while armed robbery is at the very apex of the pyramid. The rewards are amazing and tempting, but when one pushes his luck too far, life smiles back at them by hitting their faces with a rotten egg. Many have been gunned down in cold blood as a warning," he said.

So the weak families like us scavenge from the dumpsites for scrap metals and plastics and bones to sell, and once you scavenge, you still have to protect your wares from the older street boys, who have a tendency to steal, so sometimes you will need protection. For you to get the protection, you have to exchange something, sharing the little you get on the streets," he said.

"Juvenile delinquency in the streets of Nairobi has grown, and the street families keep growing. We can't just rob any streets anymore. Each street has been covered and is domineered by a street family that feeds from it and lives off it, and no other street family can interfere with another's zone. The battles to dominate and rule a certain street are always brutal and sometimes fatal, and no one family is willing to enter into another family's territory."

"What! That's scary, Makau!"

"Recently I got introduced to a secret trade, and I will show you how it operates. It requires a lot of patience and skill. My contact's name is Moniqa. She owns an expensive boutique on Tom Mboya Avenue, and she specializes in human hair." Makau's voice was starting to race with excitement. So, the deal is simple: you hang around her shop, and when she sells an expensive wig to an unsuspecting customer, you track down the customer and snatch it from them and return it to Moniqa's shop. She immediately pays you a thousand shillings. I have done this several times now, and I find it easy money. The ladies are usually too scared to react, and I simply fizzle into the crowds." He was smiling with a confident smile on his face while I stood there amazed at how dangerous the whole escapade sounded.

"I do the same for gold chains, necklaces and earrings on the streets. Once I spot one on the streets, I carefully follow and hunt down the victim, then grab and snatch off the jewelry. Sometimes it comes out bloody with a piece of the ear, but then we simply wipe that out. It's then taken to Moniqa for her to resell it. Moniqa has one of her boys who usually comes here on our streets to pick these items once we collect enough stock, which is what keeps us going and helps us survive on the streets." He paused. "I stopped rummaging through the plastics, Baraka. You get nothing by the end of the day that way!" he continued with a sense of pride in his voice.

Come, let's go. I will show you how it's done. We sat a few meters from Moniqa's boutique and waited for hours. I was already feeling like giving up when a boy came and tapped Makau on the shoulders. Makau swiftly followed him as I scurried behind them, my heart pounding hard. He pointed to a plump, well-rounded lady that was carrying a big, black polythene bag. Makau quickly understood the signal and ushered me along.

The lady was moving very slowly, so we had to slow down our pace and followed her a few meters behind not losing sight of her. We crossed several streets and came to the much busier Mfangano street, which had hordes of people moving up and down.

At that point, Makau shoveled meticulously through the crowd and was just about to grab the nylon bag when the woman tripped and fell down with a thud. Looking closely, we realized that her bag was gone. "Someone has beaten us to the trophy," Makau said.

Makau was distraught, feeling cheated.

"Moniqa is very evil. She is wicked. Why would she send two people for the same item? It must have been very expensive!" Makau lamented.

"I am not going to work for her again. This is the third time this has happened."

We were quickly swallowed by the crowd, and we disappeared and retreated to another corner of the street to regroup. Makau's anger was through the roof. "This is what stresses me up with these errands that Moniqa assigns, they are very dangerous and unpredictable. Let's get out of here!" he said as he dashed and turned towards River road.

We stopped at a shop that had no name on it. Venturing in, we found three men seated, chewing khat and smoking cigarettes.

"You are back, Makau! How are you?" One of the men said as he extended a fist bump to Makau.

"This is my friend, Baraka. This is Mustafa alias Konyi," Makau said.

I gave him a fist bump as he ushered us to sit down.

"I thought you were never going to come back here!" said Konyi with a naughty smile.

"Are you ready for an assignment tomorrow at 10:00 a.m.?" he asked with his commandeering voice, a cigarette in one corner of his mouth.

"I have a package that I need you to deliver to Dandora. I will need you to be extremely careful, as you almost messed up the last time. Okay?"

"I will be careful, I will come with Baraka," Makau said timidly.

"That's perfect. Two are even better than one, as you will raise less suspicion while crossing the bridge downstream and traversing through the streets. You know that the police are always prowling around? Don't you?" he paused.

What did I get myself into? I kept asking myself.

That evening, we passed by Horizonn Café. Makau informed me that the owners were a bit considerate. They didn't throw away the food left by the customers into the bins. Instead they lumped it all together, and every evening he had formed the habit of passing by to pick the remains. He was forever grateful to them. We carried two heavy nylon bags full of an assortment of foods all lumped together. We didn't really care about the presentation. I hadn't eaten since the previous day, and I was feeling frail, so it didn't matter to me. The goal was to get full. Most of the other eateries sold the remains to pig farmers so the options were limited.

The rest of the team slowly retreated to the den, and they too recounted their episodes. It was a ritual to share in each other's worlds and experiences.

***

The following morning at ten, we were speaking to Konyi and taking instructions.

"These are twenty stones of bhang and four hundred grams of cocaine. You have to be extremely careful. You mess up this time and I'll mess you up. My boys will be following you from a distance to ensure everything is fine."

"When you get to Dandora, next to the dumpsite there's a huge, Kenya Power electricity post, and there is a shop selling *Miti ni dawa* products. You will find two young men dressed like you working on the dumpsite, directly opposite that herbal shop. Give them the package and disappear from there immediately. Don't linger around, even for a minute. When you come back, I will pay you each two thousand shillings. Understood?" he asked.

This was a lot of money for an assignment that was only going to take less than half a day to accomplish. I was excited, and I started dreaming of making lots of money on the streets. It was a blessing in disguise.

So, we were both given two sets of bags, which we staffed separately into our sisal bags that were soiled and dirty.

We started off with our signature glue bottles to our nostrils. I was following the steps of Makau. He had done this before, so it wasn't going to be a problem.

Just as we got to the Kirinyaga Road roundabout, we were met face to face with the police on patrol. My heart was pounding hard inside my rib cage like a drum beat. They were armed and we couldn't run. They could simply shoot us and turn us into yet another statistic. They stopped Makau who confidently stopped.

"What are you carrying *kijana,* young boy?" one of them asked.

"*Wacha wewe,* leave us alone. These are plastics. Have a look," Makau said as he opened his bag. The smell of his bag turned the cops away, and they asked him to quickly close it.

"Get out of here!" they shouted, *"Toka hapa!"* I felt so relieved I followed him, hoping they weren't going to ask me to do anything.

We trudged on and avoided the major roads, passing through the slums of Gikomba Market, Eastleigh, and Mathare, finally arrived in Dandora at 2:00 p.m.

We went straight to the dumpsite, and right before our eyes stood a mountain of waste with plastics strewn all over and some nylon papers dancing in tune to the wind. Huge pelicans were graciously rummaging through the mountain of waste, searching for food.

"There is the shop," Makau said with excitement, pointing towards the *miti ni dawa* shop that Konyi had mentioned to us. At the far end, there was a power pole as instructed, and below the power pole there were two young men who were scavenging through the massive dumpsite, looking for valuables. They were our recipients just as Konyi had advised.

Just as we walked towards them, two policemen came running towards us with their guns trained at us, ordering us to stop. As we stopped, I stole a look at the two young men who had been busy below the power pole and realized they had vanished into thin air. They were nowhere in sight.

"Drop the bags," one of the men ordered us. "Put your hands in the air and turn around!"

We could hear them murmur and talk to each other in low voices. My hands had been in the air far too long, and I was feeling weary. I was wondering why the police officers were taking so long without giving us further orders. I slowly turned my neck around anticipating a bullet to fire through my head.

I was shocked and terrified to find there was no one behind us. The two policemen had vanished with our cargo. We had made it easy for them by taking all the trouble to transport this cargo this far only to be tricked and lose it. I felt cheated and abused, and I vowed to myself that I wasn't going to do it again.

Makau was crying like a little baby. "What are we going to do? Konyi will kill us, we can't hide from him. He will think we sold his cargo and we are double-dealing him."

"We must go back to him and explain ourselves" he suggested.

"Are you out of your mind, Makau? Konyi will not believe us. He will shoot us on the spot. You said he is always armed, and he always carries his gun, right?"

"Yes, he is always armed, and he shoots at will and with impunity! We have to face him. Remember what Kibe said. We are dead already, so it doesn't matter. This is a chance for us to live. We will go to him, as we still need him. If we don't go back to him, he will have more reason to believe we sold out his drugs. He will still hunt us down and kill us," Makau said.

We walked back the same way we had come, not having accomplished the mission we had been tasked to perform. When we arrived at Konyi's shop, he was anxiously waiting for us. Furious.

"How did it go?" He asked

Makau was trembling and sweating profusely, "Some two policemen accosted us on the dumpsite and—"

"And took away my drugs? Right? Save your breathe!" Konyi interjected, reaching out for his gun. He pointed it at us angrily. I looked down and started mumbling my last prayers. I could feel my pants getting wet as he rumbled.

"Next time if you have to work for me, I will not entertain such levels of incompetency."

"You made me get back my drugs from those two imposters. They were not policemen, but luckily enough, you were being watched all along, so my other boys recovered the cargo from the two men who accosted you, and they were able to deliver to the client, so today you will escape with your lives but you will not get your pay as you didn't deliver the task!"

"Now get out of here!" He thundered.

We scampered for the door and ran out of his shop, our hearts hammering after that near-death experience.

"That was close, Baraka! We almost lost our lives again in the hands of those thugs at the dumpsite and in the hands of Konyi!" he said, gasping for air. "Is this how you die every day on these streets Makau?" I asked.

"Yes, and other days are tougher, sadly—much tougher! Living here is by chance, and today we were lucky to have escaped with our lives. These drug syndicates are dangerous and brutal. I wanted to run away and go back home to my mother, but the thought of Kibe's bullet going through my head scared me stiff. I had no option but to stay.

That night back in the den, I asked Kibe to attach me to someone else. I had nearly died in my first encounter.

CHAPTER NINE

I woke up with every part of my body aching. I didn't know where I was, and I couldn't explain how I had gotten there. The darkness around me was scary, and the strong, stale stench of formalin awoke every sense in me.

I tried feeling my garbs only to realize I was naked. My feeble heart begun to dance. I stretched my hand to my left and held something that felt like a human head. I wanted to scream, but I couldn't. At that very moment, I saw something lurking in the glaring darkness. I could feel every hair on my head rise with each thought that crossed my mind. At that juncture, I heard the door swing open, and a hand switched on the lights. I sprang up from the slab. I had never seen so many bodies around me. I was in the midst of the dead!

The man who had opened the door quickly closed it behind him, leaving me engulfed in the acrid smell of death. As I screamed inside the room, I could hear him scream back as his footsteps quickly disappeared into the cold silence of the night. With the silence I could hear a pin drop, it was hushed and as quiet as the true passage of stars. But in this emptiness, I was not alone, or was I? No, I wasn't. He had seen a ghost, and I too had seen a ghost and I wondered loudly which one of us was right.

When I looked again at the room, some bodies were strewn on the floor and still leaking fresh blood. I screamed some more. They came in all sizes—some big, some small—but they all looked scary. The pain had quickly fizzled out and turned into a mental torture, there seemed to be a fresh injection of adrenaline into my veins that made me hypersensitive.

I screamed at the top of my voice, shouting and banging the door, hoping that the ghost that had tried opening the door would come back and open it again, but all my cries simply echoed back, turning my own cries into bloodcurdling banshee tunes.

It was Kibe's words ringing in my ears: *We are all dead, and living is by chance!*

Now I knew what death looked and felt like, and, no, I wasn't dead.

My voice was now coarse and irritated. Without another option, I braced myself, sat down on the bloody floor, and waited nervously, hoping that the door would be opened. It was a long wait. Finally, after about five hours of mental torture and fatigue, I heard the footsteps of what sounded like three people coming towards the door. I decided not to shout so as not to scare them away and risk prolonging my stay there.

The room wasn't empty . . . or was it? No, it wasn't. It was full of death, and I was the only one alive. I had had nightmares but not something close to such horrendous levels. This wasn't a nightmare, was it? It was happening in real time.

My big toe had a tag—a tag of death that read, "Unknown." A sordid statement. "Young male found dead on the streets along Moi Avenue!" I couldn't relate to this statement. It boggled my timid mind, and I couldn't recollect what happened. Had I suddenly lost my mind?

"What am I doing here? Why am I here? How did I get here?" I asked myself.

I was having sudden amnesia, and I couldn't seem to recall anything. There was just a hazy recollection of someone pounding continuously on my head and distant chants of, "Kill him! Kill him!" The chants got louder, and my head was starting to ache. I wanted to scream, but I restrained myself, fully aware that I could scare the morgue attendants the second time. As I gathered myself, the scenes slowly unfolded in my memory like a distant ebb peeling away the ocean from the shore. At first it was slow, but then the tide of emotions and events flooded into place, putting my mind at the very eye of a stormy scene. I saw myself crying out in dire pain. I was terrified, and I wasn't daydreaming. The pain was real, and my whole head was aching, scarred with a large cut across my earlobe. It quickly dawned on me that this wasn't a dream; it was happening right before my eyes. I had narrowly escaped death, and in the process, the merchants of death had put a tag on me.

At last, I recalled what had transpired.

It had been one of those early afternoons that we casually went out into the streets to search for food and valuables, just like always. I was in the company of Njoki, who was now heavily pregnant. I had been attached to her after my scary escapade with Makau. I had expected less dramatic adventures with Njoki.

We sat in the alleys of River road for about two hours, watching hordes of people tread back and forth on the streets, each one of them seemingly lost in their own world. Njoki had a keen eye on the trophy, and for the past few days, I had relied on her precision. She was skilled, indeed, having refined the art of sieving from the crowds an easy and worthy target.

She quickly elbowed me when a lady who was carrying a small baby on her back passed by. The lady was sweating like a leaking roof, carrying a heavy load on her head, and her child was hanging precariously on her back—a sign that she had been walking for a long distance. She held the string of a tiny, red purse in her left hand. The baby was crying, but the lady was moving on briskly, seemingly in a rush, as if to catch a bus.

"That purse has money in it, Baraka. Go for it," she said, prodding me.

I had learned how to quickly scan the environment around me with laser precision. I had been enjoined to a mistress of this trade and her immersion lessons had been daringly successful.

But before I went for it, Njoki had sprung into action and grabbed the red purse from the woman's hands. Unfortunately, the purse had a longer string that she had wittingly tied tightly onto her waistline, running into her undergarments. Njoki had snatched from the lady with the ferocity of a wounded tiger and her energy had caused the poor woman to come down with a thud, her baby falling off from her back and her load tumbling from her head. Her baby fell on the other side of the road, crying in pain and almost getting trodden by the heavy human traffic. A few people hopped over her.

The woman sent out a shrieking sharp cry that permeated the noisy air around us and quickly caused heads to turn. She was hysterical as she cried out, *"Mwizi! Mwizi!"*

Am I a thief? I silently asked myself.

Njoki had stumbled on the load that came off the lady's head, and she too came down with a thud, hitting the ground on her stomach. Hurting herself and her unborn baby, she cried in anguish, touching her protruding stomach.

Sensing trouble, I quickly dashed to run away but someone with a big torso and with the skin of a rugged frog blocked my way with his sturdy foot toppling me down.

The crowd descended on me with kicks and blows as another section of the crowd beat up Njoki. She was pregnant but no one cared! She was a thief, and her day of reckoning had come.

A section of the crowd descended on her with merciless blows, hitting her everywhere, including her stomach. We all cried in pain, but her cries sounded more desperate. There was no way of escaping.

I was now bleeding profusely, and I strongly felt that I was losing this battle. I had been screaming, pleading for mercy for the last thirty minutes, but the crowd kept increasing, taunting, "Kill them! Kill them!" And the beating grew harder as more hands joined the fray. I innocently cried out for my mama, but the rowdy crowd didn't seem to understand that language.

"Mimi ni mama yako?" one man with a burly torso was shouting at me. Surely, he wasn't my mother. He didn't have to remind me that.

The crowd was baying for our blood—the innocent blood of our youth.

But was I innocent? The innocence in me had in a few days turned into something else—a gel of delinquency that was flowing into untested waters that were now swelling up to swallow me whole. I had been carried away by these waters. I was drowning—going down the drain—and my wailing turned into short painful coughs, bleeding my lungs out.

I was fast losing my hearing and my body was now numb to the pain, but I could hear someone shout; "Bring a tire, and let's burn these two thieves!"

Within a fraction of a second, something heavy fell on my head. I was forced into a humongous tire, and the crowd wasn't relenting. They hit me more, ready to squeeze the last breath from my lungs. They turned me into a contortionist. I didn't know I could be one, but my bones suddenly could bent at will as they forced me into the inner part of the tire. Then as fate had it, I felt something that smelt like petrol being sprinkled on me, and at that moment I knew that my time was short.

Many times, I had wished to die, but this was not one of the ways I had imagined my life coming to an end. I was on the verge of taking my last breath. I could feel my spirit leaving my body and saying to me that it was time. The pain in my body was excruciating. I had sunk low in the gutters, but this was the lowest I had come.

I could see the hand of death more clearly, beckoning me, and I didn't even have the strength to rise and hold his arms. Even so, he had the audacity to come closer, extending his ugly hands. I could feel his dark hand firmly holding onto mine, raising me up. He wanted me to accompany him on a journey that I had always dreaded but I had no strength left to fight him.

For a moment, in a haze of emotion, I knew I was going to die, but who would be there to cry at my funeral? What would they be crying over? What would they say while crying? In life I had lived in pain, and now I was dying in pain. I had hoped that one day things would change for my brother Isate, my mother, and I—that I could wipe away the tears that fell from her eyes, but that clearly was not going to happen. My life, indeed, had been a big joke.

I was lying in a pool of my own blood, my body was aching so badly from every core, my resilient spirit giving way, I felt my spirit rising up to start up another journey through time, then everything got silent. Suddenly my world stilled, and everything became quiet.

* * *

Suddenly I felt a strong tinge of raw pain run through my nerves with the thought of Njoki.

What happened to her? was her baby safe? Had she been lynched, as was the norm in the city streets of Nairobi? She had cried all along, shouting nothing else but, "My baby! My baby!"

But her cries fell on deaf ears. Mob justice and mob psychology was hard to control in the city of Nairobi, and the courts on the streets quickly identified, prosecuted, and meted their judgments with speed and efficiency, and the ultimate punishment was almost always death. It was done in broad daylight so as to scare off any would-be offenders in the streets, but this clearly had failed to resolve the deep-seated issues leading to these crimes.

I was nudged back to reality by the three ghastly morgue attendants who were bewildered by my presence trying to stand up, but feeling ashamed due to my nakedness.

I had been harassed, stripped off all the clothes and "killed" on the streets. One of the morgue attendants threw a white coat at me, and I wrapped around myself, shivering like a reed in the morning cold. They walked me out of the morgue. I was shaken to the core, and I was struggling to walk. I was limping as my nerves regained their sensations. The pain was real, raw, and getting worse. I was sobbing and crying out as all the memories of the past few hours came back, flooding on my mind like raging waters. My mind was chaotic, threatening my sanity.

Later the police officer who dropped me into the morgue was called and he confirmed to the attendants that he had picked me from the roadside along Moi Avenue at midnight. As they talked to other officers on duty, it was discovered that I had been saved by the Town Hall *askaris* from a mob who had been keen to decimate me and turn me into charred rubble.

I had been badly beaten up and on the verge of death. They had abandoned me a few kilometers from where I had been accosted and left me for the dead, as they didn't want to fall into trouble with the media for yet another killing. They had wanted to exonerate themselves, and as such, the best bet for them was to abandon me on the streets.

I had already lost consciousness and drifted into a coma, so when the officers on patrol saw my body lying on the street, they quickly came to the conclusion that I was already dead and they brought me to the morgue with the brief report:

"Unknown!"

"Young adult male Found dead on the street along Moi Avenue."

The two morgue attendants had weird, cadaverous looks. They had saved me from the morgue—from among the dead—but they so much reminded me of the bodies I had seen in the morgue. Indeed, we are so much influenced by our environment, and most of the time it transforms us.

I thought about my mother who I imagined was thinking about me, and the pain that I had caused her. I was weeping hysterically, but I was back to life, and the morgue attendants were busy, going in and out of the morgue and helping distraught people who had come to identify their loved ones and also to pick up their loved ones for burial.

I wanted to quickly escape from this place, it caused me so much pain to see other people wailing and crying, and I imagined how my mother would be crying over my dead body. That shattered my little brain. I needed to go to my mother. She was the only one who could truly and sincerely cry over my dead body. Perhaps along with my brother Isate. And Mr Wanyonyi might shed a tear or two.

After making several calls to the police, the morgue attendants were allowed to release me back into the world, to go back to where I came from.

"Where is your home?" one of them asked, his face stern and cold like that of death.

I didn't have a quick answer. I hesitated but jerked back to my senses when he impatiently asked for the second time, "Young boy, we don't have a whole day, we need to attend to other bodies!" Well, to him I was just another body, but I thought to myself that, no, I was not just another body. I had life. The rest of the bodies he was referring to were lifeless, but my opinion definitely wasn't going to change anything.

"Kibra!" I said to him

"What's your father's name?" he asked, his pen ready to scribble a name.

I hesitated for a second then said, "Jane Uside!"

I will write that under your mother's name, "Now tell me who your father is," he shouted angrily.

"It's Jane Uside. She is my father also!" I said defiantly. He wrote in his book, looking at me for the second time discontented.

"You can go home now. And be careful. Next time you won't be lucky enough to leave this place alive and walking," he said.

I looked down at myself, and I looked at the morgue attendant desperately. I only had the white laboratory coat.

I needed something to cover my loins and wade off the mid-morning cold. The man went back into the morgue, and a few minutes later, he came out with oversize grey trousers and a blue shirt, both of which stained with blood.

These clothes had clothed the dead, and I had been one amongst them. It scared me stiff as I dressed in the oversize trousers. Obviously enough, it had come from a plus size man. I put on the blue shirt which had a very strong stench of formalin, and the acrid smell of death was knit into every fiber of its fabric, but I had nothing more to lose. I had lost everything.

As I walked through Kenyatta National Hospital, Mortuary's gates, the mourners quickly gave way, some scampering for their dear lives to hide behind the pillars to watch a live ghost on his feet, and others stood at a distance, exchanging weird glances and talking to each other in whispers. I couldn't have cared less. It sweetly dawned on me that once again I was a free spirit. I had gotten back my freedom, and I didn't have to take myself back into the custody of Kibe, in the dungeon on the street. The stars and the elements had secretly aligned in the most bizarre way to set me free and send me back to my mother.

I was not so sure where I was, but every time I tried stopping anyone on the streets to inquire, they all ran away. They couldn't stand the smell of my body, as I hadn't taken a proper bath for days, and the blood-stained clothes that I wore probably scared them.

I feared I was going to be arrested as everyone looked at me with suspicion written all over their faces. I was a criminal, and even the walls knew it. The scars on my head gave it all away and fed into their narratives. After walking for about twenty minutes, I had to take a long detour in the woods to avoid getting into trouble. I looked like someone who had escaped from prison or a criminal who had killed someone and was running away—a delinquent vagabond on the loose. Everyone knew something was wrong with me, but they just didn't know what or how to place a finger on me, so they simply stared and held their noses close to wade off the sordid air of death that stuck with me like an evil cloud.

I got my bearing and general direction and ventured into the woods, pressing on as birdsong drifted down from the canopies. The walk through the woods was refreshing. I was away from the weird looks that I had to brave on the road. The walk was rather quiet and peaceful, apart from the rustle that my oversize trousers made. My bare feet were subjected to multiple thorny twigs that snapped and pricked my sullen feet, torturing me further with pain and raw injustice. I pressed on past the expansive bushes that led me to Mbagathi Road.

It was under construction and very dusty, so it had less human and vehicular traffic. I took a long breath and crossed it, and I could now clearly see the path that led to my freedom—back to the arms of my loving mother. Deep down, I knew I was a slave here in the slums, but having tested the walls of confinement, I looked forward to the freedom of being myself and the beauty that came with the option of dreaming that one day the chains of poverty were going to shake off and let go.

As I approached Kibra, I realized that it hadn't changed. the usually narrow alleys as usual were lined with shallow open tunnels; trenches were filled with raw sewage, and dirty water carried waste from the thousands of shacks. One had to be a genius here to locate one's shack from the thousands that were packed together like sardines in a huge sack from the Lake Victoria region.

The smell here was familiar, and I didn't attract much attention from the crowds. This was home. We gelled together nicely. My new found perfume from the morgue resonated well with the dirty trenches and the throng of bodies around me. We were family, and fate had made sure we all fitted in together nicely. We shared a common identity. It ran in our slum DNA, defining who we were. It's said when you stay with a pig, you soon desire its ways, and before long, you learn its ways, and you too become a pig. I was a pig.

So I gained a rare confidence in my steps as I trudged on home, with no one stealing second looks at me. I was dressed right, I looked right, and I smelled right. There was nothing to make me stand out, so I easily walked myself back to our home, the little shack that I had lived in with my mother.

I found out that she wasn't in. The door had been secured, but that wasn't a problem. I had learned the simple trick sometime before. I lifted one of the iron sheets on the wall, got into the room, then slowly returned the iron sheet back in place. The nails that were to secure the iron sheets in place were loosely hanging in their respective holes.

I removed the oversize trousers and oversize blue shirt that had covered my nakedness and dressed into my torn t-shirt and heavily patched shorts. I was pleasantly surprised that my mother hadn't thrown them away.

I kept the morgue clothes lumped in the corner of the room. I was going to show them to mum, and she was going to decide whether or not I should keep them!

Mama Pima was busy serving customers in her den, and she hardly noticed that I was back. Patrons were shouting obscenities at each other.

I pulled the thin mattress and lay myself down to rest. I was tired. It had been a few weeks since I stepped my foot in the city of Nairobi, but it felt like it had been an eternity.

I was awoken by my Mum who almost wailed, thinking she had seen a ghost. She had come in much later in the evening, only to find me in the room, having slept the whole day out of fatigue and mental pressure.

She jumped up and down hysterically, "Baraka! Baraka!" She was so elated, she ran out of the house to inform the neighbors that I was back.

Mama Pima and about ten patrons came from their den and taunted me as I recounted my ordeal on the streets and in the morgue. They were so inebriated they hardly followed my adventures, noisily interrupting my narration.

"You should see *Muganga Kutoka Tanga,*" said one patron, referring to a specialist witch doctor from Tanga. "You should be cleansed from the evil spirits that you carried from the morgue!" One young man with an old face said. The others too weighed in their unsolicited pieces of advice about what I should do to be whole again.

The slum witchdoctors had mushroomed into real businessmen, and their trade was blossoming, as they offered a variety of solutions to all the problems that we faced in the slums. They could treat bad luck, provide protection of one's household, and get back lost items by causing the thieves to suddenly realize the delicacy that was hidden deep in the green grass, causing them to start grazing like cows. The doctors had spells for work promotions and money making, but surprisingly, they couldn't make much money for themselves. And their hideouts were always full of people seeking sudden fortunes which never came to be, but they still returned anyway. I abhorred them, and I was always afraid of even meeting them face-to-face on the streets, and now I was listening to a recommendation that I should visit one of them? I just said to myself that that was never going to happen.

My mum wasn't listening to any of them. She was overwhelmed by the fact that I had made it back.

When we sat back on our tiny mattresses in the house, we talked endlessly. I recounted to her the gory things that we did on the streets and that scared Mum to the core.

"Baraka, you should be so thankful to God that you are still alive. You are walking dead! All this shows me that the Lord loves you and preserved you through all those miseries!" I had lost all hope of ever getting you back, and am so grateful to God who kept you even as you walked through the valley of the shadow of death!" she said.

I also recounted all the other children I had met on the streets and the lives they lived out there in the cold, and Mum was petrified. I thanked her for holding onto me and my brother Isate and for not letting us slide into the streets.

"My heart goes out to Njoki, Mum! I am not sure if she survived the horrid beatings, and her baby! Oh, her baby! The unforgiving crowd had been merciless to her!" I said between sobs.

I didn't realize how much I had attached myself to Kibe's gang. They had quickly become family. We shared so much in common. Our lives mirrored each other in many ways. At first, I had been confined to them, but eventually I became part of their lives.

Mum listened to every word that I said deep into the cold night. She was genuinely happy to see me. I was so pleasantly surprised that she wasn't going to punish me for having left home in the first place without her permission and then veering off the radar leaving everyone else in the dark.

Sitting back in my mum's embrace reminded me of the power of a mum's unconditional love. I remembered the many times she had advised me against something but at times I just did it in defiance. Somehow, she was always right, and I always learned the hard way, from my own experience.

Looking back, I should have listened to my mum's voice echoing through the shanties, reminding me the ways of life. However, I didn't listen, I had chosen my fate, and it had defined how I related with my environs.

Freedom was no longer a misplaced abstract word. It was real. It looked real, and I could smell it, I could almost touch it. I started focusing less on the environment I was living in but more importantly I started laying more premium to the people I interacted with in my environment. The love that we shared with mum was invaluable. I had from time to time taken it for granted, but when I remembered the testimonies of my friends on the streets, I couldn't believe it. I was lucky to have a mother, and I promised myself to love her, take care of her, fight for her, and to make her battles my battles. I promised myself to live to be a respectable man—a man who was going to make a difference—but again I appreciated it wasn't going to be easy. I was going to try. I was going to start yet another journey to walk into freedom, step by step, and dig myself out from where Mum had left. I had seen the dead, and I appreciated the fact that once you lie on that cold slab, there is nothing you can do. Your value is erased and sooner or later people start talking about you intermittently. Then they finally stop, and you become a distant memory.

"Mum, I have to make a difference while I'm still alive! I was dead and counted as such, and all I brought into your eyes were tears. I thought about who would cry at my funeral, and you are the only one that came to mind."

"Mum, what would you have cried over?" I asked teasingly.

"Oh Baraka, I cried every day to God to preserve you wherever you were. I didn't want you to die like a dog on the streets, no, my toil could have been in vain. All the things that I ever labored for could have been in vain. The labor pains. The shame that has carried me through life because of you could have been in vain. One day you will understand this, Son! The ridicules; the misery of not having clothes and money to feed you could all have gone with the wind. Your presence, Baraka, and smile all add value into my life, and if you had died, I too could have died soon after, as there could be no reason or motivation to live on. You have been my motivation every single day that I wake up. I always look forward to a new dawn in your life. I always thank God for you, and I know in my heart of hearts that you will outlive me to do greater things that my small mind cannot think about. That is what could make me cry over your body. You will one day tell your story and change generations!"

She continued, "To know that you had died with my dreams and you had aborted them while all my life I lived trying to incubate you, with the hope that you would birth a new self—a new generation that will for sure be new, fresh, and free to walk and tread wherever you like, however you want to do it. Free to explore life in its fullness without limits. That's what you would have denied me Baraka: the freedom to reach beyond the stars and to take your dreams beyond, to explore the untapped heights and to reach out to that awesomeness and sweet core that God has put in us, it's deep down, but when we try hard to find it; we indeed locate it, and then we realize that happiness is about living to your full potential and helping others with their own journeys as you press along."

Mum carried on in her wisdom and I sat there in her arms, listening to her soft talk. She had studied to form six back then, and she had a sharp mind, but fate had other plans for her.

The world around us didn't exist. It was just the two of us—two souls put together by design—and I couldn't have wished to be anywhere else.

Mum had lived her entire life trying to change our lives and our environment, but I hadn't realized how this had taken a toll on her. It had drained the life out her and denied her the life she so wanted to live. She had laid her entire life aside for us to live. It was a selfless, bold move and a narrow path full of thorns that she had chosen. She had gone to school and attained her A-levels, but she hadn't secured a job, so she had to endure all the thorns and thistles that were strewn about life's narrow path, and she had to tolerate the pricks and the bleeding that came with that decision. But she endured, and she had paid with her life. Nothing else really mattered. She just wanted to see us better.

She continued, "When we sit back and critically isolate the noises in our lives, then it becomes something that's within reach, but then the multiple layers surrounding that beauty and sweetness within us is covered with layers upon layers of things that we need to shake off. And as we shed those layers, we begin to grow fresh muscles to replace the old narratives that have formed our lives, and with that, we start feeling anew, both physically and mentally."

'I want to take that journey, Mum,' I said to her. She hugged me tight as our rags locked into each other. That night, Mum taught me one invaluable lesson: that even in adversity, love is the most expensive thing in existence. It takes everything to truly love someone, including laying aside your life and your indulgences for the sake of the other. That night, I lay on the tiny mattress with a different insight in my heart, a strong feeling of a mother's love. It was a special feeling that I couldn't let go. My heart tickled with excitement.

CHAPTER TEN

I t was amazing how the high walls had separated us from
the rich. They rose high above us and elegantly stood
as a stark reminder of the reality of where we belonged.
While our world was dark with smoke billowing from the
rusty shanties, beyond the sturdy walls lay mansions, wealth,
affluence, and liberty. Rumor had it that the trees there had
the old man's beards hanging on them—the lichens—as a
solid statement of the pollution-free zone and the fact that
we didn't breathe the same air.

I strayed through the leafy suburbs, and left my mind
to wander in admiration at the leafy homes, peeping through
one of the gates. I could see the well-dressed gardens: heavily
manicured grass smiling at me with elegance. I could see
the gigantic mahogany tree full of swallows and swifts, and
a woodpecker busy pecking on the hanging branches. My
feeble mind had wondered why only the master in heaven
had allowed rain only onto these lawns. I later came to
notice the sprinklers that had been synched to take turns in
gracefully curing the thirst of the green lawns that soaked
in the water. My tongue hankered for a drop to quench the
thirst that milked away all the saliva in my dry mouth.

I was astounded by how much care the grass received,
but my imagination and world were crushed when a mean
dog, clearly heavier than my tiny frame, started barking and

running towards the gate; seemingly having smelled the dirt that ran through my blood. I scampered back to the cabro-plated road down to the path where I belonged. I ran down the road with the hoarse sound of the dog barking on furiously behind me. I had developed a fear of dogs after uncle Matata released his hounds on Isate and I back in the village.

Physically I had been scared away by the dog, but my mind kept at it. Why were these people living here and not everyone? Who were they? Who were their fathers? Who was their God? What did they eat? Had they ever tasted *ugali* or *mrenda* cooked on an open fire in an earthen pot? Had they ever taken the ice-cold water that's drawn from the cooking pot that lay on a round ring of banana leaves sometimes hosting dead rats at the bottom of the pot only discovered after days of savoring the water drawn from it? Did they have children? Who were their friends? Where did they go to school? My mind raced with these questions, and that night I couldn't rest. When Mum came home that night, I insisted that she take me along to her work-place.

She told me to wait for a week, which was a long time, full of anticipation.

Finally, we walked down the path. On either side of the road, beautiful soft palms rose high to welcome the smell of freshness, serenity, and calm. After a few miles there was a high gate with an electric fence meant to scare away the would-be trouble makers.

My eyes had so much to see that I had a difficult time keeping pace with my Mum's sure-footed strides. Twice I stumbled while trying to steal a second look at a magnificent cottage whose archaic roof elicited memories of very old movies that I had watched on my neighbor's television.

Mum was adorned in her pink, oversize checkered uniform with a matching pink cap loosely tied on her head. She looked elegant. I had known all the clothes mum had and could see and tell exactly how she looked even if I didn't see her leave the house. I could always correctly guess what she was putting on, as she didn't have many changes of clothes. But this was strange, as I had never seen her in this outfit before. I giggled to myself as I walked behind her, her arms firmly holding onto mine to ensure she didn't leave me behind to indulge in my daydreams.

We made a few turns, and right at the corner of the boardwalk was the most magnificent and inviting gate I had ever seen in my life. It rose high above the walls, and its artistic, arching doors left no room for doubt about it having been the work of master hands. It had two narrow passageways on both ends and a sheltered electric bell whose socket was gold-plated.

Mum used her key to open the gate, and my eyes were awed as I entered through. With every step I felt as if my filthy feet had strayed again into quarters I was never meant to step into, and I suddenly felt a tinge of shame, guilt, and embarrassment that made me to almost step back towards the gate. As I stepped onto the walkway, I felt my steps imprinting their murky indelible marks onto the pavement, my dirty shorts and shirt loosely held by two buttons that had survived continuous use. I suddenly became aware of the smell of my unkempt hair that folded into rusty thick brown strands that were now turning into a real pollutant of this cozy aura, and my sweaty body compounded the feeling. My mum pulled me along, saying nothing.

The gigantic house stood before us with its high slanting brown tiled roof a sight to behold.

Mum made a quick step forward and stood in the doorway.

"Baraka, remove your sandals before you come in," Mum said softly.

The formal lounge opened to the dining room and the entertainment patio.

"Welcome home! My son!" she said with a wide smile.

The reassuring tone in her voice melted my fears away, and I felt peaceful.

She was now standing in the spacious entry hall of this masterpiece with the grand circular staircases right in front of us. Mum ushered me in.

I looked at her, looked at my feet again, and smiled as my feet were so dirty. I hadn't seen water for days, and my sandals had a wide hole that ensured my whole heel touched on the ground. I had patched it a few times but there was no need of doing it anymore, as it was beyond repair. There were two strands that held it in place—one green and the other one red, having been recycled from an older sandal that I had picked at the dumpsite. My heel had since developed a deep crack large enough to serve as a natural wallet for a small coin. It made no difference whether or not I removed the sandals, but mum was not the kind of person to repeat herself. Over the years, I had learned this the hard way, so I quickly untied the lose strand that circled on my ankle to tie the sandals in place and stepped into the house. The gentle caress of the thick velvety Persian rug under my feet felt warm and heavenly. It tickled the nerve endings of my feet, and it reminded me that the senses in my feet were still alive. They'd seem to have been dead for years.

The rug was largely brown, but other colors were elegantly woven in, forming beautiful patterns. There were two large windows strategically designed to allow in enough light and cheat my feeble mind that I was still on the outside. I couldn't help but notice the large curtains in each window that beautifully blended with the heavy rug, which was perfectly in sync with the maroon walls. The window panels had large, back loops with botanical embroidered designs and fancy top grommets that made each panel to drape gracefully to feel the soft caress of the Persian rug. The living room was in itself a piece of art.

Mum ushered me to sit down on one of the couches. She broke into a hearty laugh as she watched my amusement as I sank into the couch, the leather soft, spongy fabric with the serpentine spring underneath shocked my gluteal mass that had been used to sitting on a cold hard floor. On the right corner of the house was a U-section sofa with five sets of elegant charcoal-black pieces, and in the middle was a glass table with a vase that had fresh flowers. Mum was quick to point out, "That's Mr. Igwe's favorite spot in the living room!"

Brass chandeliers hung from the gypsum ceiling, and the dim light gave the living room an amazing ambience. The large flat screen Samsung television was airing an animal channel, and for a moment my eyes got glued to the honey badger as it shrewdly delved deeper into the honey combs despite the hundreds of bees that seemed to sting into its heavy fur. The images showed on the screen were like tiny crystals full of color, and they brought the badger right into the living room. It was amazing. I remembered the many times my neighbor had to dash out to fix the aerial wire that stood high above all the houses in the village as a sign of affluence, though frequently the aerial danced to the tune of the wind and almost always forgot to relay a clear signal. Instead it transmitted what my neighbor had christened rice images on the screen; making it permanently hazy and one had to painstakingly search for images in what looked like zillions of rice particles. But I had looked forward to watching TV at my neighbor's home once every Saturday, evening after working on his farm for the whole day. Now there I was in Mr. Igwe's home, watching real images come to life right in front of my eyes.

"This is Mr. Igwe, the owner of this house with his wife, Mrs. Igwe, and his two children. This is his first-born daughter, Rebecca. I am told she is currently studying Computers in America. And this is his son, Mkombozi, studying Drama in Australia." Mum introduced them to me.

From the large family portrait on the wall they looked like one happy family, and I couldn't get my eyes off the photo. I admired the smiles and the happy faces and the intelligent eyes that lay behind the horn-rimmed glasses that Rebecca wore that made her look like a quintessential nerd. On the other hand, Mkombozi, Mr. Igwe's son, had taken after his father, with his hairline showing early signs of recessions to emulate his dad's alopecic head. Looking at the picture, I could guess he didn't really need the services of his barber. But he looked larger than life, and his broad smile gave an easy impression of himself. Looking at Mrs. Igwe, I couldn't tell much. The veneer that covered her face would take me time to get through. I left the unmasking for another day.

Mum was speaking as she dashed to the dining area.

"They are one happy family! My son!" she said with a rueful tone.

She carried on as she poured some tea into a wafer-thin cup, "Mr. and Mrs. Igwe have travelled to the USA for a family reunion with their son and daughter; their son will be flying in from Australia to join them in the USA for the summer holidays and later Dubai, so they will be away for a whole month."

Mum informed me that the swimming pools were chilled and sometimes warmed, depending on the time and clients' preferences, and that they could make my amnesiac mind to quickly forget that Dubai was a desert.

"They will later go to the dancing fountain that has been trained to dance to the music that blasts from the heavy speakers!" Mum narrated. Mum had never been to any of these trips, but she had mastered those tales from Rebecca's numerous anecdotes; Rebecca and Mkombozi were the only children of the Igwe's, and they had been given all that money could buy and they had learned to eat high off the hog.

My heart leaped at the thought of staying in this magnificence for longer, but my Mum, being a perennial disciplinarian, quickly read my mind and said to me, "Son you are not allowed to come here, neither are you allowed to stay here. This is foreign to you, and you are a foreigner here."

She sighed for a moment and continued, "No, *we* are foreigners here, Son! You are here today because I want you to experience affluence—to feel it, to taste it, and for a moment have it within reach! Come, let me show you around," she said with a sense of pride in her tone.

I gulped the tea from the tiny cup in one single huff and placed the cup back on the table, wondering why the cups were so tiny. I also wondered why Mum said it took Mr. Igwe one whole hour to finish the tea. *He must be a lazy eater*, I thought to myself.

By the pool was an elegant chaise lounge. The tautness of its upholstery was mind-blowing, and mum was quick to mention the spot her boss's favorite relaxation point. I didn't doubt her! I sank into it, enjoying every moment and allowing my mind to think like Mr. Igwe for a moment, though nothing came to my mind. It was blank.

Mum led me to the garden where I met her co-worker Mr. Museno.

I was pleasantly surprised at how happy he was to see me. He was middle-aged, stout, with a short torso and a long heavy beard. He had twisted his moustache into two awesome whiskers that looked like inverted antennas that protruded from either ends of his mouths, and his balding hair, like Mr. Igwe's, stood out like etiolated vines seeking the elusive sunlight.

'How are you Baraka?" he said with his outstretched arms ready for a handshake.

"I am fine, sir!" I said. His handshake was firm, warm, and prolonged. As he continued to shake my hand, he kept saying, "Welcome Baraka. We have been waiting to welcome you here for months now!"

I was extremely surprised and so delighted to meet someone who wasn't going to judge me, and he didn't seem to be bothered by how clumsy I looked. He was just happy to see me. His act and demeanor settled a quick friendship that made me easy, as I had all along thought that mum was alone in this massive compound.

"I will be back," Mum said as she dashed back into the house.

"I have worked here for Mr. Igwe ever since I was a young man as a shamba boy, and as you can clearly see, I am no longer the young boy, he said. "I know everything in this compound from the many years that I have lived with Mr. Igwe serving him diligently and faithfully. I will show you around and you being a young man, you can achieve all the things that you see here in this farm if you start now. For me, my time is gone, and I cannot reverse the clock." He paused as a tear formed in the corner of his left eye, but he quickly shrugged it off. He had spent all his prime years on this farm.

He led me past the open patio that was made more sheltered by partly enclosing it with a trellis that was dressed with beautiful flowers.

As we turned towards the garden, a cool breeze blew my way and embraced me with a warm welcome. I could feel an elated skip in my spirit as I marveled at the beautiful lilies that responded to the wind, dancing in rhythm. It was a happy garden.

There was a small, restful hideaway beyond the patio with a bed of gravel as part of the firescaping in the garden. The pathway to the garden was aesthetic—gravel chips made an attractive mulch around the echeveria herbs and other assorted variegated flowers. There were white and yellow daisies, whose blossoms added an unmistakable sense of elegance. I moved closer and touched the roses and the lilies on the pathways. Their softness was divine.

Along the pathway, the grass had folded away into deliberate tussocks akin to the elegant water bogs in the beautiful Arbedare mountain ranges that I had read about in my science classes.

The soil was well dressed, and Mr. Museno quipped, "I cover this soil with an organic mulch of bark, chips, coarse compost, peach pips, assorted shells, and pine needles to conserve the moisture to reduce the run off and soil erosion, and to ensure its natural look."

The concrete stone walls were filled with tiny exotic marbles, which provided an exotic elegance.

"See the high, stone walls. Baraka. The archways, the pergolas, and the trellises are all made from non-flammable material to protect this palatial building from would-be fires, but the constant watering ensures the entire garden is ever green regardless of the season."

"How did you learn all this!"

"I am an old man, Baraka! Some things come with age! I have been here for decades, my son!"

I would have wanted to lie down in this garden, to soak in the fresh air, but that didn't seem to be an option. There was still so much to see. The soft garden breeze reminded me of the numerous holes in my pair of shorts.

Museno took me back to the house and explained that there were seven bedrooms. He was going to show me around the house. "This is the family room," he said, pointing at the voluminous room with exposed roof trusses equipped with a Morso fireplace with a large glass automatic door that opened towards the gardens. He took me up the elegant spiral staircase that led to the master bedroom. It had a dressing room that opened to a large atrium and a fully-fitted en suite. It had a beautiful jacuzzi with gold lining on it inscribed with the words "IGWES' PARADISE."

There was an artic small table with a chamois bag on top of it that had shiny ornamentals that Museno was quick to mention contained rare pearls that Mr. Igwe had collected over the years. Mr. Igwe's study room had wooden blinds with a private balcony that had an amazing view of the gardens; this was truly a source of inspiration that the mind needed to think.

I wondered how it felt to sit on the armchair covered with a silk arm rest that lay at the center of the room. To satisfy my curiosity, I went and sat on it, and for a moment I had a magical encounter with destiny. I felt I owned the world. I felt different almost psychedelic but Musoni quickly tapped me back to reality! "Let's go, we have more to see," he said, grabbing my hand and pulling me out of the bedroom.

As I hobbled behind him, I kept wondering; "God, why did you allow Mr. Igwe to live here and a young soul like myself to be here at such a time just admiring all this wealth? Why God? Why?"

I knew I was leaving behind a foul odor. It oozed from by dirty skin, and it would take a miracle to restore the freshness of the rooms after my visit.

"Baraka, this a fully equipped wine cellar. A private sommelier visits whenever Mr. Igwe has important guests to give them a taste of fine dining. As you can see, there is an eat in kitchen; thatched *lapa* with built-in *braai*, overlooking the sparkling pool that opens towards the delightful garden that we just visited," he said with pride in his heart as he explained.

I wanted to ask him who a sommelier was, but I kept that to myself.

"There are also secure living features that includes an alarm system and automated sliding doors leading to the carport, as you can see, but I have switched off the alarms and security systems so that I don't get into trouble explaining what you were doing here to Mr. Igwe." He gave me a naughty smile.

He pressed a button, and the gigantic sliding doors opened to a carport, and next to it was a simplex for pets, with a large kernel. It's at that moment that I heard the loudest woof. Right there in front of me was a huge, grouchy dog, wagging its tail. With her molten eyes, she scared me to the bone. She had no doubt been trained to sniff out unwanted guests like me. Her canines were poking out as she raised her saucer paws ready to strike me. Museno called her out and she calmed down, wagging her tail.

I was now tightly clinging to Museno panting like a banshee.

"Don't worry, Baraka. You are safe. She will not harm you," he reassured me.

The carport was exciting. Museno pressed a button, and the automatic doors folded away with grace into the upper pockets and exposed two heavy machines that were inside. He explained to me that the silver Pajero belonged to Mr. Igwe's wife and that it wasn't shy about consuming fuel. It was a guzzler. He also explained that the car had airbags to protect the driver and the front passenger and extra airbags on all the side windows to protect the passengers seated in the back. I interjected and asked, "What are airbags?"

He looked at me with a smile and giggled, then said, "These are bags that get inflated with air and spring out within nanoseconds of a collision to cushion the occupants of the car from injuries."

I looked at him in shock and thought to myself, *Oh, so not every car is the same?* I wondered if I would ever have the privilege of stepping into and driving in that confident machine. He also mentioned that it had air conditioners akin to the ones that I had seen in the house, and their main function was to cool the temperatures within the car, so that when the boss drove out in the hot sun he didn't have to worry about the sweltering heat outside. Instead he could cool his car and enjoy his ride, even for long hours! This was mind boggling.

After this experience Museno ushered me back into the house towards the hallway, and he said

"This is the guest bathroom. Come in. Your mum has prepared the bathtub for you to take a shower," he said.

Those were the most magical words that Museno had said since we met. Looking around the bathroom, I saw that it was fully equipped with a large walk-in shower fit for royalty. A swell of excitement filled my heart as I lay in the bathtub. Mum had fully soaped it up, and I felt sooty. I felt like I had never taken a bath all my life—that I had been walking around dirty all my years! I soaped myself silly, scrubbing all the filth from my body. There was layer after layer of dirt, and I continued soaping and scrubbing. The sparkling, pure-white bathtub turned brown and sticky with the dirt from my body having coalesced into dark clots blocking the bathtub, but I couldn't have cared less. I continued to scrub myself clean and soaked in the moment, cleaning every part of my body, including my hair. It was amazing and insanely refreshing.

Mum fetched me down, surprised me with new shorts and a new t-shirt, only to realize later they belonged to Mkombozi who hardly wore them, as he had outgrown them. Mum assured me that I could keep them and wear them home. I was on cloud nine, riding with the angels. She mentioned that Mrs. Igwe had allowed her to take the shorts home, but she was waiting for the right moment to surprise me, and the day had come.

She led me to the kitchen, where the wafting smell of delicious fish was in the air. It was at that point that I got the intuitive insight that I had never smelt the cooking of food back in our tiny room in the slums. Every nice smell was camouflaged by the heavy smell of raw sewage that generously laced every air particle that we breathed, denying us the smell of our own *ugali* and taking away our dignity. And here I was, fully enjoying every breath of air. It shocked my nostrils, being able to recognize the smell of niceness and freshness. It was incredible!

The kitchen was rustic and inviting, fully designed to have one become an instant chef. With polished concrete finishing and exposed brick walls, it left my mouth gaping. There were several cabinets that were filled with food. In one cabinet I saw several packets of rice; in another was whole bread, nicely sliced; there was an antique table by the kitchen that had all sorts of spreads—margarines and jams—with different fruit labels on each jar. I moved closer and took one in my hands. It had pictures of fresh berries that made my mouth water with excitement. There was a gigantic gas cooker with several burners, and an oven. The food in the cabinets was more than the entire stock in our nearby slum kiosk.

"Mum, what's this?" I asked.

"This is strawberry jam that's spread on bread," she said calmly with a smile on her face.

She took a slice from the cabinet, spread the jam on it and asked me to eat. It was the most tantalizing thing that had been in my mouth for a very long time. Bread was rare back at home—a rare delicacy over the holidays—and now bread with jam was like a miracle. It tasted divine, and never in my life had I ever imagined that bread could be this tasty.

Mum served the fish with a plate of rice and I enjoyed it, savoring every bite, crushing almost all the bones. She served a side of well-trimmed vegetables, with fresh mango cuts and assorted grapes with ice-cream, and later she served hot coffee direct from the coffee machine that was in the dining room. She had called me and ushered me to the coffee machine and asked me to press a button. When I did, the machine roared, and with one act of magic released a cup and filled it with hot coffee and milk. The red button turned green, and mum ushered me to pick my coffee! I had seen too much for a single day! She made me eat like royalty and feel like royalty.

"It's dusk now, Son! We need to get back home!" Mum said to me in a low tone.

'Mum, but you said Mr. Igwe is away for a month! I want to stay here a little longer, Mum!"

No, we have to back home, Baraka!"

My dreams sunk with every word that she said. I knew this wasn't home, but I had hoped she would allow me a night to indulge in the affluence—to feel and enjoy sleep in this magnificence. However, Mum was a principled woman. She had already changed back to her dress, and I didn't doubt her words that it was time to leave.

"Mr. Igwe is not here!" I reminded her but she ignored me.

I had banked my hopes on that, but it didn't earn me the right to stay, so we had to leave. I gave Museno a tight hug and thanked him for the warm welcome. He watched as we left the compound empty handed with only a small paper bag that carried my old rags. My hopes sunk with every step back home.

On our way, we didn't say a word to each other. My mind was jumbled up with every scene that I had experienced flashing back onto my mind. I was troubled. I remembered Igwe; his image was tightly etched onto my mind like an engraving on a piece of rock. I wandered back to the beautiful arrays of flowers and gardens that adorned the paths to his home, surrounding myself in the fragrance that emanated from his gardens.

Back home, I remembered the many times that I had to bear the brunt of the sun that heat up my meninges into fluidity—that coiled my freedom into a fiery furnace that seemed well determined to fry my dreams and serve them back to me. I recalled the soft hum and the cool breeze flowing from the air conditioner, and I kept dreaming that one day I would ride in an air conditioned machine and enjoy a controlled environment—an environment of choice where I wouldn't take in the caprices that nature far too long dictated to me. When I walked around, I knew there was a difference between living and just hustling by. I had taken breath for many years, but my life felt empty.

The moment we stepped onto the path that led to our dwelling, the air changed into an acrid cocktail and there was no doubt I was heading back to my reality—to a place where I belonged: a place where poverty was synonymous with and deeply inseparable from our family name. Poverty had a smell, and my nose could pick up its scent from a distance. I sat down on the cold floor as Mum drew the thin mattress that had been donated to us after the storm some weeks back. We had shared the tiny sisal mat, but after the donation, Mum slept on the old bed and I slept on the floor on the other thin mattress. The sisal mat that she had slept on for years had been swept away in the horrible storm. I dreaded the cold floor and the cold breeze that blew through the numerous open curvatures of the rusty corrugated iron sheets that were meant to be the walls of our dwelling.

On the inside, we had layered the walls with old cartons and newspapers, but over time they had been eaten up by cockroaches and rats that forgot this was to be a collective abode for us and them. I blamed these creatures for being so myopic, selfish, and poor in their mental faculties. But perhaps they were lucky, as they would crawl into a neighbor's house in search of more cartons, but I had nowhere else to go to. This was my home. And these were the four walls of my confinement. It was my reality and everything else was a dream.

I thought to myself, *Mum must be very wicked to enjoy all those things that I saw at Mr. Igwe's house and not to carry some of them home.*

She had quickly read my mind and with quick wisdom she asked me to move closer and sit on her mattress that she had now rolled out.

"Son, I am glad you got the chance to visit my workplace. I trust you learned something today—that there is a life out there beyond these rugged walls. Beyond these open sewers there are cleaner homes and environments.

She continued, "Beyond this horrendous indignity, there is dignity. Beyond the cramps that we call food, there are royal meals that people sit together around dining tables as families to dine and wine, and beyond these rugged shacks that we all crumble and muzzle into every day, there are homes where the wind still blows and sings and talks the language that our ears are not trained to understand." She paused. "Not just yet, my son! That's the irony of life, my son, but today is a new dawn for you son! You are filled with all that you ever need to be what you were meant to be in life. Just remember, you will never and you can never unwind the clock. It keeps ticking, and as it ticks, so are your dreams, so are your hopes, so is your destiny rolling into greatness or obscurity. The wheel of life keeps clanking," she said.

"Always remember the story of the lizard. Though a small weak animal, she finds room in the king's palace. You have to be strategic and to have no limitations son. To conquer your mind, don't be a slave to your emotions. Be a wild spirit in thought and ambition, but tame your indulgence. Be in charge of yourself, Son!"

That night, Mum taught me profound lessons in life—that I could be all that I wanted to be in life and that I shouldn't let inhibitions drift my hopes and aspirations. She held me close and asked me to look her into her eyes. For the first time, I saw and could feel her pain. Her eyes had seen both the two worlds. She had lived both in the two extreme worlds every day of her life in the last few years.

She said, "Son; I would like you to understand one thing. It pains me so much to walk down from that palace back into this shanty—to prepare food for royalty in that magnificent kitchen and come home to see us sleep hungry with no water to drink. It pains me to prepare those beds that you saw with huge mattresses, with the numerous layers of sheets and warm, silk blankets . . . before coming home to draw and lay our heads on these tiny mattresses that are home to bedbugs that ferociously feed on our blood. It pains me to use all those gallons of water in a day flowing down the drain while we can't even get enough here to drink. It pains me daily to look at a fridge full of foods—some imported from far-off countries—and to come home to our small kerosene stove that has been dry for weeks. The worst of all, my son, is to see you sleep hungry on this rugged floor with my conscience fully aware that there are mattresses out there that I can't afford to buy you—even just one. Those are the two worlds I live in, Son, and it pains me. I pray that your children will never see you in such a state of helplessness, where you silently watch them in the night while their stomachs crunch in pain from the hunger and they toss and turn, trying to wade off the nerve-racking cold and the stubborn bites from these seasoned bugs!"

As she continued to speak, her eyes filled up with tears. She was now sobbing, and I couldn't resist it. I gave her a warm hug and started crying over her shoulders. I could feel her pain. I could see her agony, and this day I had experienced her two worlds.

Mum continued, "I work my fingers to the bone and have denied myself everything. Look at my dress," she sobbed. "It's been torn for five long years—five long years, Son. I haven't replaced it in all that time. Look at the several patches that have made me lose sense of its original color; look, Son! It has endured a zillion washes, and I can't wash it anymore. I am not able to replace it, Son! Look at your shorts full of holes.

Look at the countless open sewers that you have to jump to access the road—the ignominy that denies us the sweet-smelling aroma of our burning *ugali* on this kerosene stove, the wind that has been trained to blow into our house only the pungent smell of stale urine. The many fires that have razed down our neighbors' shanties every other year. The flood waters carrying raw sewage that rage into this room, sweeping away the utensils and giving us an unwelcome fresh start. We cannot continue to live like this. Poverty has no dignity. Poverty is the leech that bleeds an already dying heifer. It will kill us someday, Son. It has stripped us of everything. We don't have a name—no visitors! This has to stop, Son! We shouldn't die like this. We have to live someday. I might not live in this generation. I might not live to see it, Son, but you need to start a new generation—a generation that will know there is life in the years that come with it. A generation that won't know the pain and disgrace of having to defecate in the open fields beside their children. But you have to make a choice: you have to choose the road that you will take. That's the road that will lead you away or into your destiny."

"I went to school, and some of my classmates are now professors, but I made mistakes, and have owned them up. Learn from my mistakes, Son!" she said amid sobs.

The distance between me and the cold floor had been a thin layer of sisal strings that made up the sisal mat. Every night as I drew the sisal sheet I knew that underneath lay a trail of ants that I had learned over time to respect. Attacking one of them meant an uncanny assault on an army whose retaliatory bites would last the whole night. The experience had taught me to be wise and to let those little creatures be. Sooner or later, I would hear the whining sounds of mosquitoes, which had become bosom friends, coming for an early meal. I had told myself that I was an answered miracle to their prayers. They needed to survive too. They needed to feed, and I had over time learned not to fight them but to share generously the life that ran through my veins. That night, I couldn't sleep. I became aggressive with them, trying to fight them off, and I also attacked my bedbug friends, who couldn't understand my sudden animosity towards them. I'm sure they wondered why I wasn't willing to cooperate this particular night. I had been God's gift to these little creatures for far too long, and as I wasted away my life in misery, they fattened on my blood.

That night, a deep-seated complacency that had clouded my mind was lifted. I was angry with myself for having been too naïve—for having insulted my mother, devilishly imagining her living in wealth. For not appreciating every effort she had made.

I felt sorry for the heaps of clothes she had to wash to get hold of a bunch of half-rotten chicken legs that were fried along the open sewer lines. These pieces were meant to be fed to the dogs, but instead they were well-guarded by a swarm of flies, waiting for such customers as my Mum who had become a regular. These were the delicacies that Mum snuck to the room with after saving for a whole week to afford them. The chicken legs were the rejects from the hotels frequented by the bourgeoisie. They had been deep-fried in a huge, sooty pan with recycled oil that violently roared on its base as more and more chicken heads and innards were thrown in to fry. The oil was black as tar after being recycled for weeks, and when the chicken legs came out of the oil, they too had been marionetted into black delicacies. Rumor had it that the oil was siphoned from Kenya Power transformers, but in the slum, our stomachs treated that as a non-issue.

But these had been the favorites, which I had learned to look forward to—to enjoy and to relish.

I knew I had to do something, and I had to do it fast. I had to begin a journey, and I had to start there and then.

CHAPTER ELEVEN

T hat night, my mind had wandered into a world of possibilities and with every thought of success, my heart leaped with joy. I couldn't sleep. My mind danced to the sound of the wind as it caressed the rugged iron sheets that were our abode. The clustering sounds were a stark reminder of the squalor that we lived in. At 3:00 a.m. that night, I got off my tiny mattress and crawled under Mum's wooden bed. I pulled an old blue band tin from the hole under the heavy cartons that had served as my home bank for the last few weeks. I couldn't afford to run a bank account, and I knew it was time to break my covenant with the tin. We had agreed I was only to open it during the Christmas Holidays and that I would visit a fast food joint and enjoy some real fried chicken—those ones that had been trained to summersault on grills. I had heard it was finger-licking good and laced with some secret ingredients that made it crunchy and tasty. With the balance, I would buy myself a pair of shorts and an Arsenal jersey to cheer my team through the cracks of the wooden frames at the slum video kiosk, but that wasn't going to happen. I had to end that dream. Sometimes the end of a dream is the dawn of a new one.

I took a piece of metal and forced it through the tiny nozzle that had ensured whatever went in couldn't get out, I struggled to open the tin, but with every struggle it reminded me of the broken dream. The only way to get the money out was to destroy the tin. After about thirty minutes of trying I gave it a final twist with the metal bar and managed to open it up. Several coins came out of the tin with a clutter. I made sure Mum was fast asleep, as I didn't want my next dream to be extinguished before it could even start. I counted the coins under the dim light of the kerosene lamp. With exhilaration it had taken several days to amass a total of 520 shillings from the menial jobs at the construction sites. I wrapped them carefully in a black paper bag and slid the disfigured tin safely back under Mum's bed and the black piece of paper under my mat to be my pillow case for the night.

I couldn't sleep after that. I started counting the hours of the night and appreciated how long one night can be. At 4:00 a.m. that morning, I folded my mattress and carefully slid it back under my mum's bed. I took my brown sandals. Each of them had a humongous hole that reminded me of Mt. Longonot crater that I had read in my geography classes. I put them on religiously, despite the fact that half of my feet trampled on Mother Nature, and I had since developed signature cracks on the heels of my feet from the endless treading. I stealthily walked to the door that was patched with a confused assortment of scrap metals of different industry brands—Blue band, Kimbo, Cow Boy—that had been collected over time from the dump site and patched on the door to wade off the biting cold. I opened it and it made the usual loud screech that woke my Mum from her deep slumber. Indeed, God gives sleep to they that loves Him. Mum, despite the challenges and vagaries of life, was a happy soul and a deep sleeper.

"Where are you going, Baraka? Not yet time for work!" she bantered. Her voice was still a low tone, heavy from the morning sleep. "I will explain later, Mum," and with that I disappeared into the dark alleys leading to the bus station. She muttered, but her voice was weak and waned, barely beyond the doorway. As I trudged along, I could see shadows and imaginary objects in front of me scaring me stiff to the nerve. I increased my pace and was almost breaking into a run when I stumbled on a stone and fell down with a thud, hurting my front toe that was always poking outward looking for trouble;. It pained me to the core, but the biting cold of dawn quickly numbed the pain as I soldiered on.

At the bus station I met two women with heavy sisal bags and a carrier bag each tied on their heads and rested calmly on their backs. Their backs arched like an archer's bow designed from the pacific yew. It was a true testament to the heavy loads they had to endure to get groceries from the market. They were silent as if in tune with the silence of dawn, not uttering a word to each other. I joined them in the awkward silence and waited for the bus. It was after about ten minutes later when a middle-aged man, also carrying with him a sisal bag, joined us, walking with a signature bent back. The thought of myself having a bent back scared me stiff, as I had been told you are who you surround yourself with. He immediately brought the place to life, chatting with the two women who were clad in heavy sweaters and head gears looking like Eskimos going to hunt for ice in the desert. The man was also wearing heavy clothes with a large beanie. He turned to me and asked, "Young boy; what's your name?"

"Baraka," I answered him in a low tone.

"What are you doing here in the cold dressed like that?"

I looked at myself. The shorts that I had were well-ventilated, allowing a free flow of air to aerate my bottom, creating tiny little frozen bumps. The tiny bumps were beginning to itch, as was the norm, and I scratched them, my mouth twitching in pain. My white t-shirt had shed its whiteness, and in its place were myriad shades of grey. It had multiple folds, and one could almost think it has just been snatched from a cow's hungry mouth.

I was still looking at myself, when he asked again, "Baraka, where are you going at this hour?"

I looked at him and gently responded, "Am going to the market."

"What are you going to buy?" he asked with a rugged smile folded at the corner to his mouth. I am going to buy maize to roast," I said.

He looked at me with a long gaze and put his hand calmly on my shoulders. "Why would you want to do that at your age?" he asked.

I looked back at him, ignoring his question. I said to him, "I want to roast maize. Will you please show me where to buy when we get to the market?"

He stared at me for a long time. I looked down at my feet, trying to draw something in the sand. Then I looked at him again. At that point he said to me, "*Kijana*. It's going to be difficult but if you fail you will have tried."

At that moment, a rusty brown bus pulled up. It was already full, but I wasn't surprised that the driver still stopped. That was the norm, but I hadn't experienced it first-hand. The two women were bundled in first like a bunch of cabbage sacks. The conductor was in a rush and asked us to get into the already overloaded bus. I went in after the man, but there was nowhere to sit, so we had to stand huddled next to each like sheep in a crowded pen. The bus was already sweaty with the acerbic smell of humans permeating and lacing every air particle that we breathed. Deep down, I knew my whole body had a strange dirty scent, but I couldn't compare it to the pungent smell that engulfed the bus, which was horrendous. We swayed with every single turn as the driver tried to negotiate the meandering road, which had fumarole-like cracks similar to the trails left behind by the molten rocks of Mt. Longonot. I could feel my back ache as the bus tires crunched over the serrated road. It felt like a raw cactus cutting through my back. The potholes felt so large that it felt as if we were driving through an archeologist's den.

As the bus bounced over the loose gravel on the road, we in turn smashed into each other like wheat grains on a winnowers fan being separated from the chaff. No one complained, however. It seemed like a normal process for the rest of the passengers, and it surprised me so much how one could get so used to such discomfort and torture that none could say a word in protest.

But then I quickly reminded myself that we had been cut from the same piece of cloth and that nature had a way of reconciling anything that we as individuals accepted as normal. I protested loudly in silence. The conductor's head was right next to mine, his mouth stayed open for the rest of the bumpy drive with his nicotine-stained teeth poking out in the morning cold. In close proximity to him, I could smell his malodorous mouth, which he seemed to have gargled with a dose of rotten eggs. I quickly diagnosed him with acute halitosis that needed some immediate medical attention. I had been used to the smell of sewage, but the smell in this bus was like a second skin that I wanted to quickly peel off, and I was so relieved when the bus came to a halt with a sharp squeak. I gave the conductor a twenty shillings coin as the fare and alighted. I waited for my newfound friend to alight, and when he came down, we held tightly onto our bags and joined the massive crowd that was milling down to the infamous Gikomba Market. This market had been known for fires that gutted the stalls every so often and for muggers who robbed traders in broad day light.

But here I was, putting all that behind me; having been trained by my own environment in Kibra. Such occurrences were no longer news. This was our existence.

We all flowed in one direction like a huge shoal of fish. Everyone was in a rush—their faces clouded with a cornucopia of mixed feelings hidden beneath their darkened skins. Hundreds of makeshift market stalls made from wood and roofed with corrugated rusty sheets dotted every side of the muddy street, turning it into a narrow passage. Traders and buyers haggled over the prices of secondhand clothes. I saw a plus-size woman lifting up an oversize pair of panties and stretching it to its limit. I giggled as I walked by. She clearly didn't have manners! My mother would have scolded her. Other traders were chanting about their merchandise at the top of their voices, shouting themselves coarse.

"Kumi! Kumi." one man sang, insisting the pricing was only ten shillings.

Others took turns: *"Mia ni Moja, moja ni mia!"* Making one hundred shillings sound so melodious to the ear.

The seething crowds kept surging forward, paddling through the mud. We passed by open spaces with no stalls but filled up with heaps upon heaps of rotten produce and peelings. Pelicans were already mounting onto these heaps, searching for food. There were stalls with meat hanging on hooks, dripping with fresh blood and dozens of cages with chickens uncunningly waiting in turns for their time to face the butcher's knife. They had trusted their owners to feed them, but they had only been fattened for the knife.

The smell of onions and bananas mingled wildly with the unholy agglomeration of the saline odors of the sweaty crowds giving the air above me a concoction of sorts. We passed hundreds of women who had already set up their wares: sacks full of nuts and grains of different forms and colors. The market was alive, and I was amazed at the spirit of hard work and determination on the faces in the crowds and how these people, with so few resources, were doing so much. I wasn't going to kick my can down the road anymore. I was going to act. I was going to be in control of my destiny. Destiny was calling me and here, I was dangling my tiny gluteal mass from left to right in a rehearsed rhythm, copying the voluptuous and plus-size women ahead of me as I trudged in the mud, calling my dream to life. We stopped at a huge pile of maize that was just being offloaded from handcarts. The man tapped me on my shoulders and said to me, "Baraka, this is the place to buy as much as you can and return the same way we came!" I turned to thank him but he was gone, swallowed by the colossal crowd.

I looked at two men who were selling the pile of green maize chanting in turns in a ten shillings tune,

"Kumi."

"Kumi."

"Kumi."

"Kumi."

I bent and started picking only 50 pieces. I counted 500 worth of coins and paid for the merchandise and with that I turned to leave. Unlike other traders who carried their wares on their backs, I instead put mine on my head and joined the bustling crowd.

Dawn had given way and the sun's rays were beginning to creep through the crowded alleys. I got to the bus station, and this time there were several more rusty buses carrying vendors who had already purchased all they needed from the market. I ushered one to a stop and boarded. I got back to my house with the maize and found Mum had just woken up. I explained everything to her and the decision that I had taken. She laughed hysterically at the idea but then stopped and told me to try my luck. I requested to use our broken small charcoal *jiko* to roast the maize outside along the pathway where there was heavy human traffic to and from their daily hustles and bustles.

The first day was tough as I only managed to sell eleven cobs the rest were readily munched by my friends and neighbors who dawdled at my location for the better part of the day, claiming they were keeping me company while prowling like hungry tigers waiting for fallen prey.

"Baraka, that one is burnt. Can I eat it?"

"Baraka that one no one will buy. Can I take it?" They went on and on.

When Mum came later that night, I was feeling so discouraged that I had lost part of the money as I had not sold all the cobs. We had eaten almost half of the stock. I had looked at the smoke from the *jiko* rise into the clouds, and as it did so did, my dreams spread into smithereens. My Mum added an extra two hundred shillings and said to me that she was paying for the money that I had lost. It was a kind gesture from her though not a full re-imbursement, but she invigorated my spirit and I woke up even earlier the following day to the market repeating the same routine over and over again, and with each passing day, I learned the tricks more and more, and I made more money in the process. By the end of the month, I had grown my money to one thousand eight hundred shillings, and there was no looking back. I was roasting more maize and selling more than 90% of the stock each day. It was exciting to know that I could make my own money. I bought second hand sandals—this time made from recycled tires—and my feet quickly adopted to the roughness and texture of the sandals. I kept saving my money in a fresh blue band home bank tin that I hid in a hole that I had sunk on the floor. Every single day when I was sure no one was watching, I lifted the huge cartons that secured my bank and hid it away. I removed the loose soil and banked my daily savings then secured with the carton box. I did it religiously for several days.

I had to fight off the Town Hall officers who often smashed my *jiko* for refusing to offer kickbacks or harassed me for selling illegally on the roadside. Many were the days that they ran away with my stock and I had to chase after them pleading with them to allow me to continue with the hustle. Some days I was lucky to get the stock back, and other days as fate might have it, they ate my roasted maize, and poured water over my charcoal. The Town Hall officers had become an albatross around my neck. Nevertheless, I soldiered on and kept my dream alive. I had heard of people minting money through such ventures, and this was my liquid gold. I was going to milk it.

***

I remember the date so vividly. It was December 28th, 2000, and that evening, Mum came to my business premises, running like a wild cat. She danced around the elevated *jiko* that I had raised with a three-legged triangular metal stand to match my height. I looked at her and wondered in awe what was going on. She was embarrassing me. She started ululating as crowds of people milled around us, looking at her with strange faces, some chiding her for getting drunk so early in the day and for being high on bhang which was readily available in the corridors. I had never seen my Mum so wild, and I just stood there watching her in amusement as she kept chanting, "Thank you, Lord! Thank you, Lord! Thank you, Lord!" I got concerned when Mum started sprawling on the ground, soiling her dirty garb further. In the slum, everyone seems to know everyone else so deeply. It's ridiculous, and where I was selling my merchandise wasn't so far away from our shanty, so our neighbors had also milled around us, wondering who had bewitched my Mum overnight and driven her mad.

Mum was bursting at the seams. She recovered and announced to the massive crowd, "My son Baraka, has topped the whole of western province in the KCPE exams with 593 marks out of the possible seven hundred.

With this news I found myself airborne, with the crowd grabbing me, tossing me into the air. The crowd suddenly broke into song and dance while others rushed into the nearby bushes and came with twigs which they loosely put around my neck. They took me round the slum, in the corridors, at the market place singing and dancing *Mwana wa mbere* songs! Others shouted 593! 593! More people left their wares unattended to and joined in the euphoria. I had never felt so special as I did in this moment. My heart was pounding, and I was afraid it was going to burst out. I had never felt this happy. The feeling of happiness was an amazing one, and I was afraid it was going to drive me insane. *So, someone can be this happy?* The feeling was strange, yet exciting. I was in seventh heaven. All I had known in my life was pain and misery, and now this feeling was confusing. The slum was one huge community. We embraced each other's misery, and everyone knew there was nothing they could do about it, but they talked about it endlessly and gave each other an audience to speak about the lives we shared. That was the beauty of living in the shanties. The day a neighbor cooked beef or real chicken, everyone would know, and everyone would talk about it. Forget about mum's chicken innards. They never had a scent to be relished.

After about an hour of being tossed in the air and having moved around the slums for almost two kilometers, I was finally put on the ground. The sudden attention drove my spirit into a frenzy. That evening I appreciated the statement that success has many fathers but defeat is an orphan. I instantly became a son to many, as everyone kept saying our own has made us proud. It also dawned on me that we all belong to a community, and you will know that the day you do something that's extreme, whether good or bad.

My mum had been swallowed by the crowd and I couldn't trace her. I slowly traced my way back to my business site. I couldn't believe what I was seeing. My *jiko* had been broken into pieces, and the wire-mesh that I lay my maize on to roast had been stolen, all the maize that I had been roasting, too, was missing, including the bag that still had fresh ones. It was all gone. The metal stand was also missing. Nothing was left but the maize cobs and the small mound of ash, reminded me of my business.

I touched my pockets too and all the coins that I had sold for the day were also gone. I couldn't tell if someone one had taken them or they had fallen out during the triumphant melee. I didn't allow that to dampen my spirits I ran home to my shanty and found neighbors who had pulled up their stools, flanking the open fire, chatting happily. They burst into more songs and celebrations when they saw me, carrying me around and tossing me up in an insane celebration—a collective celebration of victory. A victory against the masses, against the mighty and scary winds of fate that swept our shanties every single day, reminding us of where we belonged—in the gutters! My victory had been fathered by the slum—by the difficult life that we lived back in the village, by the environment that reminded me daily of the struggle that I had to live through, and of the battles I had faced. It was equitable and joyous to share this incredible experience with them.

Strangely, sleep evaded my trap that night. The incidences of the day lingered in my mind and stuck to my frontal lobe like a thin layer of fine glue, not letting go. For the whole night, I was denied my rest. Mum didn't sleep either. She was on cloud nine, elated and feeling so proud and dignified. All her life she had actively played the plumber, digging us out of the miry trenches of life, hoping that one day she will get us out of the sludge, and indeed she had become decorated with the improprieties of life—with the many tags of a failed mother. But she had kept digging, and the more she dug, the murkier she got, and now here she was, shedding one whole garment of indecency and putting on one thin layer of hope that her son was going to turn around things. She was justified to be happy, and she cared less what the world would think. She was going to celebrate her son. We looked at each other in the dimming light of the kerosene lamp whose light faded into the wee hours of the morning, only then running out. Mum smiled looking at me with the innocence of a little girl, and I could see a tear in her eye. It was a tear of joy.

At dawn we heard a knock on our shanty door. We hadn't slept. Mum opened the door ajar. We hadn't seen anyone visit us in weeks and it felt strange to hear someone knocking this early on our humble abode.

Standing at the door was a stout-looking old man with a round potbelly that reminded me of the village pot that uncle Matata had reduced to shards. He introduced himself as the area chief, and I marveled at why he would be visiting us at the early hour of the day. I had heard rumors that it was very difficult to see him or even book an appointment with him, but here he was. I waited with bated breath to hear what he had to say.

"Good morning, Mum!" he said

"Where is the shiny boy!" My heart almost leaped when he mentioned that

So, he had actually come to visit the wonder boy. My heart smiled.

He continued, "Mama Baraka, we want you to know that we are proud of you as a community.

So, he even knows my name! I thought to myself.

"The Leading TV station will be here at 11:00 a.m., and they will be accompanied by a battery of dignitaries to interview you, so please don't leave. We want you to be ready.

That morning we hosted the Kibra chief in our shanty and were later invited into his offices. Later, we sat at the TV station with my sandals feeling the beauty of an expensive Persian carpet and flashy studio lights. The news anchor introduced herself: "My name is Chichi. Please introduce yourselves to our viewers." She was speaking in fluent English, and I struggled getting her words.

I was feeling jacked up but I composed myself and responded eloquently to all her questions with simplicity and clarity of mind.

The station was receiving numerous calls congratulating me on the success that I had brought to the Kibra slums and that our day to shine in the slums had finally dawned. Suddenly our gutters were wafting with the freshness of roses. The evil winds that blew the smell of sewage into our shanties had forgotten to blow. Everywhere smelled strangely sweet and fragrant. Yes, slender and voluptuous news anchors with their velvety tight pants and sports jackets had to jump our gutters full of raw sewage that suddenly smelt like fresh porridge and bend their backs, adjusting their expensive

Brazilian weaves to catch a glimpse of my humble abode. The air precipitously wafted with fresh and expensive cologne with the wild freshness of Igwe's farm. It was an amazing sight to behold. All the while, my mum stood beside me with a permanent Cheshire grin on her face. No one was going to take that grin away from her. It was her time to shine.

The powerful town clerk made a surprise visit, brandishing a ranked helicopter. With no helipads to land in the slums, we all scampered as the air below us rose in a huge cyclone of sewage dust; his expensive chopper perched on the sewage sands—the sands of time. It was amazing to see him jump over the human waste and the dirty sewage trenches to have a glimpse of where we lived. When I went to the news stand the following morning, all the headlines bore the images of the town clerk as he interacted freely with us, the commoners, at some end kiosk near our shack he had ordered a *mandazi* with tea served from a rusty spout. I marveled at the optics used to push his agenda where the perceptions as a great, humble, and down-to-earth leader were far more important than the substance of the decisions he made to change our lives. Like the other leaders, he cared far more about his appearance in the public eye than the actual substance of service; he was determined to compete with other politicians—to pull the best public stunts of all. I marveled at the thought of the fuel he had used to fly to our shanty. That amount could have fed hundreds of us for weeks. But that was not important. It was important for him to take tea in a rusty cup with us as a show of solidarity—to be seen to share in our miseries. Yes, that was important. Very important, indeed.

The TV stations interviewed me, and the morning radio talk shows were not left behind. Many offered to help in front of the cameras, but unfortunately no one came through for us. Mum and I still languished in our shanty, living the life we had always lived.

When my mum broke this awesome news to Mr. Igwe, my mum's boss, he was so excited and officially invited me to his house to meet him. I looked forward to going back to his house with a lot of anxiety. When I met him, he was more pleasant than he looked in the pictures, and he was pleasantly surprised by how unkempt I was, though he calmly advised me to trim my hair. As we took a cup of tea, he took his time and shared lots of his personal childhood life back then in Ibadan in Nigeria and he gave me pieces of advice full of wisdom. "The book of proverbs in the Bible has a special mention of four things that are extremely wise. Four little things on earth that are small—insignificant—but extremely important. Ants are creatures of little strength, yet they store up their food in the summer; hyraxes are creatures of little power, yet they make their home in the crags; locusts have no king, yet they advance together in ranks; a lizard can be caught with the hand, yet it is found in kings' palaces. So, nothing really can stop this journey that you have started. keep the spirit and keep moving."

He told me to be strong and to allow the greatness in me to shine. He was so proud of me, and he promised he was going to increase my Mum's salary by three thousand shillings every month, and that he would try as much as possible to assist my Mum towards payment of my school fees.

I thought to myself at least one man is trying to make a difference in my life, and I thanked heavens for him. All the other people had celebrated my success in front of cameras but that was it! It was a selfish world.

***

A few weeks later, Mum came home with a letter in her hands, and she was so elated. She asked me to open it, and to my amazement I had been admitted to Chavakali High School. It had always been my dream school, and it was such a great moment for me. I fell onto my knees and thanked God for the opening. Indeed, He meets the desires of our hearts, and He is full of surprises.

The letter had a whole list of items that I needed to buy, including a mattress, blankets, sheets, toiletries, books and assorted stationary, two pairs of uniforms, shoes, a hockey stick—yes a hockey stick—and a metal box or a suitcase, and they had indicated on the letter that they would inspect to ensure one had all the items on the opening day. The fee for the first term was twenty-six thousand shilling, and the thought of this figure paralyzed my thinking. I had toiled roasting corn for weeks, and I had only managed to save 7200.

One morning, I woke up early, slid into my sandals, took the admission letter, and stuck it into my pocket. I arranged the 7200 nicely into a black nylon bag and put into a brown envelope. I was going to bank all the money I had saved to the schools' account as per the admission letter. My heart raced with excitement at the thought of how Mum was going to be pleasantly surprised to note that the burden of the school fees had been reduced, albeit by a small figure. I walked farther down towards the stage anxious and tensed at the same time. I had never carried so much money at the same time. My eyes were fixed on my envelope and I held it tightly with my grip.

I boarded a *matatu* that was going to the central business district and I was terrified at how long it took us to get to the CBD. It was a long ride. I alighted at the bus station and stood there for a few minutes, trying to trace my location while admiring the hustle and bustle of the city. Everyone was seemingly busy with their own lives. In that moment of confusion, two young men approached me. One pushed me forward as the other one grabbed my brown envelope bag. I fell, hurting my wrist and waist. In a nick of time the two had been swallowed by the crowds, and I couldn't tell whether they had run in front of me or behind me. But one thing I was sure of, I didn't have my brown envelope. My whole savings had gone. All the money that I had woken up in the wee hours of the night to save had gone. All the money that I had saved denying myself sometimes even dinner to sleep on a hungry stomach too had gone. I remembered the long hours I had to stay standing with my feet aching from the pain underneath while fanning the fire to evenly roast the maize, the determination to sell had stirred me on. The many days and weeks I braved the sun's heat with my mouth dry and cracked from the hunger pangs, denied my own maize, because all I wanted was to sell and save. The numerous struggles with the officers. Now all that work had been snatched from my hands, in broad daylight. I stood there still, frozen in time, devastated. My world had come to an end. I tried screaming but my voice was coarse, and my wailing only came out as a shy whisper that was swept away by the bustling city. I didn't move for hours. I cried my heart out like a lost baby in the same spot till I couldn't cry any more. I had now developed a very severe headache, and I felt as if my whole head was cracking and breaking into two, the pain was real. The veins on my hands were visible. They had formed crisscross patterns on my head and on my hands, seemingly ready to drain the little blood that was left inside me. My eyes were sore and itchy out of hours of continued scratching.

My world had crumbled in moments. I regretted having made the decision to come alone to the CBD with all my savings in one envelope.

Why didn't I tell my mum about this?

Perhaps she could have been so proud of me but the thought of her spending the money on food when we slept hungry made me not to talk about it. I had kept the secret all to myself, and now here I was counting and languishing in the hazy world of my loss. They say only fools learn from their mistakes and I had been foolish enough to learn the hard way.

"Stupid boy, you will never amount to anything!" It was Uncle Matata again, speaking into my ears.

I gave up on my dream of going to school, and I wanted to end my life. I wanted to be forgotten in a world that had been so cruel to me. Despite the many attempts that I had made to change things for the better, this defeat was the toughest to stomach. Then it dawned on me that for the time I had lived on the streets as a street urchin. I remembered the escapades that I had been involved in, and I felt remorseful to realize the many families I had caused pain by my actions—the dreams I had shuttered and the families that I had broken. I had been part of the broken system. It was dusk when I stood up to go back home, having lost my admission letter and all my savings. The world around me was spinning, and I was moving in circles, totally shattered.

CHAPTER TWELVE

I got to our shanty that evening with my eyes drenched in misery and all my hopes dashed. I had wanted to get out of this shanty, and school was going to be my conduit, but here I was, up a creek without a paddle, my head biting and my dreams sunk, dead in the water.

I entered the shanty, and the moment I saw my Mum, I broke into tears. I was hysterical and inconsolable. I was not the type that shed tears. Life had taught me to be tough that real men never cry—and I had been determined to be a real man, but here I was, broken and shred into pieces as the tears flowed freely. I wasn't man enough to stop them.

"What is it, Baraka?" Mum was shaking me frantically demanding to know what happened.

"What happened to you?"

I couldn't bring myself together to speak. My tongue hung on the roof of my mouth totally dumbstruck.

My mother held me close for several minutes, not uttering a word as I sobbed, not able to bring myself to look into her eyes.

"I lost all the money!" I said softly in an incoherent voice.

"Which money are you talking about Baraka?" Mum asked

"All my savings are gone, Mama!" I responded sobbing some more. "I went to the Nairobi central business district to go and pay part of the school fees, but two men accosted me and snatched the money from me. All of it, Mama—a whole7200 shillings."

She cried out, her hand holding close to her mouth. She now was in shock.

"I knew you were saving your money, but I couldn't imagine you had saved that much Baraka," she said amid sobs.

She was devastated, and she just didn't know how to respond, but being the Mum she had always been, she said, "It's well son!" I looked at her, but I could see she was deeply disturbed by this sad news.

In the morning, she took me with her to her work place, as she was scared that I could hurt myself if I was left alone. This time around, her boss Mr. Igwe, was at home.

He had a wide, gentle smile on his face that was very welcoming. He was wearing a pinstriped suit with a dazzling royal blue carnation in his lapel. He looked elegant.

It was a déjà vu moment as I walked through the living room to the dining area, where Mr. Igwe ushered me into a chair.

"Feel comfortable, Baraka, and congratulations on your great achievement in your KCPE exams," he said in a soft voice. Within no time, Mum dashed to the kitchen and came back with two wafer-thin cups that she had mentioned the last time I had visited were Mr. Igwe's favorite, and she filled the two cups and placed some wafers on two side plates. With that, she left and went back into the kitchen.

Mr. Igwe took a deep look at me, his eyes trailing from my unkempt hair to the rough soles of my feet. I suddenly became self-aware of my dirt. Here I was, stepping on his expensive rug with filthy feet. The silk Persian high dense rug had an extra soft touch that gently caressed my feet with its velvety feel. It looked awesomely woven by skilled, artistic hands and at the center of the rug was a huge stenciled note "WELCOME", which offered a warm and inviting feel.

After a long silence he said, "Baraka,"

"Your mum has told me all about the success that you attained. Well done. Congratulations."

"Thank you, sir," I responded.

"Your mum also told me about the business venture that you had and all the efforts you made to hustle and save some money towards your school fees. It's very unfortunate you lost all your hard-earned savings to someone who deserved none of it," he continued.

"As promised, I will assist your mum in whatever way that I can to help you start off your schooling."

Those were the most musical words I had ever heard in my adult life. I fell down on my knees to thank him tears rolling down my cheeks.

He quickly reached out and picked me up, his hands soft and gentle like a sponge. I had been used to my Mum's sand paper hands that could potentially file a knife.

He sat me back on my seat and carried on.

"Your eyes see together, they blink together, and they cry together. They are one in sync. Your nostrils know no competition. They smell together and take an equal share of both bad and awesome smells. That's how you were designed to be—in sync with yourself. The left ear hears the same thing the right ear hears and it doesn't choose what to process and what not to process. The jaws are paired to chew in tandem. You have been paired up with destiny, and you need to unlock it. There is the old cliché that only a fool learns from own mistakes.

"As adults we do make many mistakes. Your parents may have made some mistakes in their lives, and I don't want you to repeat those same mistakes. Please kindly chart your own course into life—into your wildest dreams. Dream on, and let your dreams take you to the place you want to be. Then, finally get yourself ready, and start on the journey to take yourself there," he said, and with that he stood up and walked into the carport and left. As he walked out he was said, "I wish you all the best Baraka. I have another important business meeting that I have to attend to."

The second physical encounter with Mr. Igwe had pushed my dreams further and stoked my fire..

As we walked back home to our shanty, I was fully aware of the environment. The streets started to doze off under the mauve jacaranda blossoms spreading their purple fragrances to calm my nerves. And as they swayed, I swayed back. I smiled at one branch, and it responded in kind, dropping a flower in a zig-zag dance to express nature's love. I hopped across the road and grabbed it in my fidgety hands. Its soft, velvety touch caressed my hard, cracked hands, which seemed to have been cut from steel. All around me, I was embraced by beauty and bliss, and it was awesome. High on the jacaranda trees, the birds noticed and felt my happiness, and they responded with barrels of laughter, celebrating with me. The wind, too, could feel my happiness, and it gently blew through the holes in my shorts, giving me a tickle.

I trudged along, looking back and smiling at myself, hoping that one day the smile on my face could be replicated by the smile of the nature that gazed back at me, truly responding in kind. It was showing me an expression of pure love that was not easy to find. It couldn't be measured. It went beyond measure to the very deep core of my existence, and I felt a dance in my spirit, realizing that my heart had taken to a dance—a dance of life—a place I had never been to and I was afraid of turning back from this elegant scenery.

I was back in seventh heaven, there was now someone who was willing and ready to assist me chase my dreams, and I said to myself I was going to chase them hard.

Later that evening in our humble abode, Mum was saying to me, "Son, you know I have made mistakes. Looking around, you will see these shanties are run by desolate women—mostly single mothers. No dads. Only absentee fathers. And the only thing that reminds these women about the men in their lives are the children that they left behind. We have to bear the burden and brunt of the society that calls us names and tags us as immoral, we are the yardstick of what immorality looks like. That's not who I'm raising you to be. I'm raising you to be responsible—to take charge of your own life and be a man! When you grow up, be a man. Don't be a deadbeat dad. Cut the cycle!" She continued. "I have saved some little money for you, and tomorrow we will go and buy your metal box that is required for your school.

Mr. Igwe has promised he will assist to pay half of your school fees, and I will save all of my salary increase towards your school fees."

"Thank you very much. I love you!" I said, apologizing for the mistakes that I had made and for the times I had not lived up to her expectations.

Many had made empty promises, but here we were on our own, and I thanked God for one man: Mr. Igwe, who had come through for us with actual support. I had made news in the whole country. I had attended many media interviews and I realized it was just to further a cause. There was nothing in it for me. It was just to fan emotions and excitement to the general public that a pupil from the slum could write his exams successfully and outperform thousands that had privilege. Many had sent in congratulatory messages. They had raised my hopes to the mountaintops, only to let me off to the cracked and rugged terrain, rolling down back into the valley where they had picked me. On my way up, I had experienced the beauty of the mountaintop but on my sudden way down, all my hopes were dashed and broken by the unforgiving terrain. Fame came at a cost, and way down the terrain, I had to pay for it. But here there was one man who was standing out of the crowd and willing to give solid and sustainable assistance to enable me to pursue my dreams. Just thinking about Igwe and his words led me down to my knees, and I cried to God with thanksgiving.

***

The journey from Nairobi to Chavakali High School in western province was treacherously long, and the buses were sooty and rugged. We arrived at the country bus station in the early evening that Sunday, and we were quickly bundled into one old bus by the riotous thugs that strategically posed as bus attendants. My metal box, a basin and mattress, were all thrown to the overhead carrier of the bus and secured in place with a sisal rope, the overhead carrier of the bus was just as overloaded as the inside of the bus.

The air in the bus was suffocating; a dozen people had already vomited and the whole bus had an acrid smell. There was a lady seated next to me who seemed to have inhaled an overdose of sulfur dioxide, and her bowels released it in small but toxic portions. I was afraid the dose at which she was administering the fumes was going to kill me. I had now mastered her art; every time she twitched to the left, I knew she was ready to release more, and in turn I prepared my poor nostrils to receive the dose. And she also mastered the trickery of pretending to be surprised and irritated, readily willing to partner with me to search for the culprit who was polluting and shamelessly farting in the bus. But I was certain it was her, and I didn't see why I should be involved in her theatrics.

We passed several towns with the passengers dozing off. Some slept and had weighty loud dreams while others simply drifted off to escape their emotions.

It was going to be a rough ride along the 420 km stretch to the western part of Kenya. We had two scares where we narrowly missed a head-on collision with an oncoming trailer. The visibility was poor, but I guess the driver was too exhausted, and he dozed off and veered off the road multiple times. Just after Nakuru, there was a loud explosion, and the bus lost control and veered off the road, but somehow the driver managed to bring the bus to a halt. We all alighted, and the bus conductor announced it wasn't anything to worry about. It was simply a blown-out tire. We were asked to come out into the morning cold, which we braved for about an hour. Then we were back again on the road to continue with the journey. We survived three such blow-outs, and at one point, the bus ran out of fuel and the bus conductor had to board a motorbike to get petrol some twenty kilometers from where we were stalled.

We only arrived the following day at 9:00 a.m. in Chavakali town, having survived a grueling twelve hours on the road. When we alighted, our feet were feeling heavy from the exhaustion of the journey, but this was my big day, and I wasn't going to allow anything to dampen my spirits. We took the path that led to the school with Mum carrying the metal box of books on her head, bearing the full weight, but she couldn't have cared less. The dream was closer, and we were going for it.

As we approached the gates of Chavakali High School, I felt as if my feet were treading on the clouds. I was over the moon. There, right before me, stood the magnificent gates—a doorway to my freedom. There was a big sign that read "MOTTO: STRIVING FOR EXCELLENCE."

We were asked by the guards for our admission letter, but we didn't have it as it had been stolen when the two young men had accosted me, so we had to wait for another hour before the senior teacher could come to verify from his master list that indeed I had been invited to join the school.

All the items on the checklist were verified, and I was admitted to Chavakali high school on Monday, February 5, 2001.

There were so many students, some in front of their family cars, enjoying lovely moments with their parents. Some were sharing a meal of chicken from a massive hot pot and exchanging happy smiles. Some had the audacity to sit on the roof of their cars with their take-away coffee cups, munching humongous burgers.

Mum's mouth was dry and cracked. We hadn't taken a meal since the last evening when we boarded the bus and the hunger pangs were real, cutting through my stomach like a raw cactus. My mum noticed my worried face and turned to speak to me.

"Son, I am proud of you. You excelled despite the odds being stacked against you, but that was a good starting point to light your path. That ray of hope has shone onto your pathway, and you have seen the light. Let it further brighten your dreams and make you all that you ever wanted to be. You have the opportunity. I may visit you from time to time, but I am not sure when we are going to see each other again. Stay true to yourself. I know you will make it, Son!"

Her words sounded decisive and full of hope. They calmed my spirit and opened a window through which I started seeing the future. She gave me the warmest hug ever and said to me, "You have entered this school as a pauper. A beggar. A nobody. A street urchin. A wanderer. But you have the opportunity to change all that. Don't let it slip through your fingers. When it goes off to the wind, it will never come back to you. It will be blown into smithereens, and the tiny pieces will never be recollected. Once you lose this chance, it's gone."

"Remember the many interviews that you did both on radio and on TV, and the many people who celebrated with you without actually offering assistance. Such is life. Stand up for yourself, and go for what you believe in. Don't depend on others," she said.

She turned to leave, then surged back and pressed my hand. In it, she had a twenty-shilling coin. She told me to buy whatever I liked with it, and with that she stepped out to go. Deep down in my heart, I knew that was all the money she had. In my mind's eye, I could see her weary and battered legs having to endure another twenty kilometers of the hot rugged sand and gravel along murram road to find a place to lay her head for the night and be ready in the wee hours of the morning for the winding bus drive back to the city.

I didn't move an inch. I gazed at her tiny frame as she went through the gate. She had been healthy back in the day, but Mama was looking different, and the claws and vagaries of life had turned her life into a tiny frame that could easily be swept away by a lazy whirlwind. She must have read my mind as suddenly she turned and waved goodbye. I watched in anguish until my eyes could only see what looked like a tiny object disappear into the distant marketplace.

I collected myself and took up my metal box, carrying it on my tiny head towards the dormitory. It was starting to drizzle, and as I walked, I left patches of my tiny feet in the wet soil beneath. I dragged my heavy shoes along, hurting my sore toes further. This was my first pair of shoes, and my feet were burning and longing for freedom. I wanted to remove them immediately, but I had no choice. I scampered in the rain past the big rusty chapel with a dome roof sinking from the weight of the rotting twigs and leaves that had grown on it into a pile, with a large spread of algae greening its walls.

I zoomed past the huge hallway that was beaming with students holding their plates and scrambling through a narrow entrance into the dining hall to be served, oblivious of the rains. On the side of the hallway I could see senior students exchanging hugs and wearing confident smiles as they grinned at each other.

There was an old wooden sign with several arrows pointing in different directions. From the dripping rain, I could read Elgon, and I scurried on in the direction that the sign ushered. I got to the dormitory and dashed into the entry pouch. Its moss-laden pillars were patched from the peeling paints that had braved years (or maybe decades) of existence. There was a prefect standing at the door, and he quickly asked my name and directed me to the cube that I had been allocated.

I had never seen so many metal beds at the same time. I unfolded and flung out my tiny mattress and lay it onto the wire-meshed bed and sat on it cheekily. It made a screeching sound as I sank with it into a bow shape. I spread my plain single pink sheet onto the mattress and smiled at my new home with satisfaction filling the core of my heart. For the first time in my life, I truly owned something: a metal box, a mattress, a blanket, and one sheet. Other boys were rushing outside into the rain, but I was too tired and too excited to go out. I took off my shoes and slipped them under the bed, then gazed at the ceiling which hosted an arcane web skillfully spun by multiple spiders.

***

Mum had told me many things, but none of them prepared me for the things I experienced for the next few days. My fellow students had come with their boxes and suitcases full of shopping and carried fried delicacies that they munched on for days. They spoke fine language and talked and shared stories about holidays with their parents and the cars they drove back at home and the kind of foods that they ate. Wisdom soon taught me not to be party to these gatherings that only daunted my soul and reminded me of my poor, empty, and boring life.

My fellow students complained about everything and anything. Either the cabbages were raw, or a mixed meal of beans and maize had been laced with a dose of kerosene. Rumor had it that the kerosene laced food was meant to keep us docile like tethered mules, but to me, school was my livelihood, and I had never really known a day that I was assured three full meals. I ate the raw cabbages and the other foods that my colleagues considered cattle feed. They would pour these items onto my plate, and I soon got christened "the tiny pig." I behaved like one, but my fatty cells were dead, and no matter how much I ate, my tiny, skinny frame remained unchanged. It was the riddle in the school, and my peers discussed writing a thesis about it.

As I lay on my tiny mattress, my sniffy nose caught some magical aroma that wafted through the whole dormitory. I started counting my blessings, humming at the thought of how this school was going to serve such delicacies, but my thoughts were quickly shattered when I realized that the savory smell was coming from one of my fellow students cube who had come with their boxes and suitcases full of shopping and carried fried delicacies that they started munching. I watched them as I salivated, taking my taste buds to the extremes of forced endurance.

They avoided me like the plague and kept the social distance. My immediate cube mate that was on my lower deck threatened his friends that he was going to move out of the cube if I didn't leave first, but I decided to play deaf to his chants. On my second week, I went back to my cube and found my mattress dripping underneath with all of the cube members taunting me and shouting that I had wetted my bed and that I had to move out. It was so humiliating that I dashed out of the dormitory amid the roaring laughter and insults.

I later realized it was my cube mates who had schemed and hatched the plot to embarrass me before the entire dormitory. That night, Anyore, the tallest cube member (with an obese torso) came with a basin full of cold water and started pouring it onto my bed.

I sprung up from my bedside and held him by the neck and bunged his head on the metal bars of the bed several times, hurting his head. He sent out a shrieking cry of pain with his round head bleeding profusely from the cut, and the whole dormitory milled to our cube to see what was happening.

I was puffing with all my senses alert like a wounded tiger, and my heart was pounding fast and furious, ready to hurt him more. Everyone looked at me in awe, failing to comprehend how with my little frame I had been able to restrain this massive boy with a sunken belly. They cheered as I rattled on! I was burning with rage.

"If you ever do this again, I will squeeze the life out of you! I will kill you! I threatened!"

Anyore dragged his fat torso out of the cube, involuntarily wiggling his colossal backside as the boys chided behind him, calling him names.

"Coward!"

"Loser!"

"Good-for-nothing pig!"

It was my lucky day, and I felt heroic. I walked into the classroom that evening feeling excited that I had pulled that brat in his rightful place.

My classmates talked to each other in small groups and exchanged quick glances at me. I pretended not to follow their conversations, but I eavesdropped while perusing through my biology book. Then the class suddenly went quiet. I raised my head, and right there at the door stood Mr. Tisho, our dormitory master who was on patrol.

He immediately called out, "Baraka! Why do you want to kill someone! I will teach you a lesson tonight. Come with me," he said. He took me to the staff room threatening to expel me from school for causing trouble. Anyore was also summoned and we were all treated to twenty strokes of the cane that left our backsides sore.

I felt it wasn't fair as Anyore was well cushioned with the excess fat that lined his backside, yet he cried out like a little baby with every stroke of the cane. We were both given stern written warnings that if we ever fought again we would be kicked out of the school. The mention of being kicked out of school was chilling. I couldn't imagine it! I had to be calm.

In addition, we were forced to clear and slash a whole lot of grass around the teachers' quarters. It took me about two hours to clear my portion, while Anyore, despite his size, couldn't do the work. His hands soon developed sores. I looked at him with pity as I walked away, leaving him to work on his part, his body sweating like a pig.

This one incidence elevated my status in the dormitory, and no one tried to disrupt my peace in that cube ever again. We didn't see eye-ball to eye-ball with Anyore ever again, and we alternated our presence in the cube.

CHAPTER THIRTEEN

S chool was interesting, and Chavakali quickly became my home. I tried my level best not to get into trouble. I found math particularly troublesome, but my teacher, Mr. Wamalwa, couldn't let me go. He believed that I could still make it in his subject and therefore paired me with Mugero, who became my bosom friend and study partner. He taught me the things that I didn't understand. I had a natural gift with Biology, and I could teach the rest of the class and continue from where the teacher left off. We had a super teacher who was beautiful, and most of the time the boys in their innocence spoke of her beauty, their eyes following her every step.

Mr. Nabwire, our English teacher, had been sent from above. His amazing vocabulary could make it around the entire globe twice, and he articulated the subject with profound skill. The staff was amazing, and everyone did all they could to ensure we were on track. The trouble was, when you didn't pull your weight—when you found yourself on the other side of the school rules—you were all alone, and the whole school would know you were punished. It was the culture that had taken root and preserved for years.

We did the first term exams, and when the results came out, I emerged in the top ten out of 218 students, coming in at position 5 out of 218—something to be celebrated.

We were paraded during the closing day and given five new books, a dictionary, and a geometry set.

In addition, I was appointed the academic prefect of our stream. This came with more privileges, like taking an extra cup of tea in the evenings after preps, and also not having to queue where other students would ordinarily queue, as for water in the dining hall during meals.

As we packed our bags, marking the end of our first term, all the students were so excited, but I was filled with anxiety and lots of questions, as I really didn't know where to go. After debating with myself, I decided I would trek "home" to join my elder brother, Isate, who had been employed as a bartender at the infamous Corner Mbaya pub, a local pub in the marketplace where all the moneyed people in the village came to drink their lives away.

He had been given a small room in the pub and that acted as his home. To access his room, we had to go through the pub, which was a jungle of loud voices with revelers shouting their hearts out in noisy conversations that competed with the loud *Lingala* music that was playing from the four strategically placed speakers in the four corners of the bar. I could see a skimpily dressed young lady parked high on a high stool with one of her legs crossed to expose her inner thighs, and in front of her was a man with a big pot belly patting her back and tossing back a drink and laughing happily. As we walked through the pub, I could see every vice in this little space that Mum had taught us to avoid, but Isate seemed to have embraced this lifestyle with his life. He seemed to have sold his heart to the devil.

The teachers in our village were considered very wealthy, and so were the tea farmers. Once they received their annual bonuses, they could troop to corner Mbaya and lodge with harlots who came from far and wide to milk their savings.

After a few days, the patrons would have to check out of the corner Mbaya lodge with their pockets empty, and the harlots would vanish into thin air from the market and only re-appear fully repackaged during the next annual bonus. This cycle went on and on every year.

My brother welcomed me to his tiny room. His door opened with a loud squeal from the old rusty hinges. The chamber had a table, on which sat a full ashtray, and several liquor bottles littered the floor. There was a bed and a bunch of dirty clothes strewn all over it, along with several cartons. I wondered what was in those cartons. There was a plain mattress, two chairs, and a light green curtain that separated the bed from the sitting area. There was also a small cooking area that had several sooty *sufurias* and a small, green cooking stove. The room reeked of alcohol and cigarette smoke; I was almost suffocating. My brother reached out to the only window in the room and opened it, sensing the frown on my face. It was a huge wooden window with an old whitewash that was now peeling off like a layer of dandruff.

My first night with my brother was noisy and chaotic. I couldn't sleep. Mostly we sat on the bed, and whenever I could sit on it, it would screech so loudly. I had to master the trick of sitting down gently to avoid the loud sound that came with every movement on the bed, as it would squawk back in protest. It was a spring bed with a tiny mattress on it that formed a bow in the middle, arching my back. Whenever I tried to sit down, I would simply sink into it. The walls in the sitting area were fully covered with a white net that was turning brown from the accumulated dust that loosely hang on it. There were several Bob Marley and Lucky Dube posters hanging on the walls. I could see several stickers on the wall and the door. He had one sticker on the door that said, "Knock on the next door!"

In the right corner of the room, a fly was busy struggling for freedom as a spider quickly and skillfully entangled it further into its web to secure a meal. The floor was cracked, exposing patches of sandy layers beneath it.

I soon realized my brother had totally changed within the past few months that we hadn't stayed together. He easily mixed with the patrons who were mostly old men. Women too flocked the club, and it was indeed a sin jungle. The pub was one of the few story buildings in the market, and the two upper floors all were lodges. On Fridays they were always fully booked. The pub was noisy from its loud music, and my brother was one of the waiters who sometimes also doubled up as the cashier, so he was rarely back in the room, and most of the time I spent alone, trying to immerse myself in the books, but the loud music, the commotion, and the frequent fights made for a disruptive combination that spun and blended my dreams into a cocktail of sorts.

One evening my brother came with a girl into the room.

He looked at me and said, "This is my girlfriend. Her name is Namaswa. Namaswa this is my kid brother. His name is Baraka."

The girl stretched her hand and greeted me. "You are welcome," she said

She got me thinking. I thought I am the one to welcome you—why was it the other way round?

I got my answer immediately when she placed her small faded handbag onto the bed and folded the light green sheet to expose the entire room.

Clearly, she was not a visitor here. She started washing the utensils and even prepared tea that we all drunk. She later prepared *ugali* with beef that my brother quickly bought.

"So, my brother has been having money as we starved?" I thought to myself. Since the last one week we had not had such a special treat. Isate went ahead and bought a big one-liter Fanta orange soda that we gladly shared together like one big family. All along, they were giggling and teasing each other and at times tickling each other into hearty laughs. It was annoying, the games they were playing here. Mum would have not approved of what they were doing. I shyly looked away as they played their games. I stayed focused on the *ugali* and beef that they weren't so interested in eating. It was ironical that Isate could spare a plate of *ugali* and beef.

We sat there for about one hour when my brother Isate gave me a few coins and told me to go and buy a sieve. I looked at him and asked, "But we have a sieve!" He looked at me and answered, "That one is too small. Look for a bigger one."

"Can I do that later?" I asked.

"No. go now!" His voice sounded firm. It was a command, So I quietly walked out, and per my custom, I went about the task at hand with speed. I rushed to the market place and looked for the biggest sieve that I could find and rushed back, only to find the door closed from the inside. I knocked severally, but there was no answer, though I could hear commotions from the room and my brother giggling and Namaswa laughing hard. I peeped through the gaping holes in the hinges and saw my brother had unbuttoned his shirt and was kissing Namaswa. I dropped the sieve under the door of the room and walked away.

My brother had changed. He had started living the life of the patrons, engaging in illicit sex with different girls. He got to a point where he stopped introducing them to me. It was needless, as there were so many. They had become nameless—faceless—and he grew more shameless by day.

I saw his situation was getting hopeless. I had learned the trick: whenever I saw him, I waited to confirm that he was alone. If he was in the company of a girl, I simply walked away out of the room to roam the marketplace for hours. He also drank beer and spirits, and his eyes had turned red with blood vessels bulging underneath his pupils. He was no longer the Isate that I had known growing up. I had trusted Isate to a fault, but not anymore. He was now a stranger.

The straw that broke the camel's back was when Isate came to the room one day with a girl that he quickly introduced as Bella. "Bella, this is Baraka, my kid brother. You guys have fun. I'll be back."

And with that he left. We didn't utter a word to each other for almost thirty minutes. I could only watch her from the corner of my left eye within measured intervals. I almost collapsed when Bella moved from her armchair seat and moved closer to where I was seated on the bed. She put her hands on my shoulders and smiled. I felt a strange shrill of warm blood run through my veins, turning my knees weak. I sensed trouble. She was moving closer and touching my neck. There was something in me that had died, and I preferred it dead. Her touch ignited an unfamiliar sensation that ran through my spine and tickled my nerves. A thin layer of sweat was beginning to form into tiny droplets underneath my armpits. My heart was beginning to race, thumping out of the ribcage, and my breathing was becoming erratic. I was in an unfamiliar territory, and I knew I couldn't fight. I would lose the fight as I was ill prepared. I had always been told by my mother that if you can't fight run.

I rose up and stormed out of the room. Bella was calling after me, "Are you afraid of me?" I didn't answer but I had vowed to myself that I would not come back to that place ever again. The environment was hostile and lethal to my dreams.

I needed an alternative, so I walked across the market, soliciting for jobs, but there was no one willing to assign me any role. Most of the establishments genuinely didn't need any assistance in what they did. I finally convinced Ifeza, who was a successful businessman in the market place, to let me take care of his makeshift kiosk during the night and to fetch water for him from the stream and assist with washing the dishes during the day.

It wasn't easy, but he reluctantly agreed, as he was going to pay me five shillings for every jerrican that I fetched from the stream. Washing the dishes and guarding the kiosk at night would be my payment for free accommodation in his kiosk at night. It looked like a good deal and I agreed to it.

I started work immediately, and the following day I picked up my small bag that had my books and checked myself into his kiosk. The kiosk was made of wooden logs and massive rugged chunks of bark that had been salvaged from wood millers. It had a jagged look. The iron sheets lying on the flat low roof forced the customers to slightly bend to access the food kiosk. One section had been converted into a kitchen with three sets of large cooking stones that served as cooking stations. I peeped into the kitchen, and half a dozen women were at work. One was struggling to turn pulp into a huge mass of *ugali*, and her head was sweating profusely from the heat. She seemed to care less about the sweat readily pouring into the massive *sufuria* of *ugali* that she was preparing. She was at work, and nothing was going to stop her. One other woman was fanning the fire, her eyes clearly immune to the cloud of smoke, and another woman was busy cutting tomatoes with her head facing away to wade off the irritating onions. Several customers sat on the makeshift wooden seats made from long poles sunk in the ground. On each end a frame joined the two poles, and adjacent to them was a table made of more poles sunk in the ground and joined together by a rugged beam to serve as the table surface. There were about eight of these benches, and by the way customers had squeezed themselves in, I could tell one bench could sit at least eight people, four on either side. It was a busy kiosk. There was no bed, but Ifeza had promised me there was a mattress that had to be rolled and stashed away every morning, as I would be sleeping on the earthen floor. I thanked him, rolled my sleeves, and got to work.

During the day, I would brave the scorching sun and fetch water from the stream amid torrents of ridicule from the girls. I was the only boy going to the stream to fetch water and carry it on my head, and I didn't have time to listen to their ridicule.

By the end of the vacation, I had saved one thousand shillings, with which I bought myself a bar of soap, two kilograms of sugar, toothpaste, and some rolls of tissue. The rest I kept as pocket money. I thanked Mr. Ifeza, took my bag, and trekked to school. I had promised to be back, and he said he would be looking forward to when the schools closed for the holidays.

School was a place I could truly relax. It was my new home. The graffiti and the stale smell of urine in the latrines and the urinals didn't bother me at all. I now had a latrine that I could use, and that's all that really mattered.

Every last Saturday of the month was a dedicated day where parents and guardians were allowed to come and visit their children. It was the most depressing Saturday of the month in my school calendar. I knew in my heart of hearts that Mum couldn't afford to come and visit me at school, and I had learned to painfully live with the fact that I also didn't have any other relative who was loving enough to come and pay me a visit.

During the visiting hours, I would remain in class and continue reading, fighting off the loud fact that my peers were spending quality time with their parents. One day, I couldn't resist the temptation of walking to the field to just have a feel. I promised myself that I would convince my heart to be patient—that Mum was still on the way and that she would be joining us.

I went to the field walked to the gate and checked through the dozens of parents' names that were listed in the visitor's book, looking for my Mum's name, but I couldn't find it. I gazed outside the gate as far as my eyes could see and saw images of her in the distance, only to realize it was all in my mind. So, I decided to take a walk towards the field, and I saw the most traumatizing episodes of my life in school. The head boy master, Gunyali, was sitting with his mother and father parched on top of their Ford ranger double cabin like a hungry chick waiting for its mother's regurgitated food. He had a disposable coffee mug in his hands and was biting on a huge pizza when our eyes locked.

I pretended not to have seen him and briskly walked by. Dozens of students were sitting in the shade across the field, sharing meals with their parents and other siblings who had come along with them. I started to run. I didn't know exactly why I ran, but deep inside of me, I was burning with rage and frustration. I got to my classroom and broke into tears. It was after a whole hour of losing myself in misery that someone tapped me on my shoulders.

I quickly looked up and wiped my eyes. It was Donga, and he had come looking for me. Donga was rich. He had all that money could buy, and he lavished himself, eating like a king in school. He prided himself in having a choice about when and why not to eat the school's food, as he could get himself an alternative. He could buy our pieces of meat every

Thursday and Monday during dinner and in return give out a piece of his *ugali*. He always got what he wanted

"Baraka, why are you crying?"

"I am not crying, Donga!" I answered, trying to put up a brave face, but my eyes betrayed me. They were all reddened.

His parents had visited him and brought him so much food, so he invited me to join him at his cube so that I could have a taste. I wanted to say no—to remain there and soak in my misery—but, again, who would resist an invitation from Donga?

He had the swagger. He commanded so much respect in school—and fear in equal measure. He bought his way out of every situation in the school, and there was nothing in the school that one could win against him. He lived an idyllic life that was admired by all the students. We had become acquaintances over time, and I had helped him to understand biology and chemistry from time to time for small favors like buying me bread and offering me some change once in a while.

When we got to his cube, I saw that he had also invited other students, and we dined like kings. His parents had brought him royal food from a fast food joint, he explained to us patiently as he opened the packages. "This is a complete package. It contains four dips and twelve boneless chicken strips and a double grandee cheese box. I'm sure we will enjoy it."

My mouth was watering at the mention of chicken, and I couldn't wait. That's the only item I heard and understood from what he had said. The rest was foreign to my ear.

Donga took the second box and continued, "This is the double box crunchy bun filled to the brim with tasty mayonnaise and a hearty portion of lettuce. Such a huge sandwich, eh? And this, here, is grilled chicken Caesar with grilled salad laced with tomatoes, Provencal peppers, and parmesan cheese. You will love it. And this is the dessert. After the main meal, we will treat ourselves to these delicious caramel shakes and these creamy peanut butter shakes. As you can see, there are . . . one, two, three, four, five, so, there should be enough for all of us to enjoy."

It was amazing. Donga was greatly loved, and his parents ensured whenever they visited, they brought him more than enough so that he could share with his friends but still have enough for himself. I counted myself extremely lucky to be part of his inner circle—to enjoy and have a glimpse into the life of wealth.

I ate and indulged in goodness, and for a moment I forgot my problems. That invite made such a difference and made me feel like I too belonged, and it bonded my relationship further with the mighty Donga, the chosen one—the darling of the school.

He had grown in wealth, and he had learned wealth by name. They spoke the same language.

"The breeze here speaks a language that your poor ears cannot understand son, not just yet!"

I remembered Mum's voice at Igwe's compound.

But I could see that Donga understood this language of the wind. Wealth knew him by name, and he wasn't afraid to show off what money could do. If you were his friend, he treated you like a king, and everyone in the school admired him.

During game time, students would mill around Donga and hear him relate episodes of how he went with his dad and mum to Muthuga golf club in Nairobi, where they were life members as a family. How he himself was an amateur golfer who had participated in the several junior championships.

The gods had blessed Donga with a sharp mind. He was one of the best students at Chavakali. He was a walking dictionary at school. We had christened him the Encarta—the walking encyclopedia. He taught us about the Muthuga golf club and the way it was an exclusive member only club.

He taught us about the golfing arsenal—the irons, the hybrids, the wedges, the drivers, and the putters—and we were hooked to his stories like glue. We didn't want to leave, and every day we came back to learn more. It always seemed one could learn a whole bunch of things by sitting with Donga—more than one would learn in the library reading, though he was a voracious reader himself.

As we ate the crunchy chicken, he showed us his album, and I got the first rare opportunity to have a glimpse of his life in pictures.

"Here we had gone to Abu Dhabi in Unites Arab Emirates with my dad to watch the Formula 1 Etihad Grand Prix. Here we were standing at the rooftop lounge. As you can see, we had a panoramic view of the whole F1." His face beaming with joy and pride.

Oh yes, he deserved to be happy and proud. I admired the next picture that he was now holding in his hands.

"And this is my father," he said, holding the picture next to his chest and giving it a kiss. With that, he passed it around for everyone to have a look and admire him and his dad. Indeed, they were having a great time together, dad and son. It was amazing. His dad was tall with a heavy torso and a well-trimmed beard. He was wearing a cowboy cap.

When it got to my chance to admire the picture, I looked at it and just stared at it, pain all over my heart. *Am I jealous of Donga?* I asked myself.

No! Baraka! You cannot do that to yourself. My feet were forcing me to stand up and storm outside, but my heart was demanding me to be strong.

He was raising up another picture, and he and his dad had mounted onto a horse in a large stadium. I had never seen something as glamorous as that. He was explaining, "In a horse racing game, we have the jockeys who mount the horse, and they wear the silks. The jockeys have bits, which are pieces of metal that are controlled by a set of reins, which are made of either nylon or leather that are securely attached to the bits . . ."

We all marveled at every explanation. Donga opened our minds and hearts to opulence, and he shared a window of his life with the clique of friends he respected. You were lucky if he recruited you into his group.

Fisi Okusimba, the school rascal, couldn't touch Donga. All he could do was to spit nasty jokes, but as Donga was loved, many other students always lined up to ridicule Fisi on behalf of Donga. Fisi's face was rugged, pocked with groves that made his skin look like an old frog, and he couldn't win a touting competition.

Donga didn't have to fight for anything. He was the lucky one, indeed.

I counted myself blessed to be in his circle of friends, and that day I was experiencing wealth and having a taste of it. It was indeed a new day.

And we would also just sit there and enjoy the golf in our minds. He was a great storyteller, and he charmed us with his explanations. Instead of going to run the five laps of honor around the football pitch, a whole bunch of students would just sit there and soak in Donga's world. He lived in a different world—a world unknown to us—and we admired his world. His dad had a knack for cars, and he was thrilled with adrenaline high sports, so he had taught Donga the life of horse racing and the thrill that came with car racing. This had taken him and his dad all the way to Dubai on two occasions. Even in our wildest dreams we knew it will never be possible to experience his life.

I continued to support him in biology and chemistry, where he was a bit weak, and he continuously improved in his performance. We became very close friends, and we learned a lot from each and improved each other's performance.

CHAPTER FOURTEEN

I was now in the second term of form two, and Mum still hadn't channeled my school fees to the school. That was the fifth week, and I had begged the accounts clerk to give me some time since my mum was for sure going to remit the funds, but it just didn't happen. I took the courage and went in to the principal's office to reason out my case after the deputy headmaster had read out my name and asked me to go home to fetch the school fees.

"No, we cannot allow you any longer in school with this huge balance, Baraka. Please go home and explain to your Mum the urgency of clearing this balance!" Bwana Agavah said. "I have given you a lot of time, but unfortunately your mum hasn't pulled her weight, so you have to go."

His words cut through my soul like a raw cactus and stung my nerves like a nestle. I could see my future coming down tumbling. I went back to my class, head low like an envelope, and my self-esteem crumbled like a useless paper that had been thrown out the window. I packed all my books with tears flowing freely from my eyes. My desk mate Benard Mwenesi watched desperately, totally helpless. He hugged and told me that all was well, but I knew deep down that it wasn't well. The rest of the class watched in anguish, wishing they could help, but they couldn't. This was a tall order, well beyond their reach. I left the school, not sure where I was going and not sure when I would come back.

I trekked all the way "home", my eyes red from crying and my vision hazy. Twice I was hooted at by motor bikes for having blindly walked back into the road. My world had been shattered, and all I had ever hoped for in this life was fast crashing down like an avalanche. I was terrified.

The only hope was going to be Ifeza. I was going to explain everything to him, and I was going to beg him to take me back into his kiosk.

I went back to where Ifeza's kiosk was and I was astounded the kiosk wasn't there. It was now an open space. Was I lost or was I dreaming?

Was I losing my mind? Was my brain playing tricks on me? No, it wasn't a trick. I had stayed in this kiosk for several weeks, and I couldn't miss it. I stepped up to an old mama who was selling vegetables and asked her, "Mum, where is Ifeza's kiosk?"

"Oh, aren't you aware it was demolished by the municipal council several weeks ago? They claimed it was built on a road reserve!"

She was still saying something, but I was gone. I could only hear her voice as a distant trail. I couldn't face her. My eyes were filled with tears of pain, and my heart was broken in pieces, and now the wind was ready to blow the pieces away.

I sat on a piece of rock by the roadside and covered my face and cried my heart out for hours, not knowing where to go and not having anyone else to turn to. I gathered courage and got back to my feet and wobbled like a drunkard. Yes, I was drunk in my emotions. I went to one of the customers I had supplied water to in the past. Her name was Mama Ndeda. She had a posho mill, and behind the posho mill there was a small room. I knew her to be a widow, and I went to her to try my luck.

I found her seated at the entrance of her posho mill, her only inheritance from her late husband. Her brothers-in-law had turned against her, and they wanted to get all that their brother left behind, claiming she didn't have a right, but she had fought for her rights with skill and an iron fist in a velvet glove. That's the reason she still had this posho mill. Otherwise, it could have been taken away from her.

She knew me, and when she saw my face, she asked me to sit down. "Baraka, why are your eyes so red? What happened to you?" she asked.

I couldn't bring myself to talk. I simply looked at her with a blank face, speechless.

She too understood the color of pain, as she had seen its strokes rock her boat many times, she let me calm down by allowing me to sit there next to her without saying a word. After about thirty minutes, I narrated my story to her, and she said she would allow me to use her small back yard room on condition I find a way to go back to school.

I was so thankful to her. I dropped down prostate on the ground in a thankful gesture, but she quickly chastised me and asked me to rise up. She said in a low tone, "Life is not easy, Baraka, and it will never be, just live one day at time!"

She showed me the small room that had nothing apart from a tiny mattress and a blanket, five twenty-liter plastic jerricans, and several empty sacks of maize. It also had a small, green kerosene cooking stove.

She gave me a small tricycle padlock and a tiny key tied to a sisal string and went away. I slowly closed the door, but in its innocence, the aging hinges produced a very loud screeching sound that reminded me of my brother Isate's door at the pub.

When I closed the door behind me, I was overwhelmed with emotions. I went to my knees and turned to the only father I had known since I was a child—my father in heaven. I prayed to him, and I thanked him for this little room, as it was now truly my home, where no one would bother me. I could cry in misery wherever I felt like it. There would be no barriers and no limitations. I could sense freedom. Then I went back onto my knees and lamented harder. The way I didn't have an earthly father like Donga. Who would take me to some of the places Donga had been to?

Will I ever have a glimpse of Donga's life? I silently asked myself.

I was angry, tired, and hungry when I slumped onto the tiny mattress and slept for the night.

There is the old cliché that however long the night is, the morning will still come, and indeed morning came. It was refreshing to wake up with a small room all to myself and at the same depressing to know that I was fast losing the chance to ever achieve the things that I had hoped for in my life. That dream was actually coming to a halt, and I had to defer my ambitious future. I had tried to call my mother, but the operator always came back to me saying that she couldn't get through to my mother. Once the call had gone through and the other person on the other end had been asked if they knew me, they had responded in the negative, and my world would come tumbling down. There was no way I was going to reach my mother.

I was so worried. I didn't understand why she had not sent in money to my school. She had always sent in two thousand shillings faithfully—directly to the school post office through the Bazaar—and suddenly she had stopped.

I didn't know what to think of anymore. I had gotten to a point where my life's ship had hit the high tides, and I was caught in a stretching storm. I didn't know the way out. In spite of the headwinds, I knew one thing for sure: that I had to keep steering my ship, because it was liable to sink. It was depressing.

I checked around the room for any sign of food, but there was nothing. I opened the stove to check whether it had kerosene, only to find the tank had been dry for months and the wicks totally dry like a piece of wood that had sufficiently been exposed to the January Kenyan sun.

I stepped out of the tiny room, my stomach aching in its emptiness. I asked for manual jobs in the food kiosks, but there was simply no one who was willing to even start that conversation of employing me.

I met one lady with a thin frame. She was carrying a yellow jerrican balancing on a round piece of cloth that she had cleverly molded into a ring to cushion her head from the weight of the water.

I stopped her and asked her where she was selling the water and whether she could allow me to do the work with her. She shrugged and ignored me, as my little frame could hardly carry a ten liter jerrican, but looks can be deceiving.

I followed her, prodding her further, and she reluctantly agreed that I should accompany her. We went to a shop that turned into a water shop, with dozens of jerricans and drums full of water. She gave me a twenty-liter jerrican and asked me to go with her.

She had mastered the turns and twists of the slippery path that led to the stream. She walked with a slight twitch in her left foot but that didn't seem to deter her. She had the momentum, she had the speed, she had the grit, and she had the hunger to fill the drums. And so, we worked.

"Many have tried this job, but they couldn't manage. Let me see how far you can go!" she said as we made yet another turn.

When I got to the stream, we had to struggle to fill our jerricans, as there was no elaborate order regarding whose turn it was to fetch the water, so it ended up being survival of the fittest, with pushing, shoving, and even hair pulling. It was chaotic, and I quickly learned how to fight to fill my jerricans.

We filled in our jerricans, and after the tenth trip to the stream, my head and neck were aching from severe pain. I wanted to quit, but the voice of Mama Timina kept reverberating in my eardrums: *Many have tried this job, but they couldn't manage.*

No, I wasn't going to be yet another statistic to her. I kept telling myself, *I have to fill the drum.* Each drum could take twenty jerricans, which meant that I had to make twenty trips to the stream on day one for her to pay me. She gave me one hundred shillings, and it was rewarding. I went to the kiosk and treated myself to a whole plate of beef and *ugali* and a cup of tea. It was rewarding. I walked back into the small room and collapsed onto the tiny mattress. The unforgiving cold night embraced me and reminded me of the dark days on the street, but I quickly reminded myself that this was different. I had four walls with which to protect myself. I curled myself up and slept.

For several days I struggled, working super hard to fill the drum and make the hundred shillings. Some days I made even more. Sometimes the sun was so hot that I felt it was going to fry my meninges into a thick paste. I had to wade off the annoying ridicule from the girls who chided me and called me names, calling me a woman, a girl, a coward.

Still, I saved as much as I could from every day, and with the rest I would buy kale and cook *ugali* for myself to serve as lunch and dinner.

I had been out of school now for about six weeks and my hopes of ever resuming school waned with each passing day. Poverty had made a covenant not to let me go. It had entangled me into its intricate web, and my options seemed to die with each passing day.

One day as I was taking water to Mama Timina, I heard someone call me.

'Baraka! Baraka!" a sharp familiar voice cried out.

I checked and saw it was my Aunt Makali. Her husband worked and lived in Nairobi, and she frequently travelled to Nairobi.

I walked towards her with my head low. She had the resources to help me go to school, but she couldn't help. She had decided she wasn't going to help. Her children were all studying in well-known high-end private schools in Nairobi.

I couldn't tell the last time I had seen her, "Baraka what are you doing here with that jerrican? Aren't you supposed to be in school?" Her voice sounding sarcastic.

"I was sent home from school to come and get school fees, but I haven't managed." I said piteously

"How long have you been away from school?" she asked

"Seven weeks and two days, Aunty," I answered her.

I stood there in shock as her face beamed with a heavy smile as if she was celebrating some lottery win. She had wanted nothing good for our family and naturally she hated us.

I thought she had changed. She looked at me and giggled. I turned to walk away but she reached out and held my hand back.

"I met your mother last month," she said.

My heart skipped a bit as I looked straight into her eyes with anticipation.

"Your Mum came to beg for food from our house. She said she had been jobless for several weeks. Baraka! I could help you, but your mum is too proud and she is careless. She had vowed in her entire life that she will never come to me for assistance, and all along I have been waiting for her to come. When she finally did, I gave her a piece of my mind! I reminded her of the things she had said in the past, and I sent her away! Who is she? She cannot talk to people like that. She should know people!" Aunty Makali was still talking but out of protest I walked away on her.

She had the audacity to insult my mum and remind her of her ills of yonder years when the earth was still flat. I felt annoyed. I could have punched her nose but that could have attracted a terrible curse and I didn't want any more curses. I already had enough troubles to deal with.

Her words about my Mum being jobless answered and settled the most difficult question that I had been asking myself—why mum was no longer sending my school fees. But what had happened to her job? Was she fired? What did she do to get fired? She had been diligent with her work and honest. She couldn't have stolen anything from Igwe. No way. She couldn't bring herself to that new low.

That night, I was terrified. My heart sunk into the gutters of this world, and I was sure I wasn't going to find it again. It was broken into tiny pieces. All that I had ever worked for and dreamt of achieving—the dreams of changing the life we had been living—were blown into oblivion. Just like my report card that uncle Matata has reduced to confetti years back.

That night, I couldn't sleep. I stared into the darkness—into the open space of the roof—and my mind trailed from the memories and escapades I had in Nairobi in the trenches. The mortuary scare and the near-death experiences that I had and that terrified me. The only hope of changing that past had been school, but now that was behind me. It was all gone with the winds. The winds that now blew my way were wicked, and they had been trained to blow my way and to take away every iota of joy from my life.

I didn't have anyone to talk to, consult, or seek guidance from. I was alone. I admired the many families that I had seen in school laughing and giggling in the hands of their mums, dads, and siblings, and I drowned further in misery and pain.

I sat in one corner of the room petrified. I had cried my heart out, and now I couldn't cry anymore. All the tears had dried into marks on my face. My T-shirt was totally soaked with tears. I was in pain, and I was frightened. I was having severe migraines, and I was afraid my head was going to burst. I was now sweating from the sweltering heat that came from the low roof. I didn't move an inch for the whole day. I was confused, and all I wanted now was to die. No one cared for me in this world. It didn't matter if I lived or not; all would be the same. My mind had given up. I had tried to turn around my life, but it had proven to be one heavy burden that an innocent young soul like mine couldn't carry.

I prayed to God, asking him to take my life. I had prayed to him before, and He had come through for me, but this time I was praying for him just to take my life and lead me to rest. I was tired of living alone in this loneliness that life had diligently pushed me into.

I rolled back into sleep and hoped never to wake up, but still I couldn't sleep. My mind was completely shattered. I couldn't think. It was so hazy that I couldn't even tell the time.

It was on the second day when I stepped out for a short call. My feet were weak, my skin was dry, and my throat felt so parched that I was wondering if I could speak. I was feeling dizzy, and the moment I stepped into the sun I collapsed. I woke up later to be told by Mama Ndeda that I had lost consciousness for almost three hours. She was shocked by my frailness.

"What Happened to you, Baraka? You want people to say that I killed you?" she protested, her face turning black and her eyes blazing with fury.

"I will not allow pity partying in my house, you either rise onto your feet and go out there and work or I will kick you out of this house," she shouted. It was a stern warning and she meant every word that she said.

"You will have to report to me every morning to be sure you have woken up, understood?" she said. And it was a command, she left me with no option but to struggle to dig myself out of the hole I was in.

I couldn't imagine being kicked out of that room, as that meant I would have nowhere to go. So, I had to rise to the occasion. I remembered the words of my primary school teacher, Mr. Wanyonyi, who loved to say the only way out of a hole was to stop digging. I told myself that I would stop digging and start thinking of how to get myself out.

I went back to Mama Timina and we continued fetching water and making sure the drums were full. Every empty drum was an inspiration that more was needed. In the evenings I would immerse myself in my books and get lost in the worlds they created for me. All in the hope that one day as I saved the little cash that I got I would get back to school, no matter how long it was going to take, I was determined that one day I would go back.

I missed the whole of second term, and by the time the third term of form three was starting I had still not raised enough money to take me back to school, so I kept filling the drums and kept my dream alive by studying in the night.

One day, I met Mr. Wanyonyi, who was deeply troubled by my predicaments, but unfortunately he couldn't do much to help, so he took the responsibility of visiting me often and coaching me on how to study sciences. He also brought me old books and magazines, which I voraciously read and discussed with him whenever he visited me. By the stroke of genius, he introduced me to many books and biographies of successful personalities who had undergone a lot of pain to get to where they were, and as I read the books I asked for more. They consumed me to the core and kept my mind positively engaged. I realized that I could get access to tens of hundreds of mentors. I could interact with them and answer some of nature's questions without having to travel to them. It was a great window that Mr. Wanyonyi opened into my life. He brought me books to do with art, science and robotics, animals, soil, and business. It was refreshing to learn, and the more I read, the more I wanted to know. I grew an insatiable appetite for books. My vocabulary grew by leaps and bounds within a few weeks. I loved the fact that I was not reading to sit for an exam but I was just curious to soak in the knowledge. The village in me had stubbornly occupied half my brain but the exposure to these books opened my world to a bigger world full of life and possibilities.

"Baraka, you cannot afford to live a guessing game with your life. You have to be in control, and the stars will align to shine on you," he said.

Mr. Wanyonyi himself had transitioned from a primary school teacher and was now teaching in one of the local high schools after taking an advanced Higher National Diploma course in education at the reputable Kenya Science Teachers College. He became an instant success at Kigama Secondary school, and his students outperformed their counterparts from senior schools in Western Kenya. He had taken it upon himself to nurture me—to mold me as his son—as that was all he could offer me. He counselled me from time to time and encouraged me to dream on. He was priceless.

"Discipline and hard work will open doors for you, Baraka. Don't let your current state define your capabilities!" he said.

He became my guardian angel and confidante—. He was a believer, and he ensured I went to church and I prayed. He wanted me to recognize the power of a deity in my life—a higher being than myself—and he taught me the ways of God. He taught me how to live for other people and why it was important for me to work hard to break some cycles in my life. Most importantly, the cycle of indignity that came with abject poverty that I had sunk deep into.

One afternoon, after about thirty-two solid weeks away from school, I was still busy delivering water to the customers that Mama Timina had instructed me to. I went into Mrembo Salon, which was the best salon in Mudete market. I was busy emptying my jerrican into the big tank when I had someone exclaim my name; "Hey you! Baraka! What are you doing here?" I quickly recognized the voice and I turned to confirm who was calling. Right there at the salon was my best Swahili teacher at Chavakali high school, Madam Nasimiyu. She had plaited her hair into beautiful braids and she looked stunning. Her feet were immersed in a bubbling basin with a frothy white mixture. She was having her pedicure.

My jerrican dropped from my hands and the water spilled getting everyone to stop and look my way. The owner of the salon, Mama Miheso, was the one working on Madam Nasimiyu.

I was petrified to see my favorite teacher and to meet me in such a situation. My body was sweaty from the day's work, my hair had not been cut for weeks, and my t-shirt was torn and stained with misery. She was shocked, as I was one of her best Swahili students.

She took her feet from the pedicure basin and came to where I was standing. My time had frozen. She gave me a warm hug as I stood there numb, not saying anything. Her presence alone brought me to tears as memories of school and my wasted dreams flooded my mind.

There is powerful communication in silence. I stood there still not saying a word, then after a while I informed her in a feeble cracked tone that I had been sent away from school to go and fetch school fees, but as I had nowhere to go to, I came to Mudete, and the only job I could land to fend for myself was working with Mama Timina to fetch water from the stream and sell to the traders at the market place.

She was overcome with emotions and she gently rubbed her eyes with a soft napkin. After a short talk with her I bid her bye and went back to my room. The thoughts of Chavakali High School wouldn't leave my mind. They lingered on, and I couldn't focus on anything else that evening.

It was a week later when I was busy delivering water into the drums, Mama Timina came to me so excited. She was gasping for breath trying to calm herself.

"I have news for you Baraka!" she said.

I had been used to receiving bad news, and I didn't care anymore how it was delivered. I preferred someone to go straight for it.

"I have just met Miheso, the owner of Mrembo salon. She has instruction from Madam Nasimiyu to look for you and to ask you to go to school tomorrow with all your books ready to learn!" she said her voice full of excitement.

That was the best news ever, but I had some unanswered questions. They all came out of my mouth at the same time. What about school fees? What about Mr. Agavah? What about my mattress, bed, and my uniform? I was jumping up and down with exhilaration.

"Just wash your old uniform, pack your books, and inform Mama Ndeda that you will be leaving back to school. It's that simple! She has accommodated you and been so kind to you," she said. But it wasn't as simple as she was trying to make me believe. This was great news.

I thanked Mama Timina and rushed into my room. I quickly washed my uniform that was old and torn and put it in the sun to dry. I went and broke the good news to Mama Ndeda who was equally excited and happy for me. I couldn't reach Mr. Wanyonyi, so I wrote a note and left it with Mama Ndeda to hand it to him next time he came to visit. In the note I informed him that I had gone back to school under the instruction of Madam Nasimiyu.

CHAPTER FIFTEEN

The following morning, I started the journey back to school with many more books that I carried with me. This time around, I paid thirty shillings for the bus fare to Chavakali, as my metal box was full of books that I had been studying gifted to me by Mr. Wanyonyi. I couldn't manage to carry them on my own for that long trek to the school.

I went straight to the staff room to meet Madam Nasimiyu and I was shocked to find that all the teachers were aware of my plight. I was asked to greet all the teachers in the staff room, including the principal Bwana Agavah.

Madam Nasimiyu stood up to speak. "Thank you all teachers for listening to Baraka's plight and coming to his rescue. You might not understand what you have just done, but your generous contributions will enable Baraka to clear his school fees balances for form two and the whole of form three. Baraka has demonstrated hard work and resilience, even in the most difficult situation. I got his full story from Miheso, the owner of Mrembo salon in Mudete market, and I must say I was truly moved by his story. And to you, Baraka, we trust you, and we know that you will continue to work even harder and improve on the scores that you have recorded in the past. We all wish you the very best!" she paused.

I almost fainted on hearing this great news that the teachers had dug deeper into their own pockets to pay for my school fees. It stuck on my mind like a distant dream far away out of my reach, appearing under a gauze, foggy and insanely unreal. But it was happening. It was no longer a dream. It was an amazing act of kindness, and it moved me to tears. My class teacher, Mr. Nabwire, stood up and gave me a warm hug, and he assured me that the school was going to do everything to support me to ensure I completed my studies and that he was going to personally arrange for catchup lessons by pairing me with other students to recover the time I had lost.

I couldn't believe all this was happening. Things seemed to move very fast, and the pages in this life chapter were turning faster than my mind could process.

Madam Nasimiyu was speaking. "Form three second term exams will be starting in a month's time. You don't need to worry, as when you close school we will make arrangements at the teacher's quarters for you!"

I couldn't believe what Madam Nasimiyu had just said but it seemed that was something that had been discussed at length. Mr. Agavah also promised to introduce me to the school counselor who would take me through a series of counselling sessions.

To my surprise, Madam Nasimiyu handed to me a package containing two sets of uniforms and a sweater and a new pair of shoes. She asked me to change before going back to the classroom.

She also gave me a meal card that would last for the term and with that they asked me to work hard and make their efforts count. A meal card was a coveted item at Chavakali High School.

I gave them my promise, tears flowing freely from my reddened eyes. This time, they were tears of joy. *God does listen to prayers*, I told myself as I walked towards the ablution block to change into the new uniform. Indeed, God had wanted me to reach a point where I would no longer depend on myself but just Him.

I felt a newness flow through my spine as I walked back into form 3A. It looked as if I had been away forever. I had missed almost thirty-two weeks of school. I had missed form two's end term, form three's first term, and now form three second term was coming to a close.

The whole class burst into a frenzy as I walked into the classroom with Mr. Nabwire beside me. Everyone was excited to see me back, and I could tell that from the happy faces. My deskmate, Benard, stood up and came and gave me a warm hug. It was a reunion.

"Welcome back, Baraka!" Benard said.

Mr. Nabwire ensured that I got space and a locker to store my books, and he assigned me back to my old and best friend, Benard. He was the best student in English, and he was already working on his second manuscript of a fiction story when I left way back in form two. We had a lot to catch up about.

He helped me to arrange my books, as all the other students looked out in curiosity. They all had many questions that they wanted answered at the same time.

Mr. Nabwire quickly noticed the anxiety, and he announced, "Baraka had a challenge with his school fees. That's why he has not been able to attend classes for almost a year now. I ask that you help him as much as possible to catch up to get to where you are," he instructed. "Comrades power!"

"Power!"

"Comrades power!"

"Form three A eeeh. Form Three A aaah!"

He chanted with the class and set our excitement to a new high.

Later during lunch break, I was accompanied by the Elgon Dormitory captain, Lihanda, who assigned me a bed and a mattress. This time, I had all form three students as my cube mates and we treated each other with mutual respect.

Many students had changed, but most of the rascals had grown tougher and more aggressive, especially towards the form ones and the form twos. Anyore had lost half his weight after joining rugby team and he was one of the top players in the team. Donga had continued to flourish, and his grades had greatly improved. He was one of the top students in sciences in the whole of form three, Benard had completed his first novel, and he had submitted it for publication. It had been several months, but he was confident that his work was going to be published.

The infamous Fisi had become more aggressive, and he was well known in school as the trouble maker who turned other people's lives into a living hell if you crossed his path. His bitterness with Donga didn't seem to have ended. In fact, it seemed to have grown and was waiting to explode. They couldn't have been more different, with Donga having all the money and living large in school and with Fisi living from hand to mouth, harassing the form ones and soliciting money from them to sustain his miserable lifestyle. And his grades were nothing to report home. That was his Achilles heel, and everyone trampled on him during every verbal fight to tame his wild tongue that spew unspeakable vitriol.

We sat every evening in groups, and I was amazed at how everyone was willing to help take me through the different subjects.

I had Moreno, who was well versed with numbers, take me through accounting. Andrew, whose comprehension of science principles was unmatched, easily unraveled the mysteries of chemistry and physics in simple packages that I quickly soaked in. He was a natural teacher. Joseph was gifted in mathematics and sitting with him for an hour, I achieved what I could have learned by myself in a whole week. His help was priceless! Victor was the walking atlas; Benard and Gerard's prowess in English had been refined to new levels. We had been taught to understand subjects based on principles and not based on cramming and rote learning. We read to understand, and we had one principle that we applied in all the subjects: if you can't explain it, then you haven't learned it. And every student was always eager to grab every opportunity to explain a principle in biology, a principle in chemistry, or physics. It always made learning such fun.

The whole class was equally surprised when I taught them some of the principles I had also learned from my home library collected from Mr. Wanyonyi. Most of the principles were beyond the things that we learned in class and outside the traditional topics that were taught in class, and it amazed everyone how knowledgeable I had become in the last few months I had been away.

Most of my classmates had expected that I would have nothing to offer, but they were extremely surprised when I delved deeper and explained to them things they didn't know about marine science, about new advances in modern medicine, literature, space science, the history of art, and the great business principles and innovations in the recent decade that had changed and transformed the world.

I easily found my way back into the tutoring class, a clique of students who taught others in the different areas where they were really good and exceptional in their mastery of the subject, and my area was biology. Indeed, when you read widely and consistently, there is no limit to how much knowledge you can gather daily.

Donga was a member of our clique, and his mastery of geography was outstanding.

One evening, we sat with him in the corridor, digressing from the subject. He started digging deeper to know what had happened to me. I was reluctant at first to open up my story to him, but he had been more than my friend. He had supported me in many ways and made me feel I belonged. I trusted him and for the first time in the school I opened my life to a fellow student.

I told him all about my past and escapades that I had experienced in Nairobi—my life on the streets, my mother's miseries and the fact that I didn't have someone to call dad. All the time as I told the story, he just sat there, not saying a word. He looked shocked, terrified, and troubled. Finally, he said, "Baraka I have always had a gut feeling that your life mirrors my life in many ways. I know you might not understand it, but one day when time and chance allow, I will tell you!"

His words left me with many more questions than answers, but he was my friend and friends needed to trust each other. The bell signaling the end of the prep time rang, and we were shocked by the way the night had just sped by. We picked our books, bid each other good night, and proceeded to lock away our books before proceeding to the dormitories.

I got special attention from the teachers who from time to time wanted to know how I was coping with my studies. The school principal, Mr. Agavah, introduced me to one of the school counselors, Mr. Kamonya, who used to visit the school every Tuesday to run the schools' guiding and counselling club, he added a lot of value to my life and gave me hope to get back on my feet and keep my dream alive.

Three weeks sped by, but the experience and love I experienced was amazing and simply refreshing. Chavakali was family, and there was no better place to be other than school. We sat for the second term exams in form three, and I waited for my results with bated breath and so were the teachers. It was combined pressure.

The results were always announced on the closing day of the school on the parade and the top ten students would be called forth and awarded with books and geometry sets, dictionaries and other tokens in front of the school and given certificates. In most cases, it was never about the gifts. It was just so fulfilling to hear your name being called forth and to be awarded in front of all the staffroom and all the students. Nothing could replace the inspiration that came with it.

For the whole of form one and form two first term, I had been one of the top five overall students, but I had been away and I had little hope of gaining back my position in that category.

They had already called out the names of the form ones, and form twos had been awarded. And now it was the turn to award the form threes, my heart was almost throbbing out due to anxiety. They always started with the tenth person. The senior Master, Mr. Okutoyi, was reading out the names Celestous Njoroge, Benard Mwenesi, Baraka Uside..............."

I couldn't believe it—that I had made it to position seven out of 220 students. My heart was pounding faster as I walked to the front row. The whole staff room was shouting in a frenzy, and the whole of form three and form four students were cheering. Mr. Okutoyi had to stop calling the names. I walked to join Njoroge and Benard amid the thunderous applause. He had to wait for almost five minutes for the cheering to stop. Then he continued with reading the rest of the names.

No one believed I still maintained the streak of great performance whilst I had been a way for almost a year. My secret was with Mr. Wanyonyi. He had made a tremendous difference in my life and mentored me in a profound way. His efforts had borne fruits.

I received my award of an Atlas and a dozen two hundred-page exercise books, I was overwhelmed with emotions, and a tear of joy was forming at the right corner of my eyes. Donga had also outperformed himself, and he had come in at position four out of 220. He too was elated, riding on cloud nine.

I was called into the staffroom and received further congratulatory remarks and encouragement. I had become a community project, and I enjoyed the love everyone was extending to me. It was invaluable. In my heart I thanked Mr. Wanyonyi who had kept me on the track while I was away from school and taught me priceless study habits—especially the desire to understand concepts deeply.

That closing day, as all the students went to their homes, I was assigned to Mr. Nabwire's staff quarters. He was going to be away from school during the holiday, visiting his extended family in Nyakatch village. I took my metal box suitcase and moved into Mr. Nabwire's house. It was spacious with a TV mounted on a stand and a music player secured in place at one of the corners of the room. There were several portraits of Mr. Nabwire, his wife, and two sons hanging on the walls. The sitting area had several chairs that could seat perhaps ten people at the same time. He showed me one small room that had been reserved as a servant's quarter. It only had a bed and a small table and two chairs, the room was self-contained, and Mr. Nabwire left me with enough foodstuffs to last me till he came back. He wished me a good time and reminded me to utilize that time to read and learn as much as I could.

He shut the main house and left. For the first time in my life, I didn't have to worry about what I was going to eat or how I was going to get it. I had all the food I needed. I thanked God for the opportunity and promised myself to learn.

When we resumed the term, I didn't have to worry. I simply transitioned from the staff quarters back to the dormitory. My grades had really improved, and that same year, the school offered me bursary. When I got to fourth form, I received a full scholarship from TOTAL oil company that cleared my form three and four school fees. All I needed to do now was to study and make it happen. The scholarship gave me back life and exposed me to the great efforts done by corporates to make a difference in the lives of struggling families with their CSR programs. Meeting the CEO of TOTAL Africa to receive the scholarship was the most inspiring thing to ever happen to me as a learner. I was going to remain forever grateful for their selfless act—their desire and drive to make a difference.

It was going to be a herculean task to rise to the high standards everyone had now set for me. They were not going to settle for less from me, but I knew deep down I had no options but to arise and make a difference in my own life and the lives of other people.

I actively participated in athletics and won several awards for our dormitory, and in the school's science congresses, I competed to the national level. Indeed, God had rolled away the reproach from my life, and He was working overtime to take my shame away.

It was the first visiting day of third term, and as usual I wasn't expecting anybody to visit me at school, so as was the norm, I stayed behind in class as I imagined the fun my fellow students were having with their parents.

Benard my deskmate came to class panting, "Come and see for yourself Baraka!" he quipped. I was one person who stayed calm under pressure, but the anxiety in Benard's voice was unsettling.

He grabbed my hand as we ran through the corridors and towards the gate. There were dozens of students crowding around the gate astounded.

Fisi, the rascal, was amongst them.

"What's going on?" I asked Benard.

He said something, but I couldn't hear him. I was surging forward to have a clear glimpse of what was going on.

When I got closer to the crowd I couldn't believe my eyes. There was an old harassed man with a weather-beaten face that looked older than his age. The skin on his face had folded into deep furrows that took his smile away and turned his face into an old jagged face. Fisi was shouting, "Guys, come and see Donga's dad! This man says he's Donga's dad! Guys, can you believe it?"

"Donga is a conman. He's been lying all along to us," he rattled.

I was petrified. Was I dreaming? I had met Donga's mother and father on one occasion, and I had seen them in the many pictures that they had taken on numerous trips abroad together.

No, this couldn't be.

But looking closely at this old man's face he wore a heavy resemblance to Donga, though Donga's facial features were more refined and he looked healthier and more polished.

Fisi reached out to the old man and asked, "Did you say you are Donga's dad? Of course, you can't be. That's a bad joke, old man!" Donga is rich, and you poor thing cannot stand here and purport to be his dad. Perhaps the closest you can be is his distant . . . uncles' uncle. That's the only explanation for your resemblance," he said sarcastically, and the whole crowd bursting into laughter.

"Please help me talk to my son, Donga. Can someone call him for me please?" the old man desperately asked, looking very frail and sickly.

Was this true? And if so, why would my close friend hide it from me. Why? No, this couldn't be true. My mind was overwhelmed with chaotic thoughts. I had to help, but I didn't know how.

Fisi continued touting the old man and inciting the crowd of students, who subjected the old man to an awkward barrage of ridicule. They demeaned him, and they laughed their hearts out at their own cruel jokes.

I knew one of the places to find Donga, so I rushed into his cube at the dormitory and fetched him. I didn't tell him the reason why I was calling him out but I simply dragged his hand telling him to come quickly. He trusted me, so he came along though confused and irate as I wasn't telling him anything. We soon got to the crowd of students still milling around the old man. The crowd had now grown into so many students, ranging from form ones all the way to form fours.

When Donga arrived at the scene, he locked his eyes face-to-face with the old man. The old man beamed with joy, and he put on a very wide smile. He stepped forward towards Donga's direction with a limp in his left leg as the students watched in utter shock.

Donga was the school celebrity. Everyone knew him. His face had turned pale, and his eyes were blazing red with anger written all over his face.

"My son!" the old man shouted, limping towards Donga, who seemed frozen in time.

He reached out his hand to greet Donga and Donga gave the old man a massive push that made him to fall on the ground with a thud.

He fell to the ground crying in pain, "Son, why are you doing this to me? I have missed you all these years! Please I want to talk to you."

"You are not my father. Please stop embarrassing me, and go away. Never come back here again!"

"So, this thing is your father, Donga?" Fisi said sarcastically while dancing in a whirlwind frenzy, clapping his hands hard. There was a heavy laughter from the crowd. Others just watched at this interesting event as it unfolded, horrified.

I was bewildered. I didn't know how to behave in this scenario. Donga and this old man were two worlds apart, and they couldn't mix. It was like water and oil. This couldn't be a son and his father. There was something utterly wrong.

There was total confusion on Donga's face. Fisi had now helped the old man to rise on his feet. He pushed him towards Donga demanding an explanation about what was going on, "Donga, why did you lie to us all these years about your dad? Look at how frail he is. You need to take him to hospital."

Donga was filled with fury. He slapped the old man and pushed him away. He struggled through the hundreds of students who had crowded to see what was happening, and he ran towards the dormitory, leaving the old man behind.

I was totally confused, and I didn't know what to do either. The whole crowd of students was left with their mouths agape, wide open in shock, but Fisi was amused. He was ecstatic, moving up and down as if propping up a cheering squad in a murky game of rugby. He continued to ask the old man more questions. This was going to be real fodder for him. He had found a real revenge to the many months Donga had stolen his thunder.

I reached Donga's cube, but he wasn't there, so I stormed outside and searched for him everywhere. I walked into the tall grass next to our dormitory and found him sitting down with his head between his legs and his head covered with his sweater. He was crying and in deep pain.

I had never seen my best friend in such agony. I shook him, but he didn't respond. He just kept sobbing. "Donga!" it's me Baraka!"

When I called out to him, he gently lifted up his head and for the first time at Chavakali High School, I could see the larger-than-life Donga deep in anguish. I had never seen his tears. His eyes were red and swollen, and he was constantly scratching them in pain. I knelt down beside him and gave him a warm hug, allowing him to cry over my shoulder. I didn't know what else to do. After that, I sat there next to him and allowed him to cry. He couldn't utter a word, and neither could I.

Finally, after about two hours, I helped him to rise to his feet, and we walked to the dormitory. The time for dinner had already elapsed and we therefore had missed our meals. We had to walk to class.

Every step to class was like a walk that took eternity, with every step magnifying itself almost into loud thuds. I walked him to his class, and as he entered his classroom the whole of form four C burst into laughter and jeered him.

Fisi was his classmate in Form 4C and he had trained all his arsenal like a wounded tiger, waiting in hiding for a counter attack.

Fisi quickly rose to his feet and started chanting: "Donga the cheat, Donga the con, Donga the masquerade!"

The class was laughing in ridicule as Donga covered his face in shame. He went down to his seat and covered his face. He wanted the ground to break and swallow him.

I left for my classroom, knowing very well how difficult it was going to be for Donga.

For the next few days, Donga didn't have anywhere to run to. The whole school was talking about him. He had slipped into infamy and his celebrity status in school was quickly peeled from him, thanks to the concerted efforts that Fisi sustained.

No one, including myself, could explain what had transpired on that Saturday. It remained a jigsaw puzzle in everyone's mind. Only Donga could explain it, but he had remained numb on the issue. It was a chapter in his life that he didn't want to open.

Every day, I reached out to him during the breaks. As had been the norm, we always waited for each other, and we had made it a tradition for me to go to his class immediately after the bell rang so we could walk together to have our tea break. During lunch and games, we could spend the time together and during discussions, we could alternate between our classes, as he was my study partner—a friend and a brother to me.

But things changed so fast. Donga stopped going for the breaks. He didn't want to have his meals, and two days in a row, he had hardly eaten anything apart from a cup of milo that he took in the morning and at night. It worried me to the core, and I reported this matter to our guidance and counselling teacher, Mr. Kamonya, who quickly reached out to Donga and arranged for a session. But all the same, Donga was not ready and willing to explain his predicament. He preferred to remain silent. His parents were called to the school and they were informed of the dire need but unfortunately, they were out of the country on business, and they could only visit the school the following weekend.

It was the eighth day after that Saturday incident. That evening after preps I rushed to Donga's class and found him alone in class, as he preferred to leave after everyone else had left.

I walked him out of class and went and sat under the mighty mugumo tree. The whole sky was incredibly clear. It spread above us like a mighty blanket spangled with glimmering stars giving it a sparkling shine. The beetles were at it, vibrating their membranes and wings as they buzzed by over our heads. What looked like a dragonfly zoomed past our heads. The croaking sound of frogs coming from the distant end of the field seemed to be the only loud sound determined to disturb the otherwise silent night.

We sat down on the bulging roots of the mugumo tree. "Donga, you know you can empty yourself and tell me what's going on. Please tell me what's going on? I am deeply disturbed, and I have not been able to concentrate in class for the past several days. I am deeply worried about you. What's the matter?"

Donga looked at me in the dim moon light, we sat there in silence for a couple of minutes, then he answered with a wintry restraint;

"Baraka, indeed you have been a special friend—more like a brother to me—and we have learned so much from each other. Our lives are a reflection of each other in many ways."

"My story is a long one, and I might never be able to tell you everything. What I would like you to know is that I have reached the brink of my life, right at the cliff and am afraid I am going to topple over."

"No, please don't say that, Donga. What's going on?" I prodded further with heebie-jeebies filling my nerves.

"My life has been complicated, Baraka, I was born in a family of nine brothers. I was the last-born boy of my father. My father was very poor, and he couldn't take care of our family. He was a peasant farmer, and when my mother got pregnant, my father was furious with her, and he threatened to chase her out of home for bringing her such an embarrassment and an extra burden that he couldn't carry. He had been furious, and he reportedly beat up my mum during her pregnancy—so badly that mum was scared that she was going to die. So, she ran out of her matrimonial home and went to her maternal parents and stayed with my grandmother until the time she delivered me.

"One month after delivery, she fled and left me at the hands of my grandmother, who had no choice but to wet nurse me with her breasts. I suckled my grandmothers' breasts as nature might have it, but my grandmother couldn't take care of me fully, as she too had been abandoned by her sons who had migrated to other areas in search of better lives, and her daughters were all married, but they never came back home to visit her. So, the area chief took me to the nearby Fadhili children's home, that was being run by the Anglican Church, and after a few months, I was adopted into the family of Donga.

"Donga and his wife had been married for over twenty years, and they only had a daughter who, unfortunately died in a tragic motor racing accident. They were so distraught that their world had crumbled after the death of their only child, and they didn't know what to do, as Mrs. Donga had developed complications after delivery and that had caused her uterus to be removed so she lost her ability to have another child, and Donga was a well-respected man who valued family so he couldn't bring himself to take another wife.

"He had to strongly resist the pressure from the community to remarry. Donga could hear none of that, so they decided to go for adoption, and after several months of searching, they adopted me into their family. They took me as their own, and they gave me back my life and raised me in wealth."

"One day as a teenager, as I was cleaning and arranging dad's files and documents, I bumped into a file that contained weird letters and adoption certificates, and on those certificates, I found my name.

"My world tumbled and turned upside down, as I couldn't imagine the two people that I loved the most in my life weren't my biological parents. They had adopted me!"

I was keenly listening to him as his husky voice trudged on. I could see he was really controlling himself not to breakdown.

"I was not born as the Donga's. I was adopted to be a Donga. That realization turned my life around. I confronted my dad, and he explained the whole scenario and my life and how I ended up at Fadhili children's home, and I couldn't believe what my biological dad had done to me!"

"I was astounded—furious with my biological dad! I appreciated the Donga's even more, as it had taken a stroke of luck for me to be rescued. Otherwise I would have died at that early stage of my life. We visited Fadhili home several times, and I was forever grateful to the proprietors of the home to have rescued me, and I promised to always be part of them to ensure other people benefited from their selfless cause.

"Unfortunately, I developed a strong hatred for my biological dad and harbored lots of bitterness against him. I couldn't tell how to get rid of it.

"The proprietors of Fadhili home had maintained contact with my biological mother, and when they heard news that she had died, they informed the Donga's. To my surprise the Dongas had maintained a relationship with my biological mother, and they supported her from time to time and sometimes shared my pictures with her to show her how I was doing. Indeed, a mother's love is eternal. It's priceless. It's worth exceeds that of tanzanite. The Dongas had the courage to allow me to tag along to what was meant to be my home. I met my biological father and my other siblings—eight of them—in the most awkward encounter: at our mother's funeral. I was not allowed to talk, but when I saw my dad and the stark semblance that we had, my hatred for him grew by leaps and bounds.

"We had an awkward first encounter, and he shamelessly said that I was his blood. I could have killed him there and then, but I had been raised to be well mannered and polished and to handle my anger. From that day, my biological dad started to follow up on my existence and wanted to claim me back into his family, but I couldn't bring myself to the thought of going back to a family that had rejected me even before I was born, to strangers from birth. I wanted to keep my distance.

"Unfortunately, my biological dad got obsessed. He started stalking me, and I was utterly shocked to learn that he was aware I had been admitted to Chavakali high school," Donga said amid sobs

"Now he has killed me the second time. This time he has not only killed my dreams but he has taken my dignity away in this school. He has stolen my identity the second time, he has destroyed my future the second time, he has ruined everything that I have worked so hard to build, and no one will be able to understand. I cannot stand to face him, and now I cannot stand to face anyone in this school anymore. My ego has been crushed and given to the dogs. I have lost myself for the second time and I don't know how else to recollect myself."

We were both holding each other's hands and crying out our pains. I couldn't tell him fully my story. That could wait for another day, it could only add to his sorrow and bitterness. I had established a support system for myself that helped me to get through the worst times, but he needed urgent help. He was sinking fast into depression, and he had completely lost his balance. I wished the Donga's were here. The situation could have been different, but here I was with my best friend and with no idea how to help.

I didn't realize how time had zoomed by. It was already 2:00 a.m., and we didn't realize we had been sitting under the mugomo tree for hours as Donga poured his heart out to me.

I encouraged him to be strong—that help was on the way and that it was going to be okay. The biting cold and whining mosquitos had been our companion through the tough conversation that we had just had.

I walked Donga to his dormitory cube in the silence of the night, walking by several cubes with my fellow colleagues snoring and some dreaming their lives out loud.

I went to my bed and those wee hours of the morning dragged by. I couldn't get off my mind on the conversation and the miseries that my best friend was going through. I wanted to run to his class teacher, Mr. Shikuku, and explain this predicament to him, but the morning just didn't seem to come.

First thing in the morning, I went and looked for Mr. Shikuku, who was also our mentor in the school. He was a very kind teacher with a listening ear and a broad heart, and he had built us into solid young people in many profound ways.

Mr. Shikuku was shocked as I recounted what had happened and the conversation I'd had with Donga the previous night. We immediately went with him to fetch Donga in his classroom, but on reaching his class, he wasn't in. We searched for him in his cube, but he wasn't there either. I took Mr. Shikuku to the garden where Donga and I once sat on the day his father visited the school, but he wasn't there.

During the breaks, he was nowhere to be seen. The whole school was alarmed, and during lunch hour, all the form fours were summoned to go out in search of Donga— to comb every part of the school.

"Muturi, the dormitory captain, came running, panting and shocked to his core. "Donga is . . . dead !! Come and see, guys," he stammered.

Everyone started wailing while following him, scared stiff. I followed suit with a sudden spasm of pain and cold twinge of blood rushing through my veins. My body was starting to shake and I was starting to feel weak at the knees. I fervently hoped that Mutwiri was wrong.

Mutwiri disappeared behind the chapel and right there on the path that led to the farm my best friend's lifeless body hung on a large jacaranda tree.

I stood there, shaken, stuck in time, dazed in disbelief. My fellow students were now shouting and wailing and jumping up and down in a frenzy, but I couldn't move myself to do anything. I just stood there my eyes transfixed on Donga. It was a heart-wrenching scene to watch the body of my friend dangling in the gentle breeze that swept through the trees. A woeful pandemonium engulfed the whole school after this tragic discovery, leaving a trail of misery in every path that led to our tender hearts. I was tongue tied, and in my heart of hearts I didn't know whom to blame for this misery. The wind in the gardens at school had always spoken and blown as it wished, but this time it filled the air around us with the smell of death—a deadly breeze that caused my nerves to shiver, despite the sweltering heat. I wanted to turn back the clock, but I didn't know where it was hidden, I wanted to go back in time a few hours ago to the conversation that I'd had with Donga. How could life be so cruel?

CHAPTER SIXTEEN

Donga was the richest and most monied boy in school. He had all that money could buy. The entire school admired his lifestyle, and even the teachers treated him with gloved fists. He got away with mistakes other students paid for with bare knuckles.

He had access to social media on his phone that he took from the school custody during holidays, and he could update his profile pictures—his lifestyle and numerous trips to Dubai, kart racing in Rwanda, safaris in the untamed Maasai Mara, and trailing mountain gorillas in Virunga. Swimming lessons with his dad were strewn all over his social media platform. His life on social media was a wild flower for all to admire and cherish. He was adored by many and followed religiously by his fans who liked and commented generously on his posts.

But this lack of identity and his biological father's re-emergence in his life exposed a part of his life that he had guarded closely and none of his friends knew about, including myself. All we knew about him was that he was the lucky one—the chosen Donga, the celebrity—and when this grey part of his life had been exposed, he couldn't cope with the stress and ridicule that came with it.

After his rugged dad had visited him in school and after he denied him, saying he didn't know him, he was chided, and he felt out of sync. The school he'd known was gone. His celebrity status had been lifted like a veil, and the thin veneer couldn't hold it anymore. The ground had shifted, and he began sinking. He couldn't concentrate in class. He lost his friends, and he soon realized that all of his relationships had been bought with his money, and they were all cosmetic apart from the core clique that had stayed with him.

The Donga family had everything money could buy, and they had given Donga all that money could buy, and he had been taken to all the places money could take him, but one thing that he couldn't get away from was his identity or lack of it. He wanted to identify with the rich. He couldn't stand poverty. It was a scion he had been cut from, and he never wanted to be patched back to it. He fought back with rage and brevity, and he wanted to live in wealth. And he wanted wealth to call him by name!

The smell of death was awkward and it lingered with me. I couldn't lose the sight of Donga dangling from that jacaranda tree. It hurt my mind so bad. I remembered Kibe and his gang back on the streets of Nairobi. They had every reason to take their own lives, but they didn't. Donga should have done better, and the selfishness of his act filled me with bitterness.

A few hours later a cadaverous looking man retrieved the body from the tree and it was taken to Mbale District Hospital mortuary.

Quick investigations were done and it was found out that Fisi Okusimba and two other boys were on the forefront of bullying Donga and exposing him to untold mental torture. They were expelled from school.

Two weeks later, the school arranged for all the form Four C students which had been Donga's class to go and attend his funeral. I was part of the team of his close friends that the school allowed to go and give our departed brother our last respects.

He was going to be buried in his adopted parent's home amid confusion and protests from his families' biological father. He protested to and demanded to be given their son to go and bury him. The authorities had to intervene, and the Donga's were legally allowed to bury their beloved and adopted son. Why would you want in death someone you had rejected in life? That question stuck to my mind like the flies that lingered on our tiny ant-hills of human waste back in Kibra.

We took the school bus to Eldoret town, as that is where the Donga's family came from. The requiem mass was happening at a catholic church, and his body was later to be laid to rest at the Eldoret cemetery. We arrived in Eldoret at 10:00 a.m. and joined the mass at 10:30 a.m. The pews were filled with men of honor, dressed in black and other dark colors of death. A somber mood engulfed the church.

"God be with you till we meet again." Our voice trembled as we sang this hymn.

"In the sweet by and by, we shall meet on that beautiful shore." The hymns turned our hearts into a soft gel. The preacher, an elderly man adorned in black garbs, was preaching about life and death, but my eyes were fixed on the casket that lay right in front of my eyes, carrying my best friends' remains. After he preached, we were asked to line in one file to view the body. I wasn't sure I wanted to do so, but the preacher insisted that would help us to come to terms with the fact that our friend had departed. The brown casket shined in the reflection of the church's warm ambience, with the interior of the casket lined with thick layers of white cotton crepe that draped onto the visible silk fabric underneath. Donga was dressed in a black suit and a white shirt with a black bow tie, he looked graceful in death, and my eyes welled with tears as I saw him for the last time on this earth. The half coach design of his casket only allowed viewing half of his body. Donga's mum and dad were overwhelmed with emotions, and they just sat in one corner of the chapel motionless. A few people from Donga's biological family had also attended the funeral, but none of them were allowed to say anything. His biological dad was barred from the burial ceremony, as he had threatened to disrupt the service. He had been vicious in death, yet he had rejected his own blood right from birth.

I eulogized my best friend amid sobs. It was disheartening, and I wished the minutes could just fly by, but the time hung on, increasing the intensity of the pain we felt.

After the church service, the procession left to the cemetery which was two kilometers away. It was an old cemetery with an eerie air around it. I had never seen so many tombstones in the same place at the same time. I was scared stiff as we walked past the graveyards, and some of the tombstones had inscriptions that were falling off, giving way to the vagaries of nature.

Some were moss-laden concretes and others looked recent. There was really no sound disturbing the silence of the dead—only the dry leaves crackling beneath our feet as we trod on the narrow path, clearly not walked on by many, as attested to by the long grass that was growing on each side of the path.

We got to the selected graveside where Donga was going to be laid, and his grave had already been dug and cemented. The preacher asked everyone to come closer. We surrounded his grave and sang a few hymns. He read a few scriptures including Psalms 46:10:

"Be still and know that I am God."

"Please be still and know that He alone is God." He said.

He reminded us that we are all but clay and someday, sometime soon we will all go back to the soil from where we came from.

We were the pallbearers of our departed friend, and we took the casket under the instruction of the pastor and laid it onto the lowering gear that had now been placed onto the grave. The black straps were released, and my friend's journey begun to descend into his new home. The whole place was now filled with cries of anguish as the reality sank in that Donga, indeed, was no more. Once the grave was sealed, we placed the wreath of flowers that we had carried and an epitaph that we had written for him it read, "Donga you will always remain as a beautiful memory, forever in our hearts! Shine on your way!"

With that, we went back to the bus and returned to school, our hearts terrified and filled with misery.

Indire convinced the driver to assist us with his phone, and on it he logged into his social media page. It was amazing when we looked at Donga's page; he had five thousand friends on his page and more than ten thousand people who followed him on his walls. He had posted several pictures of his happy-go-lucky life and his high-end adventures with his father and mother. He had thousands of likes and comments on his pictures with many admiring the kind of life that he lived during the holidays when he was out of school.

We saw on his page one of his friends had posted a long note, announcing to the whole world that Donga had committed suicide. His online friends couldn't believe it. They were in denial, but nevertheless they simply typed RIP. It was amazing how he had lived large on social media and how simply he had died and been buried without his friends coming to send him off. I wondered if he was going to posthumously read the hundreds of comments that were written on his page. Some of his online friends were furious and spewed vitriol onto his life, cursing his soul. They hid under the veil of the screen and typed away whatever came to their minds, not considering how their words could impact other people that read their messages of hate.

I had admired his explanations and the joy that he had consistently shared with us on how sensational social media was, and we had looked forward to joining those pages when we finished school and could afford a mobile phone, but looking at it now, it dawned on us that the majority of the relationships on social media were cosmetic, superficial, and not very beneficial. We made the stark realization that when something befalls you, it will be your family and close friends that will be there with you, not the social misfits of the society whom most people live to impress. As they say, it's like square pegs in round holes. You only show the part of your life that is successful, and you leave no trail of depression or a sense of inadequacy. Your struggles belong to you, and social media isn't interested in that part of your life. It was yours to keep. On social media, you have to be admired. That's all that matters. Most of the dark side of your life is yours to deal with, not for the world to see. There was virtual richness for all, and no one wanted to be virtually poor! You couldn't be poor in reality and also be poor in your virtual world. Never! With the applications that could take your photos and plant you in places you had never been to, how could you be poor online? Social media provided that escape from reality. It was the new virtual nicotine that drove the dopamine levels to new heights and drowned the victims into a world of fantasy.

His page was filled with condolence messages which could not reach him, and none of the "friends" went to bury him. He was surrounded by a small bunch of villagers that spent quality time with his father at the village barazas and at the common village pot where they drunk their lives away from the village pot that had been passed over through generations and the Senior Donga's friends and employees who had come to show their friend and employer solidarity.

Donga had been a celebrity in life but as fate had it, he died in oblivion and obscurity. I was aggravated by the fact that he had taken his life. Everything that he had worked so hard for, every dream that he had nurtured and watched keenly, had gone down with him to the grave. It was disheartening. He should have done better.

CHAPTER SEVENTEEN

Donga's death left a heavy cloud over our heads that stubbornly refused to dissipate. The examination week was around the corner, and we worked hard to focus on our studies and final revisions. This was a special examination that was going to mark the end of our secondary education and usher us into the next phase of our lives: college life.

We had had numerous inspirational talks from the Chavakali alumni who had gone before us, and many had launched into successful careers. They had come back as old boys to inspire us to the next level.

"The teachers have done their part, and the parents have done their part, so it's your turn to do your part. May the Lord bless you as you start your exams tomorrow!" our school Chaplain Pastor Libese reverberated through the microphone.

Finishing the examination was the most dramatic moment of my life in Chavakali high school. After sitting for my accounting paper, I felt as if a whole burden had been lifted off my shoulders. I felt a rare light moment. We were hugging each other in celebration as the teachers looked on.

I hugged Mrs. Nasimiyu and all the teachers who were available, and I bid each one of them farewell with mixed emotions. This had been my special home.

I took my metal box with all the books and trekked back 'home' to my one-room rented house and continued with the business of fetching water and selling to the business owners and saving as much as I could. The girls chided and called me names as I carried the water on my head just like they did, but I couldn't have cared less what they had to say. I had a life to live, and I had nothing to lose.

It had been two torturous months as I waited for my results with every day filled with anxiety. At last, the day came, and I remember it vividly when the results were announced.

I had gone to the river as usual to fetch water, and on my way back I was met by Mama Ndeda and a group of other women in the company of Mr. Wanyonyi all brandishing twigs fully engrossed in song and dance.

Mr. Wanyonyi was the first to spot me as I negotiated the corner with a twenty-liter jerrican balanced on my tiny head. He ran towards me and lifted me into the air, the jerrican falling off from my head and pouring the water. He was breathing frantically with excitement.

"Thank you for making it Baraka. Thank you for scoring an A! You have made us proud, Baraka! Your God has remembered you!" His words were a sweet melody to my ears, and tears of joy freely rolled down my cheeks as I remembered what I had gone through to get to this point, but it wasn't a time of pain. It was a time of insightful reflection and a true testament that we can all dream on, no matter what.

I was carried high across the marketplace like a trophy. It was a collective success. We went straight to the school and we celebrated more with the teachers, I had topped in our school and the entire western region. It was incredible! I couldn't believe it myself, but it was happening. It was no longer a dream but a reality.

Three weeks later, I was informed by the school that there was going to be a parent's day in school to receive the form ones and to bid the outgoing form fours. It had been a tradition that had been observed in the school for years, and I had been honored to give the valedictory speech after the ceremony. Awards were going to be given to the top students in various categories in the midst of all the parents, and after that, the result slips and the leaving certificates would be issued to the outgoing students; this ensured that all the parents attended the ceremony.

I was over the moon. I had to invite my mother, so I made arrangements and travelled to Nairobi by night. I arrived in the bustling Nairobi city in the wee hours of the morning and headed straight to the mini buses that plied the Kibra route.

I easily located our shack, but when I arrived, I found the door was locked from the inside. I knocked on the patched wooden door and after a few minutes, a middle-aged woman opened the door. I was astonished and I thought I had missed our door. "What do you want this early morning?" she asked.

"Is this not Jane's house?" I inquired.

"I am not Jane," she said indifferently as she turned back in.

"Which Jane are you referring to? The one at the local brew den? Please check there," she said angrily, losing her patience. And with that, she slummed the door behind her.

This had been our house. Our home.

I couldn't have missed the door as the blue band metal bars were still heavily patched on the door, they had stood the test of time.

I knocked again, but the lady didn't come out. She simply ignored my nuisance. In confusion, I walked to Mama Pima's house, which had already started serving patrons the illicit brew. I knocked very hard on the door, as it was noisy. Pombe, Mama Pima's husband, came to open the door, and he was so pleased to see me.

"Oh Baraka! *Karibu sana*, come on in!"

He ushered me into the house that Mum had warned me never to enter.

"Oh, Baraka! Welcome back!" I heard a familiar voice. It was the voice of my mum.

I watched in astonishment lacking words to say anything. I couldn't believe my eyes.

Mum sounded and looked inebriated in the early morning hours. She was serving the patrons and she went on, oblivious of the fact that I was there. She seemed to carry on as if nothing had happened. She was chatting and laughing haughtily with the patrons, making obscene jokes. She was in her own world—a strange world that I was not immediately sure how I was going to enter it and talk to her.

"Mama Pima is no longer here," Pombe said, wearing a confident smile.

His words cut through my flesh like a sharp blade. He didn't have to add anything on his statement.

Mum was the new Mama Pima. How could she? How could he have done this to my mum? I wanted to hit him on his head, but I restrained myself, hot bile piling in my stomach.

My mum was the new mama Pima and she took the title with the grace and diligence that the job demanded, savoring the freedom of recklessness that came with it. It must have been refreshing to her. She had stuck on the narrow lane for so long, and this new route must have been strange to her.

She casually passed by where I was standing and I noticed her stomach was protruding. She was heavily pregnant, and the world around me was starting to spin. My emotions turned from shock to utter bitterness.

Who was the father to this unborn child? Did the cycle start again? What happened to my Mum who had been resilient? What went wrong? I wished I could ask her those questions, but her sobriety was at rock bottom. She couldn't even strike a sensible conversation with me.

"Is that Baraaaka? How are you?" She burbled, giving me a weak, unnerving smile.

I wanted to share the good news with Mum, but she was inebriated and she couldn't have a conversation with me. She was too drunk to talk sensibly and more so she had so much explaining to do, so I tucked the news back into the pocket of my soul and saved it for another day and coiled my dignity back into my little shell afraid of peeling it off once again.

She was busy serving her patrons and hurling insults at them at the same time and laughing at her own silly jokes as the patrons touched her inappropriately. I stood there mortified and completely drained. My emotions were hurtling to hit through the roof. I didn't know where to start.

The thought of Mum and Pombe together broke my world into pieces. I wanted to whisk her away immediately from this den and take her with me there and then, but how was I going to do it? She needed care. She needed love. I had failed her! I felt a sudden rush flowing through my being, and I thought I was going to collapse. Everything that I had lived for and hoped for was crumbling right under my nose. The guilt was killing me—draining me dry.

She clearly wasn't going to make it to attend my valedictory speech. I had to celebrate my victory mostly with strangers.

The thought of calling Pombe my newfound dad was appalling and nauseating, but I couldn't boil the ocean. I had to leave. I sneaked out of the den and headed straight back to Eazy Koach bus station. My mind was boiling out of frustration. My mum had done all that she could have done to raise me right, and she had now given up at the very edge of her breakthrough. Life had taken her around in cycles and flung her into the open sewers of life to be undignified, and she had lost the battle.

Our choices have consequences and I trust you will choose wisely.

Her words came flooding onto my mind, and I felt angry at myself and at my deadbeat dad for having thrown Mum under the bus.

I was feeling a strong tinge of pain in my stomach, and I realized I hadn't eaten the whole day, but I couldn't bring myself to order for anything, so I got myself into one corner of the room and lay on a waiting coach hoping to be carried away by some wind of sleep into a different land. I spent the night on the passenger waiting bay oblivious of the cold and the biting mosquitoes. The inner pain was far weightier than anything else.

I boarded the bus the following morning back to the village praying that God would preserve my mum's life. She had taken a wrong turn in her life. She had given up hope. She had fallen into depression, and in my heart of hearts, I knew she was hurting.

My heart had sunk as one nosy neighbor narrated to me what had happened.

She gave up all hope when Mr. Igwe left back to his country Nigeria after being redeployed, and she didn't have anywhere to turn to. She had slipped back to the shanty and tried waiting at the rich city gates in the scorching sun for someone to hire her and allow her to do laundry and wash a whole six bedroom house for a mere hundred shillings per day, but most days no one hired her, and when she was hired she worked and broke her back. She couldn't wake up the following day, so she had stopped but she needed to survive. One day Pombe had fought Mama Pima and grossly assaulted her, and she had left for good, never to return, and Mum had started with a day's job serving the patrons and to do the mixing, brewing, and distilling of the local brew. She had resisted the temptation to taste it, but with time she had become an experienced and trusted distiller, a fermenter who effortlessly turned *chang'aa* into a triple-distilled magical gin. Pombe got even more clients from far and beyond the slums, and as she distilled, she tasted. She was inebriated half the time. She loved the fame that came with it. She spent more time in Pombe's den—more than in her shanty. With time, she stopped coming back to her shanty. The landlady had closed it up and confiscated her handful of belongings for rent arrears of about six months. But that no longer meant anything to the new Mama Pima. My mother had auctioned her beautiful soul to Pombe, and they had naturally transitioned into lovebirds, into husband and wife.

It's said that when life throws lemons at you, you must use them to make lemonade, but the work of squeezing the lemons is not easy. So, I had learned the taste of my lemonade and was ready to make the cocktail once again. So, I took myself up as I composed myself back to my little tiny space in Mudete in Vihiga.

I wasn't going to do the valedictory speech. I had failed, and my mind was settled. This was my lowest moment. The person that I wanted the most to attend the ceremony wasn't going to be there after all. I went to Mr. Wanyonyi and broke the sad news. He was speechless for a while and he spent hours upon hours trying to encourage me to accept and proceed with the talk and to encourage other students who could be going through a similar challenge. It took great effort to convince me back into the speech.

"Keep your chin up Baraka. Nothing comes easy! You have to fight, and you can't give up at this stage. I will accompany you to Chavakali!" he firmly said.

The day came, and I had to brace myself with my head high, despite the burdens that my little shoulders carried. I still had to put my head high. I had waited for this day with bated breath. It was my big day. It was a big day for the teachers who had played such a pivotal role in my life and nurtured me into a responsible young man. It was a big day for my mentor, Mr. Wanyonyi, and all the great men and women who had collectively nurtured me into something useful. And, yes, it was a big day for my mother, the iron lady who had taken all the shame on our behalf and postponed her happiness for Isate and I. It was a big day, and I didn't want anything to dampen the mood, so I decided I was going to smile. I was going to be happy. I was going to celebrate those people who mattered to me the most—who believed in me when no one else did, and who gave me hope and opportunity in the midst of obscurity. I was going to celebrate them.

The master of ceremonies, Mr. Shikuku, came to the stage, his voice full of excitement. "Let's all rise to our feet and welcome Baraka Uside to the stage!" he said.

The whole auditorium thundered into applause and ululations as I hugged Mr. Shikuku and gave him a hearty smile and a firm handshake as I took the microphone.

"To our guest of honor, the Provincial Director of Education, Mr. Greg Wasike, our principal Mr. Agavah, our esteemed teachers, our parents, invited guests, and my fellow comrades, good morning.

"It's such an honour and solemn privilege to talk to you during this great event in the history of our great institution. Thank you, Mr. Principal for the opportunity.

"Thank you, God, for making it possible to come this far. Thank you my honorable teachers whose guidance has been invaluable. Thank you to all our parents who were there for us and worked hard to make sure our school fees was paid, and thanks for the bursary funds. A special thank you to Total Kenya for the scholarship that they offered me to ensure I cleared my school fees. A big thank you. And a special thank you to my mum, whose spirit I carry with everywhere I go. Unfortunately she is not here with us today!

Thank you to the kitchen staff who ensured the cabbages were raw enough to fill us up!"

The hall burst into laughter.

"And to my fellow prefects who worked so hard to ensure a high level of individual responsibility was upheld in all of us. Thank you to all you comrades for making this great school what it is. You are truly champions, and we celebrate you.

It's unfortunate we lost a comrade—a friend, one of us—because of lack of identity, because he wanted to feel loved and to be loved back, yet he couldn't bring himself to accept the real scion from which he had been cut. The exposure of his father to the rest of us here in school burst his bubble, and his life crumbled, making him take his own life. Comrades, lets learn from him and let's not take this route to self-destruction. Shall we stand up and observe one minute of silence for our fallen comrade Master Donga? May his soul rest in peace."

The whole auditorium rose up, and in silence you could hear some sobs from the crowd.

I continued on. "I have some invaluable lessons from the honey badger that I would like you to carry through life, and perhaps if you can steal that secret from me, we all can make a difference and turn around our lives. As we do that, the whole world will open up to us beyond our imaginations. The honey badger has deep secrets, and I was interested the moment I saw it at Igwe's house on the National Geographic station.

"Learn the secret of positive pain. When you develop resilience and tenacity, regardless of your limitations and size, the king cobras of this world, with their postsynaptic neurotoxins, will still fear you. Be stubbornly focused on your goal, and play the part that you are meant to play, and play on hard; there are many reasons why you need to quit, but forge on in life, comrades! Life has and will always throw you curveballs—not once, not twice but several times and you need to brace yourselves to curve out of the situation and step up into action

Don't choose a metric that will hurt you; don't foolishly be the fish that tries to climb a tree or the sleazy salesman without a conscience trying to sell ice to an Eskimo. Learn to see the honey badger inside of you that will intimidate the king cobras in your life. You know the worker bee will sting you, but you remember its limits. It only has one sting, and once it has stung you, that's all it has got; remember with one and only one painful sting, its life is cut short. Despite your thick skin, the sting will hurt, but as you finally eat the honey, you will forget the pain. You will relish the victory and treasure every moment of it all. When the honey badger spirit arises in you, then you go where others have not been to. You feed on what feeds on others, and you kill and maim what kills and maims others. You develop an anti-venom to the tumultuous world that is full of venom because your system stops being ordinary. Resist the unfortunate temptation to conform, as this will surely lead to failure. Be rebellious to the norms and challenge the status quo. Not everything is cast in stone; be a free spirit with a free will, fully aware that the enemies are real and furious but awake to the fact that you are prepared. You are deliberate, and that your thick skin didn't take a day to build. It took time. That the raw confidence in your eyes didn't just appear. It's the result of numerous trials, numerous failures, and untold ridicule and critique. And those fine, sharp claws on your feet didn't just grow by accident. They're there to help you deal with the harsh realities of life. You, my friends, are resilient!"

The auditorium was roaring with thunderous applause. I paused for a moment and continued.

In my mind I was saying, *Uncle Matata did you hear that applause?*

"The honey badger will not wait for food to come to it like a lazy bird in the nest, whose tiny mouth is fully open for regurgitated food from the mother's innards. Rise above regurgitations. They are poisonous, dirty, and insidious. They come with no luxury. Don't deny yourself the power of choice—to choose your freedom to be free. Don't allow life to squeeze you between a rock and a hard place—into its own mold—as you will not fit in. You will end up in broken pieces.

Some enemies might not need your ferocious paws to fight. Engage them with your magic pouch, just like the honey badger does to calm down the bees and unsettle her enemies during her onslaught. Look out for your tail end. That has the terrific gland. The magic pouch. When everything else has been used, release the skunk in you. Then, with your thick but cleverly loose skin, confuse your enemies with your turns, so they can't get ahold of you to bite.

However, use your pouch selectively with the emotional intelligence of a skunk. It produces very little of the magic substance, so make sure your lousy pouch doesn't come out too often. Be elaborate, be modest, be gradual, be measured, and always remember: threatened skunks will go through an elaborate routine of hisses, foot-stamping, and tail-high theatrics or threat postures before resorting to spraying their lugubrious stuff into your eyes. Comrades, you have to exercise emotional intelligence and know when to use and unleash the skunk in you. Discover your pouch, learn the contents of your pouch, and be wise enough to know when to unleash it. When you are measured, you will succeed in your sports, in your academics, in your corporate life, in your businesses, in church, in whichever sphere that you will choose to pursue.

"My comrades, always remember: there are days you might not have the strength to hunt or the zeal to fight, but don't allow yourself to starve to death. Look out for the fruits and vegetables—the raw cabbages of Chavakali." I paused amid the laughter. "The berries, the roots, the herbs, the bulbs, the bark on the trees around you. They are all meant to work in your favor for your survival—for your livelihood— but this might require you to lift a stone or two—to apply some effort, to open your eyes and see the bark's nutrients. The vegetables won't just drop into your lap either. It will take some effort to get them." I looked at Isate who was seated next to Wanyonyi and smiled. He smiled back, as he knew exactly what I was talking about.

"Once your skin is thick, look out for the vision enablers, comrades. The honey guides: follow them, as they will direct you with divine speed to what you are looking for: greater realms and heights and depths. However, always remember the honey guides don't get the honey from the beehives. They simply guide the honey badger to the source, and once at the source, the honey badger has to get to work. It has to unleash itself into the danger zone—into harm's way without fear of the bee stings. And with that, it gets the honey—the sweet taste of the liquid gold—and forgets the pain. The royal honey is worth the pain.

"The honey guides are all over in this school, find them in your fellow students, in the churches you go to, in the industries you admire, and most importantly, hidden in the biographies of the great men that you admire. Find your honey guide, and you will find your hidden bee hive faster, but don't forget that the honey guide is simply a bird that knows how to fly. It doesn't have the thick skin to take out the honey for you. You will have to get in and fight off the stings from the bees on your own.

"My honey guides are all over this room, and I salute you all".

I stole a quick look at Mr. Wanyonyi, who was wiping a tear from his eye in admiration and gratitude. We locked eyes and smiled poignantly at each other. He had been there for me and given me the shoulder that I needed to lean on, but I still missed my mum. Deep down, I was lonely. I wanted to feel loved, to feel cared for, to have my mother close, and to help sort the sorrows that life had thrown her way. Deep inside I was sinking in a deep smudgy abyss, lost and alone in my own world. I was fully surrounded but in my world. I longed for belonging. I trailed a bit in my imagination and at that point I raised my head and looked in the direction of Mr. Wanyonyi, who out of love had attended the valedictory speech, and smiled at him. Whenever I stole a look at him, he nodded in affirmation, strengthening every word that I said.

"I am not an expert in life, but this is the little wisdom I have gathered throughout the few years that I have been around in this life. I have learned, have been hurt, I have made mistakes, I have triumphed, and I have gone astray many times, but I am glad that my feet are on course to achieve my dreams, and I am calling you to join in and drive your destiny. Above all, allow God to deal with you in love and to reveal the true purpose to you as to why you are here.

"Thank you, and I wish you luck in all things."

There was a standing ovation and a thunderous applause from the auditorium. Students stamped to the dais to congratulate me, parents hugged me in droves, and teachers smiled at the work they had nurtured for years with satisfaction written all over their faces. God bless their hearts with the impact on my life, they had changed my life, and in turn a whole generation moving into posterity.

CHAPTER EIGHTEEN

I received a letter to study Medical Biotechnology at Maseno University. Research had been a core area of my life, and I wanted to delve deeper into understanding human suffering and being part of the solution.

Mr. Wanyonyi had mentored me into making the correct career choice, and he had provided me with books that opened up my prism of thinking to realize that the different careers were nicely intertwined into each other.

This time I boarded the bus to Maseno, not with a metal box but with a small green suitcase that had a few pairs of clean civilian clothes and a few rims of paper and pens.

Maseno University was lush with green vegetation and pockets of deep forests with monkeys freely jumping between the branches. The serene environment was a real haven to nurture a creative mind, and I counted myself to be lucky to be there. University was so different from the experience I had in high school. There was a general carefree aura where freedom of choice was something one couldn't trade for anything else. We chose what to do, when to do it, and how to do it.

I took the constant reminder of Mum back in the den as my motivation to work harder to make a difference.

Whenever I saw the reckless lives of my fellow students, Mr. Wanyonyi's words would always flood my mind: "There are many girls out there, and there is no competition or medal to the person who has many. What matters is the person you love with your heart and are committed to. You will make a happy life together. Desire to define what beauty means to you. Make your own rules and engagements, and don't let the world define love for you. Define life and love yourself, and you will find amazing peace and direction in matters to do with love."

That morning, Prof Hardison was lecturing us on Human Physiology, but my mind was not in class. I had wandered off and anxiously waited for the lesson to end. Finally, the class ended, and I rushed outside to make sure she hadn't forgotten our prior discussion.

Her name was Kageha, and indeed there is power in a name. She looked like a princess in her natural beauty, and in every way she was elegant. Her facial features were exquisite, and her bright inviting smile made my heart to melt away into a molten state of emotions that threatened to drown me in the river of love, yet she was as humble as the grass. Her gentle yet sure gait made her elegant body to gracefully dance with every move that she made towards me. I couldn't bring myself to hold her hand as was the norm on campus.

I was too scared to touch her, and I therefore made my handshake brief. Even in that short-lived time, I could feel the softness of her velvety palms. They reminded me of my first handshake with Igwe back then.

"Kageha!" Kageha!" her best friend was calling after her. But she was already with me and we started off in a different direction towards our hostels. Everyone looked at us curiously, or so I thought. We were going to have to explain to them how our first experience together was.

I could only talk about the weather as we walked to the room. My mental faculties couldn't bring myself to discuss serious concepts and models in chemistry. While alone, I always took less than five minutes to get to my room, but this time it was a long walk as we made tiny baby steps. We got to the room, and she laughed off everything.

"Baraka, you guys don't wash your sheets. What of the curtains? That dust seems to have been there for far too long, and how do you survive on this floor Baraka? You guys can't even fold your clothes?" She saw everything that I had missed in my thorough preparation. Indeed, she was disappointed. Nevertheless, I offered her a cup of milo and a fried piece of egg and sausage and a slice of bread. She only ate a piece of the sausage, and she didn't even touch the other set of snacks that I had laboured to prepare. Deep down I was disappointed, but I knew I was going to eat all that she hadn't touched immediately after she left the room!

We immersed ourselves in discussion to get to know each other better and as we talked it was like crisscrossed tentacles that pulled us together. I discovered the beauty that lay both outside and inside of her, her tenacity, focus and love for God was amazing.

She was amazed as I told her the part of my story that she didn't know—the escapades on the streets, my high school struggles—she sat there half the time saying nothing but just soaking in every word that I spoke to her.

"Your mother is a strong woman!" she said. "I hope one day I will be able to meet her."

"Of course. Yes, you will. She will be happy to see you. She will love you instantly!" I blurted on with excitement.

"Can we now look at the chemistry questions?" she asked naughtily. I looked at her and smiled. It had been more than four hours of deep conversation, and it was time to walk her back to her hostel. We couldn't bring our minds off the emotional highs of our lives back to science to discuss chemistry, so we left that for another day.

As I walked her down the corridors of Maseno University in the darkening night, I could hear the sound of our spirits walking in tandem, and I knew I was going to walk this journey together with Princess Kageha!

That day marked the beginning of several meeting points where we discussed things about life and connected more with each other. I had never felt so attracted to someone in my entire life. I longed for the company of Kageha, and we always looked forward to the discussion times and the Christian Union sessions when we would spend time together worshiping and serving God. It was amazing. She was the most amazing person I had ever met, and she had a heart of gold, pure and undefiled. She taught me and showed me the true face of love.

I graduated on top of my class, and I immediately got a scholarship to enroll into a master's class under one of Professor Ouma's projects on molecular Biology. It was an exciting journey for me and I got lots of exposure and experience in the world of science.

I received the opportunity to work with some of the greatest minds in the world of science in Kenya and the region, as Prof Ouma's lab was a regional lab, so we hosted scientists from Ivy League universities.

It was after about six months in his lab on one warm morning when Prof Ouma came to me and pulled my hand, dragging me into his office. He was panting with excitement.

"Your God is great Baraka. I am so proud of you. You have been accepted to join Massachusetts Institute of Technology (MIT) in the USA to complete your master's program and enroll for your PhD Program thereafter. Your work and knowledge on the telomerases and the telomeres has put this laboratory on the global map, and am forever thankful to your diligence and dedication. Your papers have been accepted and published in the world's renowned peer reviewed journals and your findings presented in global scientific conferences. You will get the opportunity to work with other dedicated minds in this area of research and your cocktails may be commercially manufactured to reach a wider market across the globe."

I was jumping hysterically, overwhelmed with emotions. It was indeed a new day.

"Thank you, God! Thank you, Prof Ouma."

It had been my dream since I was a small boy that one day, I was going to be great, but it was beyond my wildest imagination that this is how it was going to happen. It was an amazing feeling. I had heard about the wonders of the developed worlds and how advanced they had been in science, but then it was mind boggling to imagine a young mind like myself was going to get the privilege of being part of the system—part of the team that was going to generate the knowledge and the data that could make a difference. I was not just going to be a consumer but a producer of new knowledge.

We hugged each other as we jumped along the corridors of Prof Ouma's lab, and the other research scientists joined us in celebration. It was going to be a great fete, and that meant more open doors for the rest of the researchers.

I went back home to meet Dr. Wanyonyi. He had also done well for himself. He had graduated with a PhD in mathematics and he was now lecturing at the Masinde Muliro University. He was fast becoming a force to reckon in the academic sphere.

"I got the scholarship, sir!" I exclaimed.

He grabbed me and carried me high, taking me round in crazy whirlwind moves. We fell down and broke into laughter.

"Congratulations! Baraka, please tell me more about it!" Dr. Wanyonyi said as he held me close by hand, giving me a firm, warm hug.

We sat on an abandoned kiosk at Mudete Market for about two hours as I narrated to him how it had all happened and how it was such a privilege to be accepted on scholarship into Massachusetts Institute of Technology to study molecular biology at masters level and thereafter to proceed to the PhD level.

"I am super proud of you Baraka and please let nothing limit you at this level. You have shown exemplary commitment, resilience, and diligence towards your goals and aspirations, and it's time to go the whole way and bring the whole world back to reality. Yes, even in this tiny village in a remote place that's probably not on the map, there are people with brilliant minds," he said with a wide grin lighting his face into brilliance.

***

I travelled the same night to the big city of Nairobi, and I met my mother. She was a bit sober, and I shared the great news with her.

"Pombe! Pombe!" Come and hear the news that Baraka has.

I still couldn't believe Pombe was my stepdad. I had desired a dad all my life, but it was hard to imagine or even call Pombe dad. He was a disgrace and the epitome of what a responsible dad shouldn't be.

I quickly noticed that Mum was no longer pregnant. I was eager to see my other step sibling—at least he or she would have had two parents—But I kept that observation to myself.

Pombe listened to the news with excitement. He quickly went back into the den and announced that all the patrons that afternoon were going to get two free glasses of the lethal liquid, in celebration of my successes.

"Let's celebrate Baraka. Everyone lift your glasses. Let's drink to celebrate the joy that Baraka has brought to us. Bring your glasses here!" he said

I could see the stampede from the patrons as they scampered and jostled for the free liquor. They were going to drink my success away, and to them that was so exciting and refreshing. In my heart of hearts, I wished there could be another way to do it, but unfortunately, you don't always get what you want in life. My success had served them yet another poisonous dose that slowly serrated their livers.

So, Mum organized a small prayer meeting for me, and she sent me with her blessings She had so many unanswered questions?

"Baraka, so who is going to pay your school fees, and where will you be staying? Will you be able to hear their language since they speak through their noses!" she said amid laughter from the patrons.

"Mum, where is the baby?" I asked when everyone had retreated back to their drinking tables.

"What baby!" she asked looking deep in thought.

"You were pregnant, right Mum?" I quickly reminded her.

She looked at me in the eye for a long time as if in a trance then she quietly said, "I lost the baby. It was a still birth! Life here in this den is tough, Baraka!" I was horrified to see the concern and the pain on her face, so I quickly changed the topic.

"Prof Ouma, my instructor, has told me that the university will send the air tickets and that I will fly Kenya Airways to Dubai then take another Kenya Airways connection flight to the USA. In total, Prof Ouma said I will spend about eighteen hours in the air before I get to America," I patiently explained to her.

She was very curious, and you could see a mother's love and glare in her eyes. She was exhilarated and happy. "Please don't forget us, Son. Some people go to America and they forget home. Please remember me!" she said that as she reached out and gave me a warm hug.

Prof Ouma organized a grand farewell party and invited my former lecturers. I also invited my former classmates from our undergraduate classes, with Kageha on top of the list and together we celebrated the success. I invited Dr. Wanyonyi to the meeting, and he gladly came to witness another phase of my journey that was just about to begin.

"I am so proud of you, Baraka, and you have, indeed, shown that as a country we have great talent—that we can bring customized solutions to the problems that we all face as Africans. Your effort and diligence is a great proof that this is a lab that believes in excellence and I am positive that the future is brighter for all the other research scientists that you are leaving behind. They too can dream big and be part of your journey, or better still, they can craft their own journeys into their own unique destinies."

I struggled to wipe a tear, then reached out and gave Prof a warm hug. We dined and allowed our minds to dream of a world full of possibilities.

With the letters that had been sent from MIT, it wasn't difficult to get the USA visa. I waited in anticipation for the travel date, and finally the day came.

I had missed sleep that night, as I dreaded the fact that I was going to be on board for almost eighteen hours. I had never gone anywhere near an airplane. They were mighty alien birds that were a privilege for a few, and I had never dreamt in my entire lifetime that I would get the chance to get on board, but here I was: that possibility was fast becoming my reality.

Dr. Wanyonyi understood fully my pain and my worries, so he offered to escort me all the way to the airport and assisted me with the check-in counters and my luggage to ensure I did everything in good time so as not to miss my maiden flight to the land of opportunities.

He helped me with all the logistics, including the customs area, but he was not going to be allowed past the customs area. He looked me in the eye and said, "Son, please carry the Kenyan flag high. I am proud of you, and I will always pray for you!" He hugged me and squeezed my hand tightly.

I felt a sudden surge of emotion run down my spine. I recalled every word that he said to me but as I entered into the customs exit area, the word "Son" reverberated in my mind and came with a huge wave of emotion. I felt it was going to sweep me off my feet. I looked back and saw Dr. Wanyonyi still standing by the metal barriers that barred relatives and friends from going beyond the set area. I raised my hand and waved goodbye to him.

He had become my family. I knew his children, and they took me in as their big brother. His wife had a big heart, and she sure couldn't be compared with anyone else that I had ever known. She was simply special, and I was extremely lucky to have known this family. Mr. Wanyonyi had assumed the role of a father figure in my life, and the time and insight he had invested in my life was immeasurable. He had made a huge difference and taught me how to be a man. I was going to be forever grateful to him. As I turned back to look into the eyes of the man who had just called me son for the very first time, I felt my heart tingle with a strange love, and tears welled in my eyes. I couldn't wipe them away. I let the tears flow freely as we waved at each other.

There was an angelic voice that was reverberating through the speakers, "Passengers flying to the USA on Kenya Airways, kindly proceed to gate twenty-three for documents check and immediate boarding."

I checked the signage that pointed to gate twenty-three and proceeded with the other passengers who wore happy, confident faces as they pulled their hand luggage.

I was mesmerized by the many shops that had what looked like high-end merchandise, ranging from perfumes and toys to chocolates and artifacts. Customers were filling these shops in droves, busy picking items and stashing them into their already bulging bags.

I was greeted at the entrance of the airplane by two beautiful air hostesses. "Welcome aboard, Baraka. Your seat is number 21A. Kindly proceed straight on your left." It was an amazing feeling, but a thin stretch of warm sweat filled my armpits as anxiety set in.

"I am your captain today, Mrs. Gaby Verhelst, and we will be flying forty thousand feet above sea level. I invite you all to sit back, relax, and enjoy the Kenyan hospitality on board. The cabin crew led by Joyce Lavusa will be more than willing to help if you need anything. I am proud to let you know that this is the first all-female crew, and we are all proud of all the great women on board!" she said.

The whole cabin gave a thunderous uproar in congratulations. Indeed, as Mandela said, "It always seems impossible until it's done." Flying on this plane was a true testament to that statement, and I felt so encouraged that there were no impossibilities. So long as one commits, one will sooner or later achieve it. The screens were running a security video in case of an emergency, but my mind couldn't focus.

The plane engines were roaring to life as captain Gaby gently announced, "Ensure you have your safety belts secured in place. Ready for take-off."

I was seated next to the window, and I was spellbound as the plane roared in super-fast speed towards the take-off. We took off into the air like a bird, and a shrill chill of fear rushed through my nerves, making me to shudder.

I was clinging to my seat and fidgeting, all the while gazing outside in utter shock as the plane took for the skies. The roads and the buildings grew tiny until I couldn't see them anymore. The clouds were now in sight, and as we cut through them, I understood what I had read about turbulence: it was like hurtling over a pothole. Luckily, it was short-lived, and we cruised beyond the skies. I was absolutely stunned to see the sea of clouds flowing like a mighty blanket below us. It was a memorable scene that my mind couldn't have imagined. I just had to see it for myself to have a mental picture. The aircraft was beyond my imagination. I admired the creation of human ingenuity—tact and skill pushed beyond limits. It was the epitome of what could be achieved when wild minds were allowed to freely think and bring their ideas to roaring life—to soar beyond where birds have been, riding on the clouds and mastering the language of the wind.

It was amazing, and I could hardly believe what was happening. I loved it as this modern bird glided by with the wind. It was mindboggling.

My immediate neighbor noticed my fidgety surprises and took her time to explain so much more about planes and flying etiquette.

I went to the toilet out of curiosity for a short call. I had to make a first for myself too. I had to empty my frustrations at the thrilling height of forty thousand feet. I ate all the food that was served, which was also a first. I tricked my mind to believe I was experiencing the old cliché of fine dining in high places. Most people on the plane were asleep, but my mind was perplexed in many ways. But in the spirit of registering another first, I also dozed off and slept for the first time high above.

I had been used to the concrete jungle that was Nairobi, but looking through the window, I could see the sublime stretches of the ocean, which looked like a long, winding snake that turned and twisted on the silent shores, culminating in an artistic expression from the grand master. After several miles, I could now see the clouds below me stretched out like a wild blanket covering a section of the skies with rain, seemingly building underneath its bowels. It would soon give in to torrents of rain, but just like this mighty piece of metal loaded with tons of human weight and cargo, I didn't have to worry about the rain. I was flying where eagles dare not go, and I could run away from the storm.

We landed in Dubai, and I had to happily endure the labyrinth of security gates and multiple counters. It took me about thirty minutes of walking through the nicely designed corridors with slippery tiles that kept my mind awake to the possibility of a fall.

Dubai was, indeed, a miracle in the desert. We had a waiting period of about five hours. As a complementary package, the ten passengers I was flying with to USA, we were all picked by a tour bus, and we drove around the city of Dubai. We were taken to the Dubai Mall and guided to the Dubai fountain. We wandered around the Dubai waterfront, observing faces.

The guide explained, "This is the largest man-made fountain in the world." There was some awesome Arabic soundtrack that was playing as the fountains graciously danced to the rhythm of the song. The fountain had been programmed to spew water into the air around us in sync with the sound of the song. It was an amazing experience. Together, we visited several jewelry shops, toy shops, and lingerie shops, and with every shop that we visited, my fellow passengers loaded their bags. They were buying gifts for their loved ones back in USA. For me, I was on cloud nine, and I didn't care anymore whether or not I had money. All I knew was that everything that was happening around me was a miracle, and God was working extra hours to make a difference in my life.

I chose to cherish every moment. We saw the manmade waterfall and the Dubai ski arena, and I was mesmerized by how humans were pushing their imagination and tact to invent such splendors. Indeed, the things that I saw around affirmed my own childhood belief that there is no such word as impossible.

"This is the tallest building in the world, the Burj Khalifa. It towers above the desert sand dunes to a staggering 828 meters with 160 stories," the guide, Mr. Hassan, said with a proud smile on his face.

I saw for the first time an elaborate electric train with hordes of people around me from different countries—

people of all different colors. It made me quickly realize the big problem that we had back at home where we saw everything in life through the prism of tribalism, nepotism, and color. Here I was surrounded by all shades of people, probably coming from a dozen different countries, minding their own businesses and doing all that they had to do.

My mind drifted to my best high school friend, the late Donga. I remembered the numerous trip experiences that Donga had shared with me, and I now understood why he had been so cultured and measured in his approach towards others. He had been exposed to different cultures and he had seen what life offered in a more open society where everyone was embraced based on meritocracy.

We were driven back to the airport after a leisurely three-hour drive through the city of Dubai, which stretched my mind beyond comprehension. We connected to our next flight, but I was too tired, so immediately after take-off, I couldn't help but drift off to sleep. I was only awoken by the captain's voice happily announcing that we should all fasten our belts ready for landing in the USA.

I said a little prayer as my heart melted with joy and anticipation. "Lord, thank you for the privilege. You are a great father. Thank you!"

I had waited for this moment, and my mind was blown away as I looked outside the window to view the amazing skyscrapers that confidently rose into the air.

"Ladies and gentlemen, welcome to John F. Kennedy International Airport. Thank you for choosing Kenya Airways. We hope you enjoyed your flight with us. For those proceeding to other destinations, we wish you a safe flight, and if this is your final destination, we wish you a pleasant stay. Thank you!" the captain said as she landed the plane.

I quickly disembarked and followed the multiple signs that led to the domestic connection flights. I had been tasked to check the boards for the connection flight to Boston Massachusetts. Everyone around me was busy rolling past with their bags while others pushed their loaded trolleys in haste. There was no chance of stopping someone to ask for something. "Baraka calm down and focus!" I said to myself. I walked past the wide alley with the granite floor that reflected the soft ambience from the hundreds of sculptural LED lights artfully encased in the gypsum ceiling, designed like a swirling wave. I walked past several counters with hundreds of passengers lined up constrained by dozens of silver bars. They were all checking in to their different destinations.

I went to a huge TV screen that was popping up tons of flights scheduled for the day. I checked through the list and after a gruesome five minutes I was able to locate my flight, Delta Airline DL5033AX that was scheduled to leave in two hours' time, so I had enough time to identify the check-in counters and also enough time to check for the boarding gates. I went through to gate fourteen and to the waiting bay, where we boarded the flight.

***

After an hour and a half, we landed in Boston, Massachusetts.

I checked out through the customs, picked up my luggage from the carousel, and proceeded for the exit gates. There was a short white man, probably in his mid-forties, that had a plaque with my name written on it. It was the most inviting and best part of my trip. It was such a relief.

As instructed by the letter from MIT, I walked up to the man, who quickly introduced himself.

"I am James, and I have been asked to take you to MIT Campus. Welcome to America, young man!" he said with a wide smile across his face.

"Thank you!" I said as I followed him down the elevator that led to the underground parking lot. It was my first time on an elevator, and I fumbled, following the footsteps of James.

Don't be in a rush to do anything. If you don't know, wait. Someone will do it and you simply follow suit. If you really are in a hurry, ask.

I remembered that advice from Dr. Wanyonyi, so when there were things that I didn't know how to do, I just had to stretch my patience and wait. There was always someone who was willing to go first, and I would quickly see and learn by observation and do exactly as they did. I found this advice invaluable in restaurants and in public places.

"How is Kenya? I hear everyone is a runner?" James asked with a slight chuckle.

"Yes, we run all the time. Daytime runners and night runners too!" I said with a giggle.

"And how was your flight?"

"Ahh, it was tiresome but very pleasant in every-other way. It was actually an all-female crew!"

"Wow, that's amazing!" James said with a genial smile.

We drove past astounding jungles of concrete and went through the beautiful boulevards. It took us about twenty minutes to arrive at MIT. The great dome exuded confidence and magnificence, giving the loud assurance that I had truly arrived. As we drove through the gates, I could feel my old self peeling off and a new sense of confidence flowing within me, ready to start another journey through time.

"Congratulations, Baraka, on your acceptance at MIT!" James said as he said goodbye.

I bade him goodbye and thanked him for his warmth.

I went straight to the admissions office.

"My name is Nicole. Welcome to MIT. Can I please have your passport, Baraka?" she said.

So, she even knows my name! What a pleasant surprise.

She ushered me to sit down as she keyed my details into the computer.

"Baraka, I sincerely welcome you to MIT. I hope you enjoyed your flights.

"Yes, I did. Thank you very much, Nicole."

She punched a few more times onto her keyboard, then raised her head and said, "Mr. Jones will help you to locate your room. Tomorrow at 9:00 a.m. you will join other fresh students for a tour of the campus and your orientation." She handed me a booklet that had a map of Boston and MIT campus. "You will find this very useful."

CHAPTER NINETEEN

There was the panoramic view of the Boston skyline, with the solid, white pillars signifying the might and magnificence that was MIT, making the administration block stand tall to symbolize the great years of academic excellence. MIT's motto "mens et manus," or "mind and hand," was very elaborate, signifying the fusion of academic knowledge with practical purpose to build a global citizenry that was focused on arriving at solutions to life's challenges.

I enjoyed the academic and all-round approach to learning in this great institution that aimed to produce pioneering frontiers in their specific fields of study. There was a large pool of professionals on the campus community that acted as advisors, coaches, heads of houses, and mentors. Indeed, help was always within reach.

In the evenings, I played basketball and jogged in the morning hours along the campus green and lush gardens.

My main instructor was Prof Tiffany de la Rouviere. She was a renowned medical biotechnologist with heavily published papers in the major scientific journals and breakthrough innovations in molecular biology and genetics. She was writing scientific articles for McGraw Hill Education, Cambridge University Press, Oxford University Press, Springer Nature, PubMed, Lancet, Elsevier, and many other publications. I was privileged to work in her lab under her instruction.

My major area of focus had been on emerging and re-emerging infections that affected global health. In the twenty-first century, Ebola, chikungunya virus, Zika virus, bird flu, and the avian flu were wiping out thousands of people across the globe. These were diseases that spread very fast and they didn't respect borders. They transcended boundaries to reach out to both young and old, rich and poor.

There was so much to do but then I settled on Cancer. I was determined to make a difference towards a meaningful contribution to contain some of these medical challenges from a prevention prism. I knew it was going to be difficult, but I had to begin from somewhere, so I decided to take the bull by its horns and settled on cancer; the mother of them all. The statistics were staggering as well, one in six deaths globally was due to cancer.

I dug deeper into the world of stem cell research, and germ cells and the normal body cells. I desired a deeper understanding of cells and their behavior, what made them behave the way they did, grow into what they grew into and what influenced and informed their deaths.

Prof Tiffany De La Rouviere and I injected several cocktails in the different models that we had identified. We injected the cocktails into mice and observed the results over a period of several weeks. We used computational modelling and simulations to modify and advance the cocktails. The results were impressive.

"We need to extend this testing to different animals, " Prof De La Rouviere said, "If this works out we are starring at a miracle that will change the world and how cancer patients are treated and managed, this is going to be big," Rouviere patted my back and genially smiled as she went inside the guinea pig lab to pick the blood samples for testing. We extended the testing to different animals; monkeys, rabbits, rats, geese and pigs in the different stages of the animal studies and we were amazed at the reproducibility of the results across the models.

We co-authored dozens of research papers from our work with Prof De La Rouviere and incorporated in Prof Ouma back in Kenya. We presented our findings in many scientific conferences in USA and across the world and facilitated many researchers to focus more on this area of study with laser ability; the more we brought our ideas together the more wiser I got, modifying the cocktails further to make them more robust and stable and also improving on the mode of their delivery into the target cells. We got approvals to proceed with human trials.

Back in Kenya the entire research fraternity was aware of my star that was shining bright. Prof Ouma's lab that had nurtured my young mind and allowed me to dream had done several interviews with local and international media to bring the story of where it all started to the entire world.

WHO constituted a consortium that we worked with to form a framework under which my cocktails were going to be produced at a high level and supplied across the globe.

The vision and the project that we had started working on with Prof Ouma in the lab was now beyond us. It had escaped our hands and caught the eyes of the major health organizations across the globe. Patients were sharing their testimonials about how the cocktails had given them back their lives and granted them yet another opportunity to life with their loved ones.

There was great evidence and hope that the dragon of cancer was finally going to be slain and buried for good using these novel cocktails.

We finally went to phase four trials, where the long-term effects and efficacy of the cocktails were going to be measured. But because a remedy for the cancer patients was urgently required, we received the necessary approvals to start administering the cocktails to patients in the same year.

I sat in high level board meetings with members from different international organizations, including World Health Organization (WHO), United Nations Children's Fund (UNICEF), United Nations (UN), United States Agency for International Development (USAID), Centers for Disease Control (CDC), and they were all amazed by this novel discovery.

A few months later, I made the announcement in a press conference that had been arranged by WHO and attended by a battery of news anchors from across the globe, covering and airing to their media houses. "We have agreed with Prof Tiffany de la Rouviere and Prof Ouma that we are not going to commercialize this cancer remedy. Instead we are giving it as a free treatment. As many children of the soil as will need it, so shall we provide." We received praise and congratulatory messages across the globe from presidents and other global leaders. Our president personally sent out a recorded video message through the media houses to register his congratulations and his deep pride as a nation.

The experience at MIT where people were eager to know how things worked inspired them to make them work better. This experience made a profound impact on my life and how I viewed my surroundings. I learned how to look at myself as a change agent and an initiator and a pioneer of bringing my thoughts and visions into tangibles—into realities that could transform the entire world and make it better. I was taught how to think of coming up with solutions through imagination and creativity, solving problems that people didn't even know existed.

Many of my colleagues thought I had a wild organ for a brain, as my imagination of possibilities in science was sensational, sometimes unsettling, and in humility I thanked God for enabling me to build my career as a medical biotechnologist. To engineer biological molecules that made a difference in managing medical conditions and challenges.

I was awarded the MIT young scholars award and given a class to teach advanced molecular biology at MIT. It was such a privilege that my mind couldn't have thought possible. In addition, Prof Ouma was invited several times to MIT as a visiting professor, as he was closely collaborating on the massive projects that we had. He helped in refining the cocktails and packaging them to ensure safe and efficient delivery to the cancer cells.

I founded the Jane Uside foundation, through which donations to fund the projects and research work that we were doing could be channeled. Millions of dollars were wired into this foundation, and politicians, businessmen, and corporates of good will all gave generously to the foundation. We were going to be able to reach out to millions of cancer patients and turn their lives around. In addition, we were going to be part of the solution by offering more scholarships and sponsorships to gifted learners from developing countries to help them achieve their dreams in the areas where their work directly impacted the societies from which they came from. I returned home to Kenya as one of the youngest holders of a Doctor of Philosophy degree. I was Dr. Baraka Uside, and together with Prof Tiffany de la Rouviere and Prof Ouma, we resolved to change the world one person at a time with a multifactorial domino effect across the borders.

CHAPTER TWENTY

A couple of months before, I had identified a farm with the help of Dr. Wanyonyi in Mudete Vihiga. I had nurtured the desire to own a home for many years, and it was time. I was filled with excitement, as I had been saving my every coin towards this dream, denying myself every other pleasure to see to it that Mum was relocated from Nairobi. From the hands of Pombe. It was depressing to see her struggle, bearing in mind that had been her narrative all her life.

So, I built a home and started making arrangements for Mum to come back home, to a place she could call her own.

I had prepared her well in advance, and she was aware of the entire plan. She had resisted and shoved aside the idea, but over time she had looked at the possibility of her life transforming for the better, and she finally embraced the plan.

The biggest huddle was getting her to forget about the den that she had now gotten used to and the near addiction that she had drugged herself into. But it wasn't too late. She still had a chance.

I travelled to Nairobi and organized a farewell party that was well attended by dozens of her neighbors in the slum. It was a happy moment, and everyone was happy for Mama that she was finally going to get a place where she could rest a bit from the hustles of Nairobi that she had known all her adult life.

Most people thought that there was really nothing to show for the years she had spent in Nairobi, but in my heart of hearts, I knew she had everything to show off. Her sons! She had laid down her life for Isate and I. That's all she had. We were her world, and she was our world.

I told her to just carry her photo album and some of her papers that survived the frequent floods that had ravaged the shanties of Kibra.

This time, going back home she didn't have to go to the country bus station to be harassed by the touts who lie in wait to exploit the desperate travelers and at times steal from them. I ushered her into my Nissan double cabin, opened the door for her, and made her comfortable and assisted her in belting up.

Before I started the engine, we said a little prayer and prayed for journey mercies. The neighbors who had accompanied us to the District Commissioner's offices where we had parked the car waved at us in admiration. It was a moment of pride for her.

Pombe didn't mind Mum going back to the village, as their cohabiting had been out of convenience. There were no attachments, so he let her go unconditionally.

I started the engine, and I could see mum's heart melt away in satisfaction and awe. She had this super grin on her face that made her look like a teenager. This was her happy day and a fresh journey for her.

Isate and his family would be waiting for us in our new home in Mudete to welcome Mum into her new house—our new house. Our new *home*.

When we arrived in Nakuru, I took mum to the highway restaurant where I bought her chicken, chips, and a coke and looked at her in awe and amazement as she enjoyed the meal.

For the rest of the journey past Nakuru to Mudete, Mum was fast asleep, lost in her emotions. I knew she was going to take time before the alcohol she had consumed in the recent months could completely get off her system.

As we approached the home, it was indeed a new chapter opening in her life. Isate had invited the local church, and the moment they saw my car snail through the narrow path that led to the house, they broke into song and dance and ululations. It was to celebrate Mum.

I wish dad was here to witness this magical moment, I said to myself. I quickly shrugged off that thought, however. It was a distant dream.

Mum marveled at everything she saw in the compound. There were fresh flowers planted all around it, a garden with several banana trees planted recently by Isate, a cow shed with a cow and a fattened heifer that were already feeding, and jubilant neighbors who wanted to have a glimpse of their new neighbor.

She broke down and cried like a little baby, and it was a magical moment. She was crying out of joy as the new neighbors hugged and embraced her. Grandma Anguzuzu was also there, mesmerized that this was happening during her lifetime. Mum had a fairly decent place to sleep, and she didn't have to run to the bush to relieve herself. there was a latrine that she could use.

CHAPTER TWENTY-ONE

I t was on one fateful day a few months later, a Thursday, that I received my most frightening call ever—that my Mum had been involved in an accident in Naivasha and I was needed there immediately. I was at work at work in Prof Ouma's lab at about 3:00 p.m.

"Prof, there is bad news. My mum is not well, and I have to rush," I said.

"What's going on, Baraka?" he asked with clear concern on his face.

"Mum was travelling back to her home from Nairobi, and she had come to pick some second-hand clothes to re-fill her stock! I have just been called that her bus got involved in a bad accident."

"It's all well, Doc. Kindly instruct Wycliffe to stand in for you with the protocols you were running," he said. "Please be safe," he added.

I made arrangements with my colleague Wycliffe and frantically collected myself up and drove home.

On my way home, I called my best friend Asamba and without hesitation he agreed to accompany me to Naivasha. That night, I appreciated how long it takes to Naivasha from Nairobi despite the fact that we took under forty-five minutes to get there for a distance that would ordinarily take me one and a half hours!

As I walked into the Naivasha District hospital my nerves were in a sordid frenzy and my whole system seemed to dance to an unfamiliar tune orchestrated by the masters in Hell. Asamba's steps were sure as we walked towards the hospital reception, and I incoherently muttered to the receptionist about an accident that had just happened. She pointed us to something that turned out to be a labyrinth of corridors more complex than a web woven in haste by a drunk spider. We finally located the female emergency ward, and in a flash, I scanned the ward, my eyes blazing like a 360-degree next-generation camera.

The loud screams of patients in severe pain wretched my tired nerves further, and in the midst of the turmoil I located my aunt who had been traveling with my mum on the ill-fated bus. The patients couldn't talk. They were screaming as if they, too, had their roles to play in the murky symphony they had joined without an invitation. It quickly dawned on me that Mum was not in this weird, forlorn orchestra. We rushed back through the unforgiving corridors and managed to locate our way back to the reception to seek further advice. We were informed that some of the victims had been referred to other neighboring hospitals.

After a long wait at the hospital, our host, a good Samaritan that had previously called me to urgently come to Naivasha, advised us to spend the night at her place and resume the search the following day. That will remain the longest night of my life. The walls amidst the absolute darkness seemed to open up scenes from a horror script, and the silence of the night was too loud to allow my turbulent mind to rest.

Morning came, and as we prepared to start off the day, the host, Mr. Gatete, advised us that as there were some fatalities, we needed to have a quick check at the morgue to be sure! We agreed to it reluctantly, seeing that there was no harm in doing that. I didn't fear morgues. I had slept in one that fateful night at the mortuary as a street child. In addition, I had walked into several morgues during my anatomy classes at the university and had handled several human organs in my hands. But this particular walk was strangely surreal. My feet were growing cold, and as we approached the morgue, Asamba looked at me and asked, "Are you sure you want to check?"

I answered him, but my words were a weak garble. I was led to the door by the mean-looking morgue attendant, who calmly opened the door, and what my eyes saw made the world around me spin.

In the midst of several other bodies, my mum lay there lifeless with her neck clearly broken, with the arteries that once ran life through her poking out—now dry, having drained all the life from her body. She was wearing the favorite blue sweater that I had just bought her.

I stood there frozen in time, dazed in anguish. The pain was real. Palpable. In my wildest imagination I had never known this level of pain existed. It was unimaginable. I was ushered out of the morgue with my eyes filled with tears. I cried over the shoulder of my great friend Asamba till I soaked his shirt. What started like short spasms of pain graduated into paroxysm coughs that caused mucus to freely run as if some floodgate had been opened.

I looked like one who had a severe flu running for days on end. Asamba and I sat by the morgue for hours drenched in pain, lost in the sea of torment. We later woke up from our arcane maze and got to our feet to face this new reality. A reality without my mother, my heroine. My champion, my *shujaa*. I couldn't imagine life without her! She had been family and everything to me, and now she was gone. She had defended me against uncle Matata, and with her limited resources she had fought the tough fight of staying afloat in the sea of life despite the many waves and tides that shoved and tossed us up and down. We clung firmly onto her, and in confidence she struggled keeping alive the hope that we were not going to sink. Not under her watch.

The seas of life had been deep and vast, and she had been thrown in the deep end, fully aware there was no chance to rest. The horizon is all we had been able to see, with no sight of the beach within reach, but she had swum on, even though Isate's weight and my own were weighing her down. But with skill and determination she had dodged the waves of life, and with her every move, the tides seemed to bring us closer to the land where we could rest our battered selves and allow our minds and souls to rest and enjoy the warmth that lay beyond the expansive waters of life.

She had been solid, she had been resilient, and she had toiled through life and carried the burden of raising two boys all by herself. And through it all, she had borne all the scathing and scars of life.

My brother and I had been determined to help her heal her scars one by one and massage away her pain and allow her to enjoy the beauty of life. We had been determined to let her enjoy the work of her sweat and to restore to her the years she had spent in the trenches digging us out.

And then, there we were. We had lost her forever. Her lifeless body left behind, her spirit had taken to flight. What was I supposed to do? To whom was I supposed to go to? How was I supposed to mourn her? My world suddenly turned crumbled.

My eyes were sore and red, as if I had washed my face with water laced with hot chili. There seemed to be tiny droplets of pain in the air all around me that dripped right into my whole being, and I was afraid I was going to collapse out of the painful weight that was mounting onto my shoulders.

Life had taught me to be tough and streetwise, but it never prepared me for this. To know that one day I could cry this much. I hadn't known how deep the wells of my tear glands were, but I now knew that they were deep, indeed, and they had run dry.

We collected ourselves, thanked Mr. Gatete and his lovely wife for their courtesy, and we drove back to Nairobi to start the herculean process of dealing with my new reality. Arranging for Mum's funeral. Asamba took the wheels as I couldn't bring myself to drive back. I could have strategically rammed into a lorry and created more of a mess, but he comforted me along the way back to Nairobi, prayed, and did everything that a great friend could do in such a terrible time. But still my heart couldn't find rest.

***

I opened the doors of my house, and every single one of my relatives and friends trooped in to pay their last respects and register their condolences. The pain was too much to bear, so we agreed we would lay her to rest in her new home at the village in Mudete the following weekend.

I took time off from work, and with Mr. Asamba we moved around funeral homes and shopped for a casket, a cross, and a wreath that we were going to lay on her grave. We also bargained for a collective package that would include transport and the lowering gear.

We took the journey the following Thursday from Nairobi and headed to Naivasha mortuary with the casket. We had a brief service at the morgue and started the final journey of taking Mum to her final resting place in the land where she had hardly stayed—.

This had been her new home, a place that had restored her confidence and self-worth—a place that had given her renewed hope for a better life. She had had a decent place to lay her head to rest and clean water to drink. There was a small backyard garden where she had already planted her favorite green vegetables. The bananas were starting to bud, and the chicken house had healthy birds crackling. Her cow—her own cow—was healthy and heavily pregnant with her second calf, and Mum had enjoyed the fresh milk from her own farm.

It had given her so much joy to know that she could farm on her own farm and eat of her own labor. Her self-esteem and worth had been restored, and she had quickly made friends with the local Friends church where she joined the other industrious women that had really helped her to integrate into the village and settle into her new home. Her second-hand clothes business had picked up quite well, and she was back on her feet.

All this was now gone. Her new journey had been cut abruptly short. And the whole village came to mourn her. When the hearse arrived, the whole village—dozens of women—broke down into wails and cries that broke and shred my soul into pieces. They had all come to mourn my mother. We shared in the pain and the anguish, and in doing so, our pain was lessened and we were comforted.

Friends and relatives from far and wide had travelled to stay with us, to help us through the pain. My colleagues from work, my church members, and my pastor, Joe, were there to hold my hand. Dr. Wanyonyi too was there, frustrated to his core, along with my teachers and alumni from Chavakali, and close friends from Maseno came in large numbers to support me during this sorrowful time. Many poured out great tributes to my mother, but there was one that took me aback—the speech by uncle Matata.

A heavy bile piled up my throat as I listened to uncle Matata eulogize my mother. He was giving his unctuous speech, saying things he had never said to my Mum when she was alive. His words made me to burn with rage. "We loved you Jane, but the Lord Loved you more. I am sorry for the paths that we crossed, but everything happens with a reason . . ."

I didn't care to listen to the other gibberish that he was spewing. My ears couldn't take the lies he was telling. I simply muted and stopped my clock. I stopped my world from moving on. He had made us suffer a lot of pain, and here he was pretending to love my mum. I wanted to snatch the microphone from his hands, but out of the respect I had for mum I restrained myself.

My brother Isate spoke to the mourners amid sobs with his family in tow. They had stayed with my mum on this farm for the last couple of months, and they were rebuilding the home that we had never had. He promised to carry on with the legacy that Mum left.

It was my turn to speak. I took the microphone, and for the first time realized that I couldn't speak. I tried to say the things that I wanted to say to Mum, but I couldn't. My eyes were fixed on Uncle Matata, and I found myself speechless.

My girlfriend was holding my hand. "Mum, you meant the world to me, and it's unfortunate you have gone too soon when you had just started on a journey to have your life back. Thank you for everything that you were to us! We will forever be grateful! Words fail me to describe you, but please know that you will forever be etched on the tablet of our hearts. Thank you, Mama! Rest easy, Mama! Soar with the angels,

Mama! Thank you, Mama! Thank you! If you are here and you have a mother, please show her love while she is still with you. One day, you will wish she was alive, but she will be no more. You will cry, but she will be gone forever! I broke into tears, unable to say anything more that.

Dr. Wanyonyi came forth in stride and hugged me. He allowed me to cry onto his shoulders, and the whole congregation was wiping the tears in their eyes to share in my misery. Dr. Wanyonyi had played the role of a dad in my life. He had been there all along—when I needed a mentor, when I needed a shoulder to lean and cry on—and here in death, he was still present. Some people are born with golden hearts, and he was one of them. He had integrated me into his family as one of his sons. His daughters and son were my siblings. He showed me love and gave me a reason to believe.

We lowered Mum's body into the grave that had been dug the previous night, and at that point, I knew I wasn't going to see her again, but she had done her best and I was glad in my heart that we had tried our level best to give back to her, though I wished I could have done more.

Back in my closet, I wrote a letter to my mum and dad. Pouring my emotions onto paper was therapeutic.

Mum and Dad,

It's so difficult to imagine life without both of you. To grope into the darkness of this life alone. Please, Mum, wherever you are, know that I will always celebrate you. I am dedicating my discoveries and cocktails to you.

Mum, you foresaw this while your eyes were still open—that you might not see this breakthrough. However, this generation will live through your eyes into posterity. Many lives will be saved for generations to come. The free vaccine and the cocktails are a gift from you to humanity, Mum. For all the struggles that you surmounted, for the shame that you suffered, for the many days that you walked with your head lying low covered in a dark cloud of shame, the guilt of raising us as rejected kids. This is a gift to all the single mothers out there, that they too can dream, and their dreams can be lived through posterity.

Truly there is nothing like a rejected kid. Everyone has a right to be here and to live life to its fullest, knowing that no one will judge them but will look for every way to nurture and tap their fountains. There is greatness that's hidden deep within us. To realize that the treasures that we so seek are engraved in us, that our souls are beautiful, that we can be all we want to be regardless of creed, whether one sleeps on a canvas or a bedbug-infested sisal mat or a king size bed, the morning will be faithful to come to us all, the sun will not care whether you ate or not. It will rise again, and you can choose to rise with it or lament under its sweltering heat as you melt into oblivion to be yet another forgotten mound of dirt.

I took a long pause, staring at the piece of paper in my hands, then I said to myself, "And this is to you my father. My special father."

"All my life, you have remained the tiny needle I so seek to find in a gigantic haystack, in the mass populace around the globe. How can I identify you amongst the four billion men out there? You never left a clue about how to find you. Will you do that now? Please, when I lay down my head tonight to sleep, please send me a signage, Father—a signage leading to your hideout.

I have floundered through life—through all life's milestones—without you. I wish you had been there when I veered off course and ended up on the streets of Nairobi. When I was circumcised and couldn't take a man's name but had to keep my mother's name. When I gave my valedictory speech, when I graduated from the University with a first class honors.

Give me your hand to hold, even if it's for one last time, though it will be my first. I promise I will cherish it. I wish you were here with me, taking this journey through time, but you decided you were not boarding with me. You left Mum to wade through the murky waters of this life alone, and she did, though you took her dignity away with you. She lost her name and her place as a lady in the society, but she trudged on.

A part of her died when you left. How do you feel, to know that she bore all your responsibilities on her shoulders? I trust you could have built your muscles while carrying us through life, but you might want to know she lost all her muscles and her strength. Our weight was too much to bear.

You left me as an open shell, and I trained myself on how to enter it, and I have hardened the shell over time, though in the quietness of the shell, your silent voice loudly lingers, mute to the many unanswered questions that I have been piling up for you. The many successes I achieved in life, after the pomp and the champagnes, I thought that you would be here to say something, but your silence lingers on. When will I hear you speak and say, "Well done my son?"

Mum suffered ridicule because you left. We suffered retrogression because you left. We have known what poverty feels like. We have seen it with our very eyes and touched it with our hearts. We became bosom friends, and poverty has embraced us. It recognized us by name and refused to go away. We fought it hard, and in the process, it took away Mum's dignity. It tore all her clothes and left her in patches. It made sure we didn't have a decent shelter to call home, but we fought on. Why did you leave, Father? Had we fought together, don't you think we could have won it faster?

We have lived all our lives in the shadows of other people, as you denied us the sense of identity and belonging. Was your shadow too small to cover us? If you had shared it with us, would it have reduced you in size—made you shorter? The other people's shadows darkened our lives, and we couldn't see where we were going, but all the same, we groped in the dark, hoping to find you along the path of life. We have been calling out your name, but in your wisdom, you've kept silent.

Thank you sincerely for teaching me how not to father my own children. Your absence has taught me a lot and made me a little wiser, and as I grow up, I promise you I will be a real man. I long for the day that I will personally get the chance to thank you and all the people that caused me so much pain, for in the pain, I found myself and I discovered the strength that lay in me to drive me to the purpose of my very existence.

You might want to know I also have a brother who is also looking for a dad that also ran away like you. Indeed, the two of you are cowards. Two men with all your strength, you decided Mum was stronger than the two of you combined? I would love to meet the two of you so you could break down this logic to me in an easy language that I could understand.

Several days passed by, and my life slowed down drastically. A part of me had been cut off, and I struggled to regain my life back. My pastors and friends worked extra time to help me with the healing process, and it went a long way, though deep down I knew too well that the pain of losing my mother would never go away. She was my life, and she always would be.

CHAPTER TWENTY-TWO

One year had gone by, and I was just recovering from depression. It was Mum's second anniversary.

Most of the time I spent talking to myself and daydreaming that I was with Mum.

Her memories and the times that we had spent together came flooding through my mind.

"Mum, tonight I remembered the fried *omena* that you prepared for me on my first day at Chavakali High School, and today I wanted to get you a treat—not on fried sardines, but something more special. I went to the pineapple building which is now the tallest building in Kenya. It stands with grace, two twin towers enjoying the fine affluence of the plutocratic suburbs of Nairobi that's now the Upper Hill area, Nairobi's new capital. Mum, they have an amazing restaurant called the Floating Hotel, and it's hung up in space, connecting the twin towers. The views here are amazing. I can see and identify our little hide-out in the Kibra slums. The signature color of the rusty, orange-red sheets has not gone away. It still lingers on, outlasting the empty promises that many politicians have made over the years, swearing to eradicate them with real houses.

I came here with the purpose to treat you to a nice meal and to spoil your taste buds. I have ordered the Celeriac soup with toasted hazelnuts & truffle oil for a starter. For the main course, we will have grilled beef sirloin served with fondant potato and a classic steak tartare that we must share. It will come with a side of velvety cheese croquettes and bacon and an assortment of Mediterranean vegetables. For the dessert, Mum, we will have the crème brulee and soft, fluffy whipped ice cream with a selection of waffles. I have chosen for you a warm, gooey chocolate fudge, topped with chocolate flakes to tantalize your soul and allow you to enjoy life's goodness.

Mum, the soup has been served, and I have held my fire and waited some more. The waiter has been asking me who my long-awaited guest is, and I have told him several times to hold his horses."

The waiter was getting impatient, so he came and asked for the third time, 'Sir, your main course for two is ready. Can I serve?"

"I took my phone in haste and dialed your number, Mum, but I got the terse response that the mobile subscriber couldn't be reached! I called again and the voice prompt from the lady on the phone couldn't connect me to you. She gave me the same response: 'The mobile subscriber cannot be reached!' At that point, I was drained, and my eyes were drowning in tears. I cried my heart out. The waiter tapped on me and gently asked, 'Is everything fine?' I quickly sat up and said to him, "Yes, sir!" Everything is ok!"

There was a woman seated next to my table, and she gave me a reassuring look and said to me, "Don't worry, sir. She will come. Ladies take their time to prepare. Your date will be here in no time!"

I looked at her and said, "I wish you were right!"

She looked at me and laughed hysterically, as she thought I was crying over my girlfriend, who had snubbed my date, but she was wrong.

I wish she could understand the sudden pain that was now running down my spine. She had no idea what she was talking about. I had not been waiting for an ordinary person. I had been waiting for my Mum, and I had ordered for two, hoping she could join me and eat at this table so I could should my appreciation after I had fed on her teat of munificence for decades. But she was not going to come. She had gone forever, and I couldn't find her! I learned that morning that your loved one can lead you to do insane things and no one will understand you.

I stood up and told the waiter that I would be back in a moment. I gave him a deposit of the bill and dashed out. I drove out into the central business district and parked at the Family Basilica parking lot and took the maze of corridors that led me to the street alleys. I met a group of clumsy-looking young men who were on a night vigil begging for anything they could get from anyone who cared to listen. They mulled around me within no time. I had been there before, and I could feel their pain. I could see their fright, and I fully understood their frustration. I quickly identified the leader of the group and gave him five thousand shillings. I asked him to take care of the entire group. He knew what to do! They were so excited, and they all scrambled towards him. The young man cried while looking at the money, and I knew what the tears in his eyes meant. He gave me a warm hug and said, "*Ahsante! Sana.*" Thanking me, I looked around and identified one young man who looked frail and frizzled, and I asked their leader to allow me to take him away and promised to bring him back the following day. He quickly agreed.

I drove back to the hotel with the young man. He was puzzled and didn't say much. When I entered the hotel, they wanted to stop the young man, as he was smelly and clearly lost. This was not his place. He didn't belong. He was a thief. He had strayed and he had to be restrained. I couldn't let them take him away, though. The ground manager heard the scuffle and the bitter exchanges from the mean-looking guards, and he quickly ran towards the concierge to find out what was happening.

"What's going on?" he asked.

He didn't wait for an answer, though. When he saw the boy, who was now clinging to me, shocked and shuttered, feeling so embarrassed and ready to run away back into the night!

He said, "No, we can't allow this boy in here!"

I softly asked him, "But why? Isn't he human? I will pay for everything he needs and takes here. Is there a problem with that??

His face darkened further, and his smile faded away. His eyes were blazing with anger, but when he looked at me and saw my stern yet calm face, he knew he wasn't going to win!

He grudgingly allowed us in and ushered us to sit in a secluded corner. He personally served us, as no waiter was willing to come near us.

"Bring our food now!" I politely called after the line manager as he disappeared into the kitchen. The boy cleared everything on the table. We had all the cutlery, but the boy chose to wash his hands in the sink. The hot towels that we were given could have turned the color of black gold, so he washed his hands, staining the sink with the dirt from his greasy hands. The water flowed graciously from the tap, and it quickly transformed into a thick gel of dirt the color of tar. He calmly walked back to our table and looked at me and joked; "I have never used these things. They will slow me down!" as he pushed away the folded white napkin that had sets of cutlery. I simply smiled at him and encouraged him to eat and eat some more. With every bite he took, he reminded me of Mum sitting there at Mr. Igwe's house allowing me to taste royalty. Now this young boy was here, as he reminded me so much about Mum and the power of unconditional love.

He told me he had been a pig feasting on the left overs half rotten foods from the bins on the street, and I could feel him! I knew and understood what he was talking about.

"I am your fellow pig!" I joked, and we laughed at ourselves.

"I desire to go to school someday," he said with a grin on his face in sync with the distant dream that he was toying with. I promised to take care of that. When we were finished, the boy stood up. He knelt down and said, "Thank you!" I quickly reached out to him and raised him back to his feet. It was the most humbling part of the evening. The other guests were impressed by the gesture, though they had murmured and moved their tables to keep a safe distance from us. Some cursed that they would never come back to this hotel again, as they couldn't imagine ever using that plate again that was touched by this innocent soul.

I paid the manager and gave him a sumptuous tip and we walked away. I realized that half of the guests at the restaurant had already left thanks to our intrusion.

We bid the hotel staff good night and disappeared into the well-lit parking lot. In town, I took him to a clothing shop and allowed him to choose clothes for himself and his friends. We later went to the late-night chemist that had a clinic and consulted a doctor, who said the boy wasn't sick. He was just weak and lacked some key minerals in his system. He gave him some multi vitamins. We left the clinic, and the boy guided me back to his street home. I was carrying the items we had bought, and I had asked a street worker with a handcart to help with the other bags that were full of new clothes and food. Their leader couldn't believe it when I asked the boy to pick the clothes and distribute them to everyone according to his thoughts when he was choosing them. It took one hour to do the distribution, and the street family was very thankful.

"I will be back. Don't get into too much trouble," I said to them as I disappeared into the dark.

That was the beginning of a great relationship with the street families. This street family linked me to other street families, and we build up a rehabilitation center right at the heart of Kibra where we created Jane's Talent Center, an innovation center and a social hall with the various former street family leaders assuming leadership positions. We started a baking school, a hairdressing and beauty salon, and a music hub, and many are the children of Kibra that have been transformed through this center. Part of the massive funds from the Jane Uside Foundation that I had established earlier on were directed towards the programs to uplift my friends from the streets.

One such gifted young man was one of the street family heads that was running the innovation center. His name was Mukwaya. He was brilliant and diligence was his second name. He came up with the idea of using Skype in the classroom, and that has transformed the center into a powerhouse. Through this program, Mukwaya mentored other street children at the center and helped the students to link and intersect with students from other countries. He formed and established a complex web of relationships and programs running across the globe across the different timelines and time zones; he has lived up to the mantra that, indeed, education is the only right owed by the society which it must freely give. Through his programs at the center, many street families have been rehabilitated from drug and substance abuse.

Mukwaya's innovative projects have transcended cultures and generations—superseded class—and stands at the heart of influence. Through his connection hub, he introduced the Skype in the classroom project, and it's amazing when you visit the connection hub and hear a Chinese school teaching Kibra children Mandarin and Kibra children teaching the Chinese key words in Swahili. The feeling of fulfillment is amazing and shows the power of will—being hungry for something and wanting it so badly that your heart focuses on nothing else but the goal.

Children from around the world are virtually transported to classrooms to learn about martial arts in China, to learn about the white and blue sharks, to get into a simulated aircraft classroom and learn about plane simulation, to learn about the North Pole and the Great Wall of China, and in turn the world is brought into a Kenyan classroom through the power of the lens and the innovative eye of technology. Students learn about why Kenyan athletes run the way they do, the great Rift Valley, the Maasai Mara, the wildebeest migration, the amazing innovations that have been done in the world of science, including test tube babies being born in Kenya (a first in East Africa), and the miracle of MPESA mobile money platforms. All of this without the children having to leave their countries, thanks to Microsoft and the wonders of innovation.

Then there was the sensational Immaculate, whose angelic voice and terrific capabilities blew minds. She had auditioned at the Safaricom Jazz academy and instantly stole the hearts of the judges. She was admitted to the academy and her talent has since opened mighty doors for her, singing in major state functions for presidents in the region and high-end corporate events. She has been amazing, demonstrating to the world that indeed nothing can bar you from daring to dream.

Truly the Jane Talent Center has built a global citizenry—children and sons and daughters across the globe who are the future leaders with an all-round exposure of different cultures and a diverse understanding of what the world is all about, that we all deserve to be here. We must leave this planet better than we found it!

I was addressing them in one of my usual Friday mentorship classes.

"You are the next game changers, people who have seen and tasted of both worlds and made the realization that we live for each other and that alone we are weak but together we are one form and cannot be derailed; we will conquer.

When the time comes, don't despise the gateman that opens the door for you every single day. Don't reward him with a dose of arrogance and curses. Remember this is someone's mother, someone's father, uncle, or aunty. They too are husbands and wives, and people call them mummy and daddy! They too have children who run into their loving arms, and all they see in their eyes is a loving father figure. While you despise them, they mean the world to their loved ones, and they are all the world to them.

Think about this, and always be there in the moment to appreciate every little effort that anyone extends to you—especially they that have nothing to gain in return for your kind actions. The people who can't pay you back with a favor for your kindness. That's a true measure of the integrity and grit of a solid human being, and that's what this center is all about! To restore humanity in the rotten world where morals have been thrown to the wind and the wind in turn has blown it away into obscurity."

I continued, "Local and international organizations have awarded this center several times for its innovations and partnered with the center to create other centers of excellence in innovation. It's well on its way to becoming the silicon savannah of the slum. Indeed, dreams should transcend our fears. Limitation is only in our minds. Even the sky can never be the limit, for beyond it lies a whole space dome to be explored.

Stay true to yourself and train your eyes and your fingers, for the battles to be won are many and the victories to be savored limitless. See the opportunities when they present themselves, for if you are not ready when these opportunities come you will say you were not lucky; while there is no such thing in life as luck. Only lack exists."

Later that morning, I was sitting in the social hall listening to Mukwaya discuss a prototype of his new innovation that they had developed with three other young minds. It was exciting.

"People spend innumerable hours on their smartphones. For sure, there is no better time to build apps like today," said Mukwaya as he powered up the laptop ready to project his presentation.

"This is a self-developed app that we are proposing to Safaricom to host. It's an app that is simple yet complex. It's going to be integrated with the mobile money payment platforms and later will be extended to the banks. The main aim of this app is to provide a vast platform for anyone here in the slum, especially to trade and do business without a physical shop. Everyone here in Kibra can trade their products and services on this platform. You will not need capital to invest in a physical shop, staff, overheads to start up something. With this app, you can start today, adding whatever value you feel you can to the rest of the community here. I realize most people here have access to cheap phones that have a camera and internet access. That's all you need to start. As a center, we will be offering free incubation services to the young people here in Kibra who would like to pioneer this project and edge themselves out of poverty. We will offer guidance and seed capital after training."

He continued, "If you have a skill in soccer, you can offer that skill and we can help you to animate your tips and skills to package it nicely to your target audience. For the great learners of this center who have already mastered French and Mandarin, please make use of this platform and offer your services to the members of this community and the schools within Kibra, and you will make money from your skills. We will animate the classes for you."

I looked at the social hall that was packed with curious young minds, and I knew in my heart of hearts that this app was going to be a game changer here in the slums. Mukwaya continued, "If you have an interest and skill in music, you can upload your music too on this platform and as people download it you can cash out of it. The options are limitless. Let your minds dream! And as we push it forward, we will open it up to the rest of the country and later to the region in East Africa and later to the rest of Africa and the whole world, and at that point, there will be millionaires who will have been raised and built on this platform!"

There was a thunderous applause from the huge crowd of youths that were listening intently.

"Any questions?" Mukwaya paused.

I looked across the room and half of the hall wanted to ask questions.

Mukwaya had made my morning, he had turned around my dreams of transforming the slum into a reality, and I was amazed at how he had pushed himself far beyond self-doubt to reach to such levels of ingenuity. Within a few weeks of the launch, the app had been downloaded by more than 500,000 users, and the numbers were growing daily, Business news channels were running to the center to interview Mukwaya and his team about the platform and helping him analyze the impact. Many corporates signed to support him, and the apps turned out to be successful beyond what we could have imagined.

"Mukwaya, you know the corridors better. Please search as far as you can go, and let me know where we can find Njoki and Kibe. My heart is troubled especially for Njoki. Was she killed? Did she survive the ordeal that we had a few years back in the hands of the rowdy mob on the streets of Nairobi? I would love to get answers to these questions, and it will be an honor to make a difference in their lives and get them off the streets."

"I know you can trace them, Mukwaya. Your links on the streets go far and wide," I said to Mukwaya.

"I will try, Dr. Baraka!" he responded.

Several months passed by after we had that conversation.

"Dr. Baraka, I have some good news!"

"Please shoot it," I replied.

"I know where we can get Kibe" he said, his heart full of excitement.

A few hours later, we were walking through the myriad alleys of Nairobi under the keen eye of Mukwaya. This had been his home, and he knew it like the back of his hand. We were hunting for Kibe, the man who had saved my life from the hands of his colleagues when I accidentally fell into his hideout. I had traced my way back to his den, but the street had been cleared and a structure had been erected in its place, so I didn't have a way I could trace them.

We did several turns deep into the corridors of downtown Nairobi and finally traced Kibe. He couldn't recognize me immediately. He looked pale, beaten, and harassed by life. Everything around him had changed apart from his signature stare. He looked weak and frail and to my estimation he needed immediate medical attention. He had gone back to sniffing glue, a testament to the fact that he wasn't venturing out on the streets for the usual escapades that would have earned him funds to afford the hard drugs.

I walked to him and gave him a warm long hug. He looked at me confused and didn't say a word for about five minutes. We just sat there and looked at each other. I tried to strike up a conversation, but he wasn't in a position to talk. He was alone in the den at the time, and we left him with the foodstuff and clothing that we had brought along, and I asked Mukwaya to mobilize and convince them to join us at Jane's Talent Center.

"Njoki, great to see you, do you remember me?" I asked

"No, I have never seen you!" she softly responded. She looked much older than her age.

I tried to remind her, but all she had was a frizzle memory of what happened on that fateful evening. "What happened to your baby. Remember, you were pregnant when the crowd caught us in the act of stealing?"

Kibe and Njoki looked at me desperately, lost in pain. Then she calmly said "The baby survived, but I had to give her up to a baby home, as I couldn't take care of her on the streets. I haven't seen her in three years."

The silence between us was palpable, I could feel their pain. It reminded me so much of Fadhili baby home and what had happened to Ndonga when he was a baby back then.

"We will trace your baby, Njoki," I promised her. They were nine in number, the group that came with them as part of Kibe's circle. We rehabilitated them at the Jane's Talent Center and assigned them committed caregivers and volunteers. They too had begun a journey through time, and I was interested to see how it would go. The effects of withdrawal from hard drugs were far-reaching, but we were willing and ready to walk with them, and we had professionals assigned to them.

Mukwaya became a sensation and a great inspiration in the slum and beyond. He inspired many young people towards a mind change and a paradigm shift towards appreciating the great worthiness that we all could get from the lovely souls that didn't have what the other cadres of the pyramid had. They were at the very base of the pyramid, and they knew the burden of life as they bore it all on their shoulders.

Mukwaya and his teams were invited to different forums across the country and the region, to music concerts, weddings, baby showers, and corporate events. And they participated in both indoor and outdoor games. His scholarship project grew by leaps and bounds as the center produced well-rounded students and they got admitted to top university colleges and technical learning institutions in the region and beyond. As they grew out of poverty, the alumni of the center became great pillars in their families, and they too were encouraged to carry one or two other families along the journey out of poverty.

CHAPTER TWENTY-THREE

I had achieved lots of success and had an almost celebrity status in Kenya, across Africa, and the world over. The discovery of how to stop the cancer cells had been an amazing turnaround in the world of science, and it was going to change the way patients were treated and managed for years to come.

And the intervention that I had pioneered was going to be incorporated into therapeutics with commercial companies estimated to mint billions out of it. However, the vaccine in the pediatrics cases was going to be given as a free vaccine that was going to change posterity. Many organizations had lined up, including WHO and UNICEF, to give the financial support that was required to produce this vaccine and launch it across the globe.

However, despite these achievements, deep down I was empty. I wanted to find closure to the mystery of who my father was.

I had answered life's notorious riddles and solved problems that had affected and traversed generations and spanned diverse geographies, but there was still one puzzle that I hadn't solved. My own puzzle. My very existence. My identity. My own paternal bloodline.

I had brought up this issue with my Mum on several occasions, but we never managed to convince her to discuss this topic.

My only hope of getting answers now lay in the grave with my mum, never to be disturbed again. I was seeking answers and I didn't know where to go.

Then, one day, I had a dream. It was so scary and surreal, yet so real.

"Baraka, arise and go to talk to Anguzuzu, your other grandma! She has all the answers you are seeking! She has all the answers that you are seeking!" Mum said, and it was an order!

Her voice was unmistakable, and the dream played out through my mind like a movie trailer. There was no mistaking what I had heard in the dream. The message was clear.

In the wee hours of the morning, I sat up on my bed, sweating profusely from the thought and confusion of the dream. I clung onto the side of the bed scared stiff. I had heard of ghosts, and I was afraid that there was a ghost in the bedroom, so I said a little prayer to calm my nerves but I couldn't calm down.

I picked up my phone and called my friend Asamba.

"I have just had a scary dream!"

"Calm down, my friend. You seem scared!" Asamba said.

"How can I calm down after just speaking to my mother after a whole two years!"

"Are you still dreaming, my friend? What's the matter? Please get some rest. Take it as a bad dream," he said.

I was not a believer in fairies. I had been trained to think logically and to avoid an emotional reaction when solving problems, but I must admit that I felt convinced that Mum had passed a message to me. How should I react to it? Should

I even react to such a mundane message? It was laughable for a scientist of my caliber and status to even think the way I was thinking.

I tried to catch some sleep but I couldn't rest. I remembered the many times that I had pleaded with Anguzuzu to share any information that she had concerning my father's whereabouts, but she had been silent and at times rowdy, not entertaining the topic at all. "And now as a young adult, accomplished, I should go back to her and make a fool of myself? No, not me. I'm not used to making a fool out of myself." I talked to myself. Anguzuzu was my mother's confidant, and my mum had made us refer to her as grandma.

The more I said to myself that I wasn't going to act on the dream, the more convinced I became that I needed to act. That morning, I missed my breakfast. I missed my lunch too, and I wasn't focusing on my work. My mind was muddled up and forcefully dragged into a zone that had always been my weakest point.

The third day after the dream, I was an emotional wreck and couldn't function, so I made the decision to drive all the way to the village some four hundred kilometers away from Nairobi in the company of Asamba, to confront Anguzuzu with the dream. I knew deep down it was an act in futility—a waste of valued time—but I was disturbed, and I wanted my mind to rest.

Anguzuzu was not an easy woman. She was old and frail but with the eyesight of an eagle, and her memory was still intact like that of an elephant. She had trouble walking and she went out into the sun from time to time to fade off the permanent cold that had engulfed her sunset years. She was alone and lonely when we arrived at the small grass-thatched hut that I once called home.

We found her seated in one of the corners of the hut with her window open to usher in the sunlight. There were rodents gliding in and out of the house at will as if they were on wheels. There was a signature smoke coming from her kitchen, a sign that she had not stopped picking her herbs from the riverside bushes that she always stuffed into the fireplace to ward off reptiles—especially snakes—from entering the house. It was a trick that had worked for her for years, and she had stuck with it.

"Guuku! How are you, I shouted!" Her ears were still intact at eighty-seven years of age, she called out "is that Baraka?"

"Yes *Guuku!"* I shouted back.

"Welcome back. Glad to see you! Where have you been? You all left me here to die. Your uncles and aunties don't come here anymore!" she was spewing out several statements at the same time.

Anguzuzu rushed into the kitchen and came back with a huge bunch of ripe bananas and sugarcane bars that she placed on the earthen floor for us to enjoy. We sat down on the floor and chewed the sugarcane that had clearly been cut several weeks ago from the farm.

"Do you still eat these canes?" I asked.

"Not anymore, Baraka, but the neighbors sometimes come to visit and they cut and enjoy them. They were here few weeks ago. That's the time they cut these sugarcanes," she said.

I was not following the discussion closely as she delved deeper into the village incidences.

My mind was elsewhere—on the dream. I needed answers! She was babbling on: "Mugodo's wife died recently. They will be burying her next week. We buried Amugune the other day, though I didn't manage to attend the burial . . ." She went on and on.

She was still talking when I just found myself bursting out. I couldn't hold it any more.

"Mum told me to ask you who my dad is and where I can find him!" I asked, my voice sounding hard and cracked and shaky, my confidence thrown out of the window.

There was a long silence as if Anguzuzu was thinking about something. Then she asked with shock on her face. "Which mum are you talking about?" she asked

"Mum, my mum. Your daughter, Jane Uside! Your great friend! She told me in a clear dream to come and ask you where to find my dad" I said.

Grandma almost had a heart attack. she started coughing desperately with a deep pain suddenly engulfing her face. She had been talking warmly with a layer of her wide smile flowing a cross her rugged face, but that faded away in haste.

"You mean Uside, approached you in a dream?"

"Yes grandma," I said to her.

"When was this Baraka?" she asked in a low tone

"Just three days ago," I said

Grandma's radiant face suddenly changed into a furious rugged face. In one single movement, she picked up the wooden stool and threw it at me. Had I not jumped out of the house, the stool could have hit my head. Asamba dashed out behind me in a confused manner.

"Get of this place, Baraka, I don't want you to torment me again with those questions and that silly dream!" she shouted.

We stood at the edge of the bushes that led into her compound scared stiff. Anguzuzu was about to charge at us again. She was agitated and panting heavily. She looked like one who had suddenly lost her mind. She had gone back to her skin of a tigress, and she was ready to bite.

She chased us towards the path that led out of her compound as we rushed out in haste. We couldn't fight her. She was clearly struggling with movement when she tripped on the long *kikuyu* grass that had formed a cassock along the path, bringing her down with a heavy thud.

She cried out in pain. Asamba turned back to go and support her back to her feet, but I pulled him forcefully, beckoning him to come along, as Anguzuzu was ready to hurt us. But it was too late for me to restrain him.

Asamba was holding grandma's hand, supporting her up as she cried in pain, almost losing her breath. I joined him with mixed emotions, and we helped her to walk to the wooden makeshift bench at the corner of her compound under an avocado tree.

We started to walk away, dejected in our souls when she beckoned us back. "I am so sorry Baraka! I'm sorry that you have to hear this from me!"

Her words poked through my nerves like a sharp needle. I exchanged a quick look at my friend Asamba, and we locked eyes in collective surprise.

"So, it's true Anguzuzu knew something about this?"

My heart was now beating hard, like a yam being pounded. I was visibly shaken, and my whole body was now trembling., Asamba was tightly holding onto my hands, waiting for the time bomb ticking away just about to go off.

Anguzuzu cleared her throat after a gruesome two minutes of silence.

"Baraka, I don't know why fate chose it this way that I am the one who is supposed to break this sad news to you!"

The word "sad" caused me to shudder, but I didn't utter a word.

"I remember vividly the day it happened. It is a sad memory that has been deposited and etched on stone somewhere in my brain never to go away. It's a memory that I can't wish away. I came home that fateful night and found your mother outside my house crying and in deep pain. I asked her what was going on and she said she had been raped."

My heart sank.

"She said she had been dragged into uncle Matata's bedroom and raped repeatedly. She was still bleeding when I arrived. I quickly went and confronted uncle Matata and he haughtily admitted having done the heinous and abominable act to your mother, Jane! He said he was going to kick her out of the house if we mentioned it to anyone. She didn't have anywhere to run, and we didn't have anyone who could help resolve the issue. Incest in our culture is an abominable act and your mother could have been excommunicated from the society never to be accepted back again. Uncle Matata knew about this tradition and so he used it to satisfy his own wickedness. He knew he would get away with it. He knew if the village elders knew about it on the day you were born, you would be thrown away in the river or given out to a stranger in a far-off village, and your mum would never have been allowed to step into the village again. She would be an outcast forever!"

"Uncle Matata is your dad, Baraka!"

The world around me was spinning, and my heart crunched. It skipped beats altogether, threatening to stop beating all together, and I could feel heavy and repeated palpitations. My heartbeat suddenly became erratic. My eyes were wide open, but they refused to see. There was a cloud of darkness all around me, my head was sucked blank by a powerful typhoon of emotions, and my nerves were sending uncoordinated synapses, making my mouth dry up and shake uncontrollably. I was suddenly sweating like a leaking roof.

From a distance I could hear my grandma's voice trailing on, "Uncle Matata raped your mother Jane repeatedly, and you are the result of his wickedness. He hated the fact that she had fallen out of her matrimonial home and that she had retracted back to her mother's house to interfere with Matata's inheritance. In protest he started mistreating her to the extent of raping her, all meant to frustrate her out of his compound. She didn't have anywhere to run to for refuge, so she stayed on, and his abusive tentacles grew stronger and weirder by day. He was determined by all means to kick her out of his compound.

Come in, and Uncle Matata will kill you one day! He is wicked. You will never understand! But I truly hope that one day you will understand how his wickedness has caused us such pain!

Anguzuzu's words said years back came flowing back into my mind. *So, she had known all along?" Who else knew about this? I* wondered.

I couldn't speak for several hours. I just sat there soaking in the green smoke from the fireplace, baffled by the news I had received. Every tiny particle of smoke from grandma's fireplace was laced with the poisons from my painful past determined to choke me. I started coughing hysterically. This was the darkest day in my life. I closed my eyes and was afraid to open them again. I was scared of what the world had in store for me.

"What of my brother, Isate?" I asked in a low shaky voice, my head still hidden between my knees.

"Isate will have to start his own journey through time to find his own father!" she said in a calm voice.

"You are Matata's secret son, and it was a trade-off for your Mum to stay in uncle Matata's compound, so we had to stay silent. He bought our silence! After you were evicted from his compound, we couldn't speak openly about it as you could be tagged as an outcast and your mum an abomination, so we zipped our mouths! Our options were limited, and we didn't have anywhere or anyone to run to for help! I am sorry, my grandchild, Baraka," Anguzuzu cried out in sincere pain. Her options had been limited by the societal norms and traditions that had relegated the place of a woman to one of timidity and subservience, and predators like uncle Matata had taken advantage, not just once but twice, maybe thrice . . . maybe many more times.

I was angry at myself and I wanted the ground to break and swallow me. I sincerely wanted to die at that very moment. I couldn't bring to my mind the pain my mother had to endure all the days of her life living in the same compound with someone who had raped her and fathered her son. The pain that she bore on her shoulders to single-handedly raise us from hand to mouth while the person who had caused her such misery enjoyed his life having nothing to worry about roaming about, verbally and physically assaulting her more, and perhaps going back to rape her with impunity, knowing fully that nothing could be done to him.

My life was torn into pieces—into wild confetti that the rough winds were threatening to blow away—and piecing it together was to be a pipe dream.

I wondered how mum and grandma had lived through life with this secret heavy in their hearts. A barbaric tradition that culture dictated had pushed me into the shell that was now my life. Didn't I have a right to know?

I wanted to curse the day I was born—the day that welcomed me into this tumultuous world, the hands that took me in at birth and brought me forth, the laughter and the chuckle of the midwife shouting, 'It's a boy!' But then I quickly realized that chuckle might have never been there. There had been nothing to celebrate in my coming forth. My mother had carried me for nine months of misery in her womb—nine months of pain that was going to last her a lifetime. Still, she had to endure double pain to push out her miseries into this world to remain a constant reminder of that fateful night that uncle Matata descended on her to inflict pain and rape away her dignity.

And this was the day that I had longed all my life to find, and he was the man I had longed all my life to know. To meet. To hold his hand, admire his smile, and to see the reflection of myself in his eyes. My father. Oh, my father! How wrong I had been.

"Why did I set out on this journey through time to find this man?" I asked myself.

I stood there baffled and dying inside to know that the man I had been looking for and desiring to know all my life had always been around me. I had always known him as my uncle, Uncle Matata, the mean uncle who didn't care about my existence, yet deep inside he knew his blood ran through my veins. I remembered the many days I went without food, but his side of the garden flourished with food, some eaten by wild birds of the air, yet I couldn't touch them. It baffled me that I had lived as a foreigner in my own father's land, in my own father's compound. I remembered so vividly the day he sicced his dogs to chase us away from his compound—our compound.

I had been denied my true identity by a man I had known all my life, my own father.

My whole world collapsed.

Had I been so naïve not to read the signs on the walls? To see that I bore his gait? That I bore his voice and his slight stammer? "No, this couldn't be. This was a bad joke!" I said to myself in denial.

I wanted to go back and re-dream, to redo the dream and get a fresh direction to my father!

Asamba sat there with me bewildered. All he could do was to give me a hug as he allowed me to travel back and forth through time.

"How was I going to break this news to my brother, Isate? He hated uncle Matata with all his life? And what of Dr. Wanyonyi? How was he going to take this news? What of my village mates who had chided me the whole of my life? Was I going back to the village to claim back my home that I had not been part of all my life?

I should perhaps have lived in the misery of not really knowing what had happened. Had Mum been very wise, and I had been naive and foolish looking for answers? I wished to turn back the clock, but it was too late.

She had been strong. How had she managed to live all her life with these truths without ever hinting at them? She was the master of the game, and I now suddenly understood why she kept all this to herself. Mothers are jewels, and she chose to fight the pain alone and to let me out of it, and for her entire life she succeeded in doing so, sacrificing everything she had for Isate and I to know peace and not to learn how to hate from her. That wasn't the lesson she wanted to pass onto us.

***

My brother Isate was furious and I couldn't calm him down. He wanted to kill Uncle Matata and feed his body to the birds one piece at a time. I could see the hatred sprouting out of him with its multi-headed tentacles ready to swallow up uncle Matata, but it was a little too late. We had to learn how to forgive. We had sought to know our father all these years. We didn't know the man who hated us (and we hated in equal measure) would turn out to be my father, so we had to forgive him. It was going to be difficult, but we agreed we were going to try.

We begged Anguzuzu to accompany us to confront uncle Matata, but she could hear none of it. She declined.

I informed Dr. Wanyonyi about this newfound information, and it was too heavy for him, but he took it in his stride and encouraged me to appreciate life and to see a silver lining in every dark cloud. And to start imagining my life with my father, a complete life that I had always desired and longed for all my life was now here. That I should put aside all the hate that I had for uncle Matata and see the love that he extended in disciplining me whenever I went wrong—that deep down he had some love for me and I needed to find it. He insisted that it was going to be difficult and that I should be prepared to live to appreciate that uncle Matata was my father and I should start to reconcile that with my inner self. It would prove a path of pure healing and completeness, and to extend my love to him and to take full care of him in his sunset years. All was not lost.

Dr. Wanyonyi visited Anguzuzu for days, begging her to agree to accompany us to reconcile and reunite with uncle Matata, but she didn't agree to the proposal. She remained solidly adamant. It was only after several weeks of continued insistence from Dr. Wanyonyi that she finally gave in.

In the company of Dr. Wanyonyi and Anguzuzu, we took the herculean task and the journey back home to a place that we had always known—a place where we had lived in fear and a place we had lived as squatters.

We found uncle Matata seated outside on a small wooden arm chair under the mango tree that had fed me for years in the past. I couldn't utter a word. For the first time I saw my reflection in his eyes. I had his eyes—the eyes that I had never looked into all my life. He looked frail and weak.

I had lived hating this man immensely, but fate had its way, and there I was, my father seated next to me in flesh and blood, not in my dreams any longer. His blood was my blood. It ran through me and ran through him too. He had given life to me to punish my mother, and it was difficult to forgive him. It took grit and effort, and the raging waters within me turned into hurricanes of pain and disgust, yet deep down I knew I had to forgive him.

"Good afternoon Matata," Dr. Wanyonyi greeted him with a firm voice.

Uncle Matata turned and looked at us in utter surprise, ushering us into the house.

I was pleasantly surprised that he was ushering us into his house, the interior of which I had never seen. "Has he changed his behavior? Or is he the same Uncle Matata?" I silently asked myself.

"Are you aware Baraka is your son?" Dr. Wanyonyi asked firmly.

I looked at uncle Matata right into his eyes! He looked at me, then to Isate, then to Anguzuzu, shock written all over his face. His frail body started to tremble.

He started off, "No, I don't know what you are talking about!"

Anguzuzu was furious. She wanted to shout and scream and threatened right there and then to scream and tell the whole village what he had done.

"I will scream and tell the whole village what you did to Jane!" she said.

"I will confess," Uncle Matata said in a low voice.

"I am truly sorry, my son, for the pain I caused you. Please forgive me, Baraka!" He started sobbing and crying out loud.

"But why, Uncle Matata? Why did you do this to us?" After a long pause I corrected myself. "Why Father?" It was the first time in my life that I was using this term to someone who was truly my biological father, and it sounded strange.

My father was heartbroken, and he was crying like a little baby. He covered his face out of shame! "What will I do to truly show my remorse?" He was talking to himself.

Go tell that to the birds! That's what I wanted to tell him, but it didn't come out.

As he cried, I cried some more, and we seemed to be drawn by our tears into collective sense of emotions that were meant to heal our pasts. I turned back to the family that I had known all my life, and I knew it was going to be difficult to sieve the good from all the years that we had lost— to know each other and interact as a family. How was I going to live with this newfound news? With my stepsister Clara that all along had been my cousin?

This life had been a big joke. A big, fat joke. I looked at myself and laughed in tears as I recalled the many times I had been insulted by Uncle Matata. The raw hatred that constantly discharged in his reddened eyes. Yet, deep down, he knew he had sired me. My heart collapsed, and my emotions rose to the roof.

He had been so mean to us, harassing my mother, yet he knew he had done such unspeakable things to her. He had ruined her life, and in return, he had ruined mine too, and Isate's.

We came together and huddled around my father in an uneasy embrace of newfound love and hate. It was a cocktail of mixed emotions. I knew I was about to set out on yet another journey through time. I had walked on this journey all my life, and here I was, right at the end of my life's pier yet starting all over again, and life was beckoning me to jump onto the deck and set sail again. However, I was afraid. Very afraid, indeed! We were all crying, all soaked in our own strange wild worlds.

My feet were hesitant and my mind jumbled, but I knew I had to start all over again. A life with my father, my own biological father. I was going to be like everyone else, to put a meaning to my identity. It was indeed a fresh start into a new journey, whose tomorrow I couldn't tell, but I was optimistic it was going to be an adventure.

I had a lot to discuss with my father. I had a lot of questions only he could answer. I turned to Isate and hugged him close, tears of mixed emotions freely flowing. He too had hopes that he could also start his journey to find his true identity, and perhaps I was going to assist him walk the path.

Dr. Wanyonyi smiled at us. He had been the true dad in my life, and I owed everything to him and thanked the heavens for bringing him into our lives. Uncle Matata had planted the seed and watched it grow all his life, and Dr. Wanyonyi had nurtured that seed through the seasons of life with the help of other great men who had stood with me to help me out of the trenches. They had given me hope and made me into a useful tool in God's hands to change generations through my discovery.

The following day uncle Matata, Anguzuzu, Dr Wanyonyi, Isate, my fiancée, Kageha, and I were all huddled together beside the mound of earth that had been home to my mother. She had been the best mother I could ever ask for in this world. She had suffered all her life, taken all the pain and shame and shut it all into her closet, never to release it on us! She had been amazing! I cried for her!

Uncle Matata was inconsolable. He was crying out of deep pain in untold anguish. He was begging for forgiveness, calling and shouting Mum's name. We bent over to him and clustered around him into one family. The thought of a new home was now ripe in my mind. We knew we had to bury the hatchet and start afresh. Uncle Matata was ready to give it his all towards this new journey together through time. There was a lot a head of us to face, and this time we were going to face the world together with my father. We were going to journey through life together.

I moved over to Uncle Matata, my father, and gave him a warm hug, and I could tell there was still some love left in him for me. That feeling was both exhilarating and frightening. His tears drenching my shirt, melting my heart into surrender and acceptance that he was my father.

I was pleasantly shocked to learn that my father had an album where he had captured and archived some of the most important events in my life. He confessed that he had been secretly following my every success, but he just didn't know how he could get into my life and reconcile.

The past lay like a dark shadow over our heads, but the light had come to peel it off. This reunion, too, was going to be an interesting journey through time for Uncle Matata, my father, yet he was excited and ready to face all that came with the new realities of our lives. I knew the journey to accepting him was going to be long and difficult. He had a whole society ahead of him to deal with, and he had questions to answer both to his immediate family and the world at large. That seemed less of a bother to him. It was our moment to come out of our closets and be free!

Freedom was calling!

Dr. Wanyonyi proudly handed me back into the hands of my father, and he walked away as a proud dad. I looked at Kageha, and her eyes were molten and dripping with love. The spark in her eyes calmed my nerves. In her eyes I could see the journey ahead. I smiled, and she smiled back, seeming to have read my mind.

ACKNOWLEDGMENT

In life's journey, you meet special people whose impact remains forever. Thanks to these awesome men and their families; Alfred Aluda, Albert Luvai, Ezekiel Mido, Daniel Mmbo, Reuben Kioko, Fredrick Anzigale, Edward Ombajo, Josephat Idah and the Chavakali high school fraternity back then led by Mrs Sai Munga Savatia. You have inspired me greatly and I am who I am because of you!

To Lucas Wafula and Erick Livumbazi Ngoda, thanks for holding my hand and mentoring me into writing this book. Many thanks indeed.

To my family, colleagues, my pastors, and friends, I appreciate you.

And to the Almighty God thanks always for the guidance.